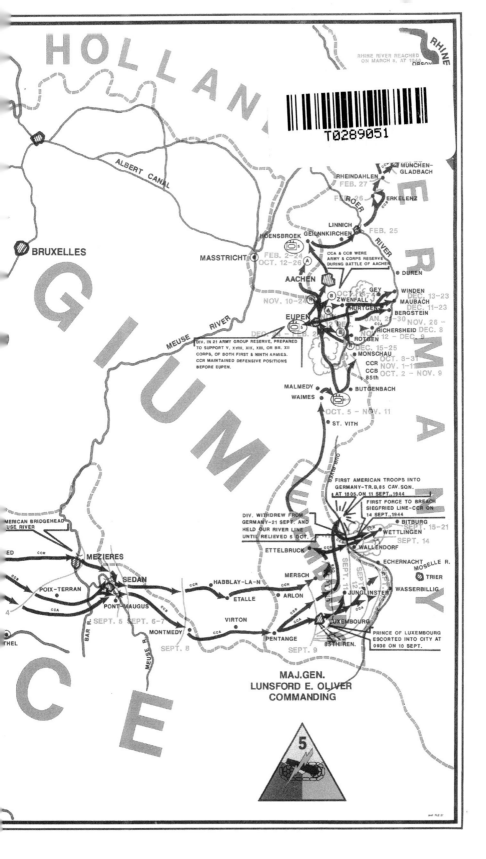

Dearest Letty

Tr. 186th Cav. Rcn. Sg. Mecz
A.P.O. 256; c/o Postmaster
New York N.Y.
7. Oct. 1944

My Dearest Letty:

Well. I hope I have time
to finish this but a guy never
knows. Anyway. I just had a flock
of letters from you and a few
other people and it is high
time I tried to answer some
of them. Everyone except you and
the family has about quit writing
to me. They can't remember to write
if I don't answer their letters, and
that is not always possible.

Say, you should have been
with us a couple of days ago.
It was Jim Madlin's wedding
anniversary and we had to do a
bit of celebrating, so we did it
with a dinner,

Dearest Letty

The World War II
Love Letters of
Sgt. Leland Duvall

EDITED BY ERNIE DUMAS

Copyright © 2011 by The University of Arkansas Press

ISBN-10: 1-55728-976-X
ISBN-13: 978-1-55728-976-6

15 14 13 12 11   5 4 3 2 1

Designed by Liz Lester

⊗ The paper used in this publication meets the minimum
requirements of the American National Standard for Permanence of
Paper for Printed Library Materials Z39.48-1984.

LIBRARY OF CONGRESS CATALOGING-IN-PUBLICATION DATA

DuVall, Leland, 1911–2006.
Dearest Letty : the World War II love letters of Sgt. Leland Duvall /
edited by Ernie Dumas.
p.   cm.
ISBN-13: 978-1-55728-976-6 (cloth : alk. paper)
ISBN-10: 1-55728-976-X (cloth : alk. paper)
1. DuVall, Leland, 1911–2006—Correspondence. 2. World War, 1939–1945—
Personal narratives, American. 3. Soldiers—United States—Correspondence.
4. Soldiers—Arkansas—Correspondence. 5. DuVall, Letty, 1920—-Correspondence.
6. Love-letters—Arkansas. 7. World War, 1939–1945—Campaigns—Western Front.
8. United States. Army. Armored Division, 5th. 9. World War, 1939–1945—
Regimental histories—United States. I. Dumas, Ernest, 1937– II. Title.
D811.D875 2011
940.54'1273092—dc23
[B]
2011034539

CONTENTS

ACKNOWLEDGMENTS

Listing the credits for this book must begin with Nancy Gately, for it was she, shortly before her death in 2010, who recognized that Leland Duvall's wartime letters had both literary and historical value. It came about this way: At lunch with other residents at the retirement home, Nancy heard her new neighbor, Letty Duvall, say that her daughter had discovered the love letters to Letty from her future husband while cleaning out the garage and that she was having fun rereading them after sixty-five years. Nancy asked if she could read a few and, having done so, insisted that they be made into a book. Letty was sure that Leland would have been mortified at the thought of thousands of people pawing around in his thoughts, but she agreed that Nancy should ask my advice. My idea, naturally, was that the letters deserved to be published and that, while he probably would not have cared one way or the other, Leland might have found some satisfaction in having them published since he had taken great pleasure in writing every one of them. Letty consented.

Connie Tisdale, the Duvalls' daughter, cannot be overlooked for having discerned that the crumbling box of letters was worth saving in spite of Letty's injunction to get rid of all the detritus at the home place. Connie's husband, Fred Tisdale, and Leland's nephew, Bob Duvall, both World War II aficionados, had coaxed some recounting of his war experiences from Leland in his declining years and saved his mementoes of the war, including maps and scrapbooks of the Fifth Armored Division's march across Europe in 1944 and 1945. Their recollections of Leland Duvall's conversations, in addition to Roy Reed's and my interviews with Duvall for the University of Arkansas oral history project in 2000, helped link the letters to the soldier's travels and experiences from Omaha Beach to the Elbe River. Confidential unit action reports from the National Archives helped, too.

My wife, Elaine, must be accorded a role. On a long car trip north, she listened while I read her a hundred letters and affirmed my hunch that people who did not know Leland Duvall would be as captivated as we were. She helped with the daunting tasks of converting the letters to type and then condensing them to book length.

It goes without saying that Letty Duvall, in spite of her early ambivalence, animated the whole project. Her mischievous humor was the inspiration that launched a thousand epistles, and it kept our enthusiasm at the right level until the project was finished, when she wondered if Meryl Streep was too old to play her in the movie.

ERNIE DUMAS

INTRODUCTION

Leland

Leland Duvall was nearly thirty-one years old when his draft notice arrived at his father's farm in the mountain valley near the hamlet of Moreland, Arkansas, in March 1942, three months after Pearl Harbor. While older men would be taken afterward, thirty-one was then the upper requirement for men to register for the draft. As the bloody Battle of the Bulge got underway in 1944, Duvall would ruminate in a letter that older men like him who had long-settled habits before the war were more impervious to the life-changing horrors of battle than the young soldiers. It may be said that every man who fought and survived had entered that war as one person and emerged as quite another, even if limbs and mind were intact, and Duvall was no exception. For him, World War II changed everything, starting with the lifelong romance that the war engendered and that is recounted in these letters. Little about his life would resemble its existence before the war except the immutable tranquility that bore him through the hardships of the Great Depression, the war, and all the daily misfortunes of life.

His self-description of a man of settled habits must have defined his emotional and social development, for it could not in any way describe the wayfaring life Duvall led before the war. He had very little formal education, and if itinerant farm labor can be called a career, it was the clearest path for a man with his upbringing in the hardest of times and the hardest of places, Depression Arkansas. His lack of schooling was not by choice. School at Moreland, such as it was, ended with the eighth grade. A youngster ambitious for more learning needed to go off and board at Atkins, a town of fourteen hundred that had a high school, but it was fifteen miles to the south of Moreland by dirt roads, which in the 1920s might as well have been a hundred miles.

By the age of thirteen or fourteen, farm boys like Duvall were expected to have acquired the muscle and agility to wrestle a mule and a double-shovel plow along defined contours, which was all the job preparation they needed. Even Arkansas's Depression governor, J. Marion Futrell, called high school a useless contrivance, a waste of taxpayers' money. Duvall nevertheless wanted to go to high school and spent a few weeks boarding at Atkins. The next year, the nearer town of Hector started a high school, and each morning he walked three miles up the mountain road to Caglesville, where he caught a school bus to Hector. Each time, he ran out of money or enthusiasm after a few weeks and abandoned the project. Still, his thirst was so acute that he read every book that he could scavenge. A younger brother would recall Leland's reading by candlelight or a coal-oil lamp far into the night from a pile of books—philosophy, history, economics, and fiction—that he obtained from lending libraries or from acquaintances. But a knowledge of Shakespeare, Kant, Dickens, or even Adam Smith would not put food on the table, so Duvall undertook a career as a farm laborer. Occasional trials with other forms of livelihood only proved the better dependability of agricultural work.

Omer Duvall, Leland's father, rented a few acres of farmland when he got married and then acquired forty acres of his own a half-mile from the crossroads community that called itself Moreland, where the rocky soil, though not like the deep, rich loam of the Mississippi Delta, could be massaged to produce a fair amount of cotton in a good season. Leland worked there and on other farms in the Arkansas River Valley. At his father's insistence, he tried his hand at teaching grade school early in the Depression. Although he was fourteen and had only eight years of school, Duvall had traveled to Russellville in 1925 with two women from the community who wanted to take the state teacher examination. He took the exam, too, and passed it with a high score, but the state school commissioner wrote on his exam certification that he was too young to be allowed to teach. At nineteen, he taught a term at Oak Grove, a community three miles east of Moreland, and a term at Moreland; but he decided he was no good at teaching and, besides, his salary of forty dollars a month at Moreland was paid in IOUs because the school had no money. Migratory labor was more remunerative.

For years, he followed the planting and harvests from the Mississippi Delta to the west Texas high plains, where he twice spent more than a year on cotton plantations and at other odd jobs left by the migration from the panhandle during the great dust storms of 1934 and 1935. It was a measure of his circumstances, Duvall would recall as an old man, that when people fled the Dust Bowl because there was little to do, he saw it as a golden opportunity. He also worked in cotton fields and gins and a sawmill in Arkansas's Mississippi County, but the vast floods that inundated much of east Arkansas in 1937 chased him home. He tried peddling WearEver cookware door to door to destitute country families in the Texas panhandle while working on farms, mainly handling a row binder, a mechanical contrivance that bundled maize and sorghum.

If toiling behind a team of horses and a row binder or a plow seemed to be what his circumstances and the economy availed a strong-limbed boy from Moreland, it was a career decision not altogether devoid of will. To Duvall, hand labor in the fields or woods was not the life of a quarry slave, to be endured but not enjoyed. It was satisfying and sometimes exhilarating work. The first remarkable thing that readers will discover in Duvall's letters to Letty Jones is his romance with the earth. It is manifest in his elegiac descriptions of winter in the wild, his eagerness to experience the adversities of the desert, his figurative portrayals of mountain splendors, wildlife, and the rhythms of the seasons, and his playful admonitions to Letty from across the Atlantic when she complained about her aches from picking cotton all day. The same rhapsodies to nature and stewardship would appear often during the half-century after the war in the vast miscellanea of Duvall's work as a farm, economics, and editorial writer for the little daily paper at the county seat and, eventually, for the *Arkansas Gazette* and other publications.

When the Japanese attacked Pearl Harbor December 7, 1941, Duvall came home from the Texas plains and worked for a few weeks at an ordnance plant at Jacksonville until his induction notice came.

The draft offered him the prospect of steady employment and, even at a private's pay, better money than he had usually enjoyed. But the U.S.

Army gave him much more than that—new worlds, new experiences, a chance to expand his learning, and patriotic contentment. While other recruits chafed at the hardships and rigor of training, especially the grueling maneuvers in the Mohave Desert, his letters to Letty Jones and probably to other correspondents expressed exhilaration with the primitive life he was leading, wonder at the beauty and harmony of the desert and forests, and a deep satisfaction with what he was learning about the mechanics of warfare and survival.

More than anything, the war gave him chances and reasons to write. And write he did—hundreds of thousands of words, from desert sands, pup tents, hospital beds, the floors of armored cars and bombed-out buildings, on stationery, tablets, and wrapping paper, by candlelight and moonlight.

Letty Jones had met Duvall in 1935, when he came to the Methodist Church on Crow Mountain one morning to help a friend from Moreland teach singing. She made faces at the teacher, and her mischievousness intrigued him. He explained years later that he thought the girl might grow up to be something special, and in his mind he "put her on layaway." He encountered her from time to time during the next six years at gospel-singing conventions at Hector and other towns in the area and a couple of times at Russellville in the weeks before his induction. He learned shortly before he was drafted that she had a serious boyfriend and was rumored to be engaged. The boyfriend was drafted with Duvall, and when the troop train neared the southern California army camp where they were to get basic training, Duvall introduced himself to the fellow and learned that the romance was over.

From Camp Cooke he mailed a postcard to "Letty Jones, Pottsville, Ark.," giving his address and asking if she would correspond with him from time to time. She wrote back that she would, and the romance blossomed. During the next three and a half years, he wrote her 403 letters and many postcards and telegrams, which altogether reached the sum of 160,000 words. Still other letters written during the European campaigns seemed never to have reached her. Mail service from the front, especially for cavalry scouts who were often behind enemy lines or otherwise separated from the unit, was not always reliable. In his letters to Letty, Duvall occasionally mentioned other correspondents, dozens of them. He wrote to his mother at least weekly and corresponded with his three brothers, two of whom also were in the army, relatives and acquaintances in three states, and other soldiers with whom he crossed paths. In one letter to Letty from France he recounted that at mail call that day he had received fifty letters, which were going to take some time to answer. The letters to Letty, which are all that survive, are sharply condensed here. They turned up after Duvall's death and her move from their home on Crow Mountain to a retirement home at Russellville in 2010. Their daughter Connie Tisdale found the letters in the Duvalls' garage.

You must imagine the determination that it took to write so much, to so many, under circumstances that were so hostile to reflection. Duvall carried a bottle of Carter's ink in his backpack along with pencils for when the ink bottle ran dry, the pens were lost, or the nibs worn out. He constantly ran out of stationery and scavenged sheets from other soldiers or from whatever paper source he could find. Writing so much to so many people would seem to most of us to be an onerous obligation, but for Duvall it was a joy, even when army censors kept him from writing about where he was, had been, or was going and what his troop was doing. He wrote furiously, rarely even scratching through a word, and with unusual grace, humor, and serenity. He always reassured Letty and probably his mother—falsely, it would turn out—that he was in little peril and was having a pretty good time of it, except from time to time for the cold and mud. He felt obliged to cheer up his mother, who had three sons in the war (one became a prisoner of war) and whose letters often revealed her depression. Only in the final weeks, as the war in Europe wound down and as he awaited the return home, did he betray any disillusionment or choler. His squadron suffered great casualties, but he hinted at it only once, and never in his letters or for many years afterward did he talk, either remorsefully or matter-of-factly, about the killing in which he had to engage.

Thus did the war prepare Duvall for what he was to do for another fifty years, which was to write. He confided to Letty that this was what he would like to do. He talked about enrolling in a journalism course at the University of Arkansas by correspondence, and he did enroll in English courses at the University of Texas by mail in the spring of 1945 when the armored division to which he was attached was chasing the German army to Berlin. The U.S. Army had very quickly realized that the private with an eighth-grade education was an autodidact ("self-uneducated" was

Duvall's characterization of his educational achievement), and it had him teaching composition, warfare, history, and foreign affairs during training and when his division was in repose in Germany and France at war's end.

Soon after his discharge, Duvall discovered that Arkansas Polytechnic College, a two-year school at Russellville, would let veterans enroll even without a high school diploma and that the GI Bill would pay for it. He enrolled for the spring term in 1946 and took a couple of journalism classes. That winter, the owner of the *Daily Courier Democrat* at Russellville, J. A. Livingston, died and left the paper to his daughter on the condition that she move back from New York City and run it for at least a year. She accepted, and the editor of the paper, a middle-aged man named Seaton Ross, quit rather than work even one day for her. The business manager asked the dean at the college, Alfred Crabaugh, if anyone at the college could edit a newspaper. Crabaugh had heard about a veteran who wrote very well. He summoned Duvall and asked him if he thought he could edit a daily newspaper.

"I reckon so," Duvall said.

Duvall went down to the paper's office and spent a day watching Ross make telephone calls, write stories, obituaries, and editorials, rip the Associated Press wire, compose headlines, and supervise production of the afternoon paper. Ross then shoved the accumulated piles of paper from the horseshoe desk into a trash barrel and put on his coat and hat.

"It's yours," he told Duvall, and walked out. No one saw Ross again, and Duvall became the editor the next day. His pay was $32.50 a week. A few years later, he saw a United Press photo in the *Arkansas Gazette* of Seaton Ross testifying before one of the congressional committees investigating American communists. The caption identified Ross as the former editor of the *Daily Worker,* a newspaper published in New York City by the Communist Party USA. Duvall told people that his journalism training consisted of one day's journalistic wisdom from a communist.

Under a succession of owners, including US senator J. William Fulbright and Clyde E. Palmer of Texarkana, the conservative owner of a string of newspapers across South Arkansas, Duvall edited the *Daily Courier Democrat* for eight years while running a dairy farm on Crow Mountain and writing a weekly feature for the *Gazette* about farming and economic developments in the Ozarks and the Arkansas River Valley. His editorials in the *Courier Democrat* did not always please the paper's owners or the townspeople. When the US Supreme Court ruled that school segregation was unconstitutional on May 17, 1954, Duvall wrote an editorial for the next day's paper under the headline "How Law-Abiding Are We?" calling the decision an affirmation of principles that were enshrined in the Constitution and saying the reaction to the ruling would reveal the nation's character. The Supreme Court, he said, believed that the nation had progressed enough toward a true democracy that it could give life to its ideals. "Time will reveal whether they were right," he wrote. He called for leaders across the South and in his own town to be calm and rational and to follow the law. The Linotype operator came out of the composing room holding Duvall's editorial between a thumb and forefinger.

"Do we run this?" he asked.

"Well, I thought we would," Duvall replied.

"Man, that'll get us in big trouble," the printer said.

"I hope it does," Duvall said.

Forty-five minutes into the press run, a delegation of city leaders arrived and told him he had to stop the press and remove the offending editorial. Duvall said he thought he would go ahead and run it. In the next ten days he wrote two more editorials condemning the demagoguery that was already surfacing in the state and arguing that there ought to be no difficulties in ending segregation in Russellville immediately. The city operated a grade school for black children, but if any of them wanted to go to high school they had to ride a bus thirty-five miles to the east to Morrilton, which had a black high school. He wrote that the Russellville high school could accommodate the black youngsters easily and they should be admitted without delay.

When the *Courier Democrat's* new owners let it be known the next year that they would replace Duvall as editor, the *Arkansas Gazette* hired him to write a daily farm column. Soon he was writing regular business and economics columns and filling in often as an editorial writer. For much of the last decade before his retirement in 1990, at the age of seventy-nine, he wrote editorials exclusively. They were most often courteous laments at government's growing obeisance to big business, whether "Big Oil" or the financial houses, which he said needed, for their own health, the restraints imposed by the New Deal after the crash of 1929. Duvall had read every major economics tract from Adam Smith to Milton Friedman, but he leavened theory with a keen understanding of human nature. When Congress deregulated savings and loan associations and the Reagan administration sent word to the institutions in 1982 that regulatory agencies would grant them extraordinary "forbearance," Duvall wrote that liberation would pretty much spell the end of the thrift industry because the risky assets they inevitably would bring into their portfolios would do them in. The crash came four years later. Eventually, some 750 institutions failed at a cost of $88 billion to the taxpayers. When a movement began to similarly lift government's regulatory hand from commercial and investment banks and other financial institutions, Duvall predicted the same fate for the banks, with far worse consequences for the country. Congress passed a law in 1999 that finally finished off the Banking Act of 1933, commonly known as the Glass-Steagall Act, so that there would no longer be real distinctions between depository banks and investment banks and little regulation of either. The ungovernable human impulse to find higher and higher profits, Duvall said, would make no scam too risky, particularly since there was an implied assurance that in the end the government and the taxpayers would save them. Duvall had retired when the bank regulation reform became law and was living in a cottage near Letty Jones's old home place on Crow Mountain. He told a visitor that he dreaded the inevitable financial crash because its consequences would be far-reaching and enduring, but he was confident that the government this time would act more quickly than had Herbert Hoover and the Republicans and that the country might be saved from another depression. The crash came in 2008, two years after his death.

Throughout his life, Duvall's writings continued a theme of his war letters to Letty Jones: an almost spiritual veneration for the soil and the natural world. At the little Russellville paper after the war he wrote a daily editorial column called "The Windrow," which is the name for brush and debris that are harvested to clear the ground for regeneration and piled in rows. The column was often a parable of nature. He would write, for example, that he had witnessed at close hand the degeneration of a family, which he proceeded to describe from event to event. It would turn out that it was a family of cardinals in his side yard, and the youngsters were being forced from the nest to test their wings. One or two would not survive. There were lessons for humans.

Dearest Letty

An early farm column for the *Gazette* described the decline of the agricultural economy in the mountains and river valleys. "In northwest Arkansas, where I grew up," Duvall wrote, "I watched the social and economic structure of communities crumble because the soil from which they drew their nourishment melted into a red slurry and ran down the steep hills to clog streams, flood flatlands and settle at the estuary of the Mississippi." In his seventies, Duvall anonymously wrote a homiletic booklet every spring for the National Association of Conservation Districts on the occasion of Soil Conservation Week; each booklet preached the virtues of protecting the soil, forests, and streams. Each journal ended with a poem, anonymous but obviously penned by Duvall, about the careful use and enjoyment of the gifts of nature. The booklets, like much of his writing, began with a parable or a biblical injunction, most often from the Book of Ecclesiastes, whose Stoic philosophy he found especially germane to his experience.

"One generation passeth away and another generation cometh, but the earth abideth forever," Ecclesiastes said, which Duvall considered a sacred injunction to men and their governments to manage their affairs so that they would leave for future generations the same legacy they enjoyed, a pristine planet.

In 1969, the 150th anniversary year of the *Arkansas Gazette's* founding, John Netherland Heiskell, the newspaper's editor and principal owner for the previous sixty-seven years, asked Duvall in his spare time to write or have written a serial history of the state's economic institutions. The magazine-length pieces ran each Sunday for most of the year and were republished in 1973 as a book, *Arkansas: Colony and State.* Duvall's principal thesis was that although Arkansas had been a territory or a state for 150 years, it functioned for most of that time as an economic colony, furnishing raw materials and hand labor for the nation's industrial engine but sharing few of its fruits, in the form of education, prosperity, or cultural and social advancement. Only by the United States' entry in two world wars, principally the second one, did Arkansas emerge from the eddies and become a real state that participated, if not fully, in the sovereign life of the nation.

Duvall was one of tens of thousands of men who were the embodiment of the transformation, who came home from the second war ordained to make their state a real democracy and make for themselves a better life. The flood of letters to the girl of his dreams, who was made accessible by the circumstances of war, record the remarkable transformation.

A word about the organization of the book. Since Duvall does not say where he is, has been, or is going, particularly after his unit leaves American soil, I have occasionally inserted a short narrative about where the Eighty-Fifth Cavalry Reconnaissance Squadron is going in the weeks ahead and the kind of fighting it will see in the hope that it may illuminate the letters.

Dearest Letty

Dearest Letty

ONE

All's Fair

When he was inducted into the U.S. Army in March 1942, Leland Duvall boarded a train at Little Rock, Arkansas, for Camp Cooke, California, a new post on a wind-swept mesa jutting into the Pacific Ocean 180 miles north of Los Angeles. Some nine thousand men converged on the camp in February and March to fill out the Fifth Armored Division. The German Blitzkrieg across Poland and France, which employed a mechanized force of armor, artillery, infantry, and air power to overwhelm the enemy, had added a deadly new dimension to warfare, and Camp Cooke was supposed to develop armored and infantry units to counter the German strategy and adapt it to use against the Germans.

At the first of August, after basic training, the division moved 250 miles to the Mohave Desert, where everyone believed they were training to chase German field marshal Erwin Rommel's Afrika Korps across Libya, Tunisia, and Egypt. Parts of the division did head for North Africa when the desert training ended in December 1942, but most of the division, including Duvall's Eighty-Fifth Cavalry Reconnaissance Squadron, stayed in the states for more training for the European campaign. It would be more than a year before they would embark for the Normandy beaches and the fighting.

Sometime on the train from Little Rock to Cooke or after his arrival there, Duvall recognized another recruit, Martin F. Drittler, as the young man who was supposed to be engaged to Letty Jones, for whom he had nursed a secret infatuation. He introduced himself and after a time asked if Drittler was still engaged to Miss Jones, whom he said he knew casually. No, Drittler replied, that romance was over. In his first weeks of training, Duvall wrote a postcard to Letty, asking if she would correspond with him. She wrote back that she would, and the remarkable exchange began. Her letters to him, lamentably, could not be saved. Although his letters would playfully disparage her former beau, Duvall would strike up a close friendship with Drittler, who was from the community of Lutherville. Duvall's letters would eventually confess an admiration for the other soldier, who fought heroically in B Company, the next troop.

Camp Cooke, Calif.
May 23, 1942

Dear Letty:

When I sent you the card I did not dare hope that you belonged to a Keep 'em Happy Club, but I am glad you do. Your letter went a long way toward relieving the monotony of a week in the Army.

One paragraph left me a little puzzled. You said, "I wanted to go to the graduation exercises at Tech, but my dog-goned ole donkey refused to take me." The puzzle was that you neglected to say who was acting as your "dog-goned ole donkey" since a certain other fellow and I are out here with the 85th Reconnaissance Battalion in Uncle Sam's fighting force. Now tell me who he is.

Yes, several Pope County boys are in camp here, but only about a dozen are in the 85th. The others are scattered around and I seldom see them. Loyd Bowden is in my company and there is another fellow with a glorious past and little future in "B" Company. He lived somewhere east of Russellville. He and I go to the show together occasionally, but I have failed to get any ideas for the Great American Romantic Novel from him yet. However, I should keep trying if you insist that I write the book.

You should see some of this country if you are interested in the mountains, the seashore or flowers. We have it all.

Our closest town is Lompoc. The word, translated literally, means "Valley of Beautiful Flowers" and it certainly lives up to the name. Many of the big seed companies grow their flower seed there. In fact, the farmers of the valley produce little else. Most of the crop is in full bloom now. Hundreds of acres abound in flowers. If you should see the valley from the top of one of the mountains it would remind you of an oriental rug whose creator had an endless variety of richly colored threads on his loom. But he is no artist so he gives little thought to the design or pattern. His sole purpose is to weave as much color as possible into the tapestry, and in this he succeeds very well. It makes a strangely beautiful covering for the earth's nakedness.

I am afraid if I let this run on you will become so bored and disgusted that you won't write again. That would be one of the great tragedies of my young life. Youth is so emotionally unstable, you know, and things like that can undermine the morale of the Army.

As ever,
Leland

Camp Cooke
June 5, 1942

Dear Letty:

It is possible that I should begin this note with an apology. It may be that you have not answered my last letter. I am taking a chance that you have and that I have not received it.

You see, I have been in the hospital for the past few days, and none of my letters has been sent over here. I don't know who has written to me and who hasn't, so I am taking no chances. I am writing all my favorite people so they won't get offended and quit me.

I have not told many people that I am in the hospital because it would conjure up imaginary pictures of pain and suffering. But this is really a pleasant place. No whistle wakes us up in the morning. We loaf around in pajamas on the sun porch and read the papers. Every two or three hours a pretty nurse comes by to hold our hand (to count our pulse).

There are a few drawbacks. The nurses are all lieutenants and are impersonal about the whole thing, and whoever heard of a private getting any pleasure out of holding a second louie's hand?

Hope you don't mind if this is a little short of my standards, but I am tired. Will try to do a little better if you should answer this letter.

Love,
Leland

Camp Cooke
June 11, 1942

My Dear Letty:

Can you imagine my confusion? My mail came yesterday, and it was the first I had had in almost two weeks. My company had been away from camp and all of my mail had been sent to them. When it came back yesterday I had sixteen letters, eight cards and two *Courier Democrats*.

Now, I ask you, how am I to answer all those cards and letters? If my dear uncle doesn't hurry and give me a pay raise, I may go broke from buying stationery.

So you have reached an age where love means nothing to you? I am a little surprised. I didn't know you were that old. But twenty is a little young, don't you think? Most people don't arrive at that conclusion until they are around eighty. So, for some reason, I can't believe it is really permanent. Maybe I can use a few convincing arguments that will change your mind when (if) I come back.

So you are an artist? Surprising, but interesting. If you were out here you could find plenty of subjects to paint. There are plenty of interesting places there, too, so you should have no trouble.

No, Bowden doesn't get drunk often now. In fact, he has few opportunities, just as the girls have no chance to sweep me off my feet. I have had only one pass, and I don't think he has had one yet. You see, we really spend our time soldiering. But it will be over one of these days.

Well, it's a little tiring to write in bed, and even though I have not answered all your letter I will have to sign off.

Love,
Leland

Dearest Letty

Camp Cooke
June 18, 1942

Dear Letty,

Had your letter today and this is what I call a prompt answer. I am trying to make up in promptness what my letters may lack in interest. It is a poor substitute, but I am hoping it will serve the purpose for which it is intended, viz. to keep your letters coming. You see, I am a selfish chap and I like your letters.

I wish I could have heard your duet. By the way, who is the other half of the team? But I didn't know you played the piano. Wish you could come out here and give me a demonstration on the piano in our day room. The boys here really murder it. Any similarity between the noise and music is purely coincidental.

Saturday is our big day, but it is not exactly a day of rest. In fact, it is a day of work, for then we have what is called inspection. The boys enjoy it so much that they describe it in colorful language. But it is not the kind of language you would expect to hear in Sunday school.

Saturday morning, the sergeant usually says, "Today we have an inspection of our field equipment." And all the boys begin to enjoy themselves so much that they are hard to control.

Then we begin trying to get all our stuff together. In fact, we only leave the shower and our cot behind. The remainder of our stuff is rolled into compact bundles and stacked in a neat pile about the size of a bale of cotton and almost as heavy.

When the whistle blows we begin trying to shoulder the stuff. Finally, we get it up and stagger out with it. We have to hike with it for a while just to show the officers that we are good soldiers. A few of the weaker men fall and fracture a leg or break an arm, but they want to weed out the creampuffs anyway.

Finally, we stop in the middle of a sand pile and the sergeant says, "Prepare for inspection," and we begin to unpack the stuff. All the time, the wind is blowing a pleasant little gale and the sand is blistering our faces. It is worse than a West Texas sandstorm.

All our stuff must be spotlessly clean, so we spread it out in the sand and wait for the officer to come by. Presently, we see him coming and take a final look at our stuff. By this time it is completely buried in the sand and we begin digging like a bunch of garden moles. We uncover a few prairie dogs in the process, but we finally come up with most of it.

We empty a part of the great state of California out of our mess kits and try to shake some of the sand out of our blanket, and the wind carries us away like a bunch of sailboats with olive-drab sails. We all get Sunday KP because our equipment is dirty.

The lights will be out in three minutes.

As ever,
Leland

Camp Cooke, Calif.
July 2, 1942

My Dearest Letty:

Your letter came Monday, but I have an acceptable reason for not answering it before now. I had six letters in the Monday mail call. I really hit the jackpot. I had first opened yours, and the others were waiting to be read when the sarge blew the whistle and called us out. We only had three minutes to get ready for a two-day trip. So I did not get to read your letter and the others until we came back today.

They took us up into the mountains for a bivouac. We climbed until eleven o'clock and they stopped us on a ledge somewhere up in the Rockies. By this time the moon had come up and we could see that our little shelf was about fifty yards wide. Above us, a cliff rose three hundred feet. On the other side of the ravine, the mountain dropped away so that we looked down on the tops of trees. Such places always deflate my ego and I felt like a bit of bric-a-brac on a corner shelf.

I was trying to think of some excuse to stay up (I didn't want to go to bed) when they put me on guard. When the others had gone to sleep, I could hear the voices of the mountain wildlife. A coyote perched on the cliff over my head and sent his howl out across the canyon. The owls held a convention in the trees, and about three o'clock some kind of a mountain cat gave out an eerie cry. And all the time a chorus of frogs were doing a grand symphony. I thought there must be a stream down there, and when day came I went down to investigate.

I found the clearest little river I have ever seen. The water was icy cold, but I went swimming and almost missed breakfast. Wish I were able to describe all this to you. It was one of the most beautiful places I have ever seen. Even if I tried to write poetry I didn't have a chance to describe the bivouac area.

Thanks for the compliment on the newspaper article, but there is really no excuse for my dear uncle, Sam, to be proud of me. I am the most inconspicuous rookie among all the six million guys.

And the newspaper was all mixed up. The other boys are both with the 307th C.A. down at San Diego. I am 300 miles up the coast with the 85th Armored Reconnaissance. We are the modern version of Daniel Boone. That is, we are scouts who ride in cars and send our information back to the main Army by radio. It should be a lot of fun.

I hope you understand that my letters must be detached and impersonal. Military reasons, you know. But don't think I don't enjoy the clever notes you write. I am only hoping you will make the next one longer.

Love,
Leland

P.S. How about slipping a little snapshot into the next letter, PLEASE?

Camp Cooke, Calif.
July 12, 1942

My Dearest Letty:

Speaking of speed in answering a letter, how is this for a record? Your letter came just thirty minutes ago. Just as I had finished it the chow ("dinner" to you) whistle blew, and now I am writing. To really appreciate my speed, you would have to know how tough the chicken was. It was so tough they didn't throw the scraps into the garbage. The government took them to a laboratory to study their potential value as a substitute for rubber.

Yes, I listen to the Hit Parade. And "Don't Sit Under the Apple Tree" is my favorite song, too. (And see that you don't.) Funny how our tastes are so alike. If you listen to Glenn Miller you know that he gives a radio-phonograph away each week to the Army camp that selects the most popular song for his program. Camp Cooke voted for "Don't Sit Under the Apple Tree" and won the radio-phonograph for the Service Club.

I hope you realize just how important your job is. You may think it is dull to tend a victory garden, hunt for scrap rubber and "keep the home fires burning," and it is not exciting. But it is just as essential as the things I am doing. Your kind of life is the thing we are supposed to be fighting to preserve. Someone must preserve it while we are away. That, more than anything else, is your job.

And don't think we could come back and take things up where we left off. It is not as simple as that. There will have to be a nucleus for us to start with. There must also be some connection between us and your way of living to make us realize constantly that it is all worth the effort. Your letter helps provide that connecting chain for me.

The job of the Army is to make a man over into a rough, uncouth and uncivilized part of a fighting machine. There is no way to resist it, no matter how gentle and peace loving you may have been. One can see this demonstrated in every phase of camp life. The mess hall is a good example. There, I suddenly find myself devouring my food wolfishly with no thought of Emily Post and no accompanying conversation. The only thought is to satisfy an animal hunger. But this is running into a boring bit of philosophy.

What I was trying to say is that your letters help me remember that civilization still exists. (Hope you don't mind if I finish on the back of the sheet. I am all out of paper.)

Have just had an interview with the company commander and I think I am coming back east to school. At least he said I would be going in the near future. If I do it will be to Fort Knox, Kentucky. If I come through Pottsville I will give you a wave. Of course, I want to go. It is a radio school, and radio is the one thing this outfit has to offer that I really like.

But I hope they pay me before I go. I have drawn less than $20 from Uncle Sam since I came into the Army. I have not had a payday since the April pay. Of course, I have had to cash a couple of checks, but if I should leave now I would not have time to get money back, and I only have a few dollars left.

Love,
Leland

My Dearest Letty:

Your letter came Monday and I hope you will believe me when I say that I have not had time to answer it until now. We have been firing the .30-caliber machinegun and it takes up most of my time. But we are through the course and I will have an easy time for a while. When we are firing for record we have to get up long before daylight and go out to the range. When we finish shooting we have to clean guns until it is too late to write.

No matter what the Morale Builders may say about what to write a soldier, just remember that anything you may write will be appreciated. Your letters bubble and sparkle with zest and life no matter what you are writing about. But you were always so darn cheerful about everything that you couldn't write a dismal letter if you tried.

Which may explain why you were always one of my favorite people. Now, don't act surprised. You always knew it. I'll agree that this is a heck of a time to mention that. One of my biggest faults has always been a poor sense of timing. I always say or do things at the wrong time. But since I have brought this up, I refuse to take it back.

Wish I could see your dog. What kind is he? You see, I am something of a dog lover myself. Which brings up the subject of Martin.

He and I often get together on Sunday and stroll about the camp. Last Sunday, we went to every exchange on the post. He was hunting a pipe, and none of them suited him. He is a likeable chap and an interesting fellow to study. One of the most precise and exacting people I have ever known. But I guess you know this a lot better than I do.

He used to mention you occasionally, as a man speaks of his great sorrow, but one day he found out that I knew you and he has not mentioned you since. I don't know why.

I guess this is a pretty bum letter but, as I said, I didn't have much time. I couldn't wait, for when I delay it makes your letters that much further apart. So please write as soon as you can, even if it is just because you belong to a Keep 'em Happy Club.

Love always,
Leland

Camp Cooke, Calif.
August 2, 1942

My Dearest Letty,

Now don't go getting ideas in your pretty head. I gather that you are thinking of joining the Army (W.A.A.C.). Take my advice and don't. It is not the ideal life by any means.

Of course, I don't know about the W.A.A.C., but there is a lot of dirty grind to this. It takes a special brand of philosopher to enjoy it. Perhaps you were only kidding.

Speaking of dogs (as you did, very entertainingly), there is one coincidence. I, too, have a dog named Skipper. He was eleven years old in April and (hold your bonnet) he is a foxhound. He is a harmless old fellow and I am sure you would like him. He wouldn't hurt a flea, but Mother says that is because he is lazy. She contends he is so lazy that he wouldn't even kick if he were dying. The other dog (yes, I have two) is not so lazy. When I saw him last he was spending most of his time chasing cats and rabbits and chewing on the Skipper's ear. The Skipper resented this and usually put an end to it by thrashing Spike thoroughly. The pup was so mischievous that he couldn't behave and always came back, but not until he staged a sit-down strike.

These sit-downs sometimes lasted an hour. All this time he would sit in the shade and look glum, pretending he didn't have a friend in the world. It was easy to see through his mask. He was merely trying to think of some new mischief to get into. Some people are like that and, darn it, a fellow can't help being crazy about them.

The company is getting ready to go on maneuvers and all the boys are excited. All sorts of rumors float around about the heat of the desert. Some say you can fry eggs by setting your mess kit on the hood of a scout car. Others say the temperature goes to 180 degrees inside the tanks. But a lot of the rumors are like the story of Mark Twain's death; they are greatly exaggerated. The weather record shows a top heat of 130 to 138 degrees. This is not as hot as it sounds, for the climate is dry.

Maneuvers should be interesting. I will hate to miss them. (I may not miss them if they don't find room for me in school.)

Too bad that your radio is out of order, but I am afraid you would never hear of me as a hero, even if you had a sixteen-tube super set. In this

Dearest Letty

Army I am just a guy named Joe. All that hero stuff is a bunch of hooey anyway. Most of it is created by ingenious newspapermen who are trying to make an honest living and boost the morale of the country, which is not necessary.

Besides, my job offers little opportunity to be in the hero class, that is, if I get into operation. In actual combat we will work our way up near the enemy lines, and through them if possible, then send back information to the main army. It is pretty much of a lone-wolf job. We do little actual fighting. The only trouble is that the other fellow has a nasty habit of bringing out his direction finder and locating the station. Then, bingo, you swallow the fragments of a hand grenade.

At that, the casualties only run about 75 percent, and with luck a chap might be among the 25 percent left.

The picture was wonderful. Thanks a million. Sorry I haven't a decent picture of myself. I am camera shy. However, I promise to overcome all that and send one. Meanwhile, I am enclosing a landscape shot taken from one of our bivouacs. I think I wrote you about the river up in the national forest. You can see it in the picture, which was taken from the bluff overlooking the valley. You can also see some of the scout cars down in the valley. They should give you some idea of the size of the valley and the height of the bluff.

I didn't know I was part of a three-cornered drama with you and Martin at the other corners. Please tell me about it. I am always in the mood to listen.

Love,
Leland

Camp Cooke, Calif.
August 4, 1942

My Dearest Letty,

Surprised?

You shouldn't be, if you will only remember that I write you at every opportunity and on flimsy excuses. This time I have a plausible reason. Here it is:

I will be moving from Camp Cooke in three or four days, and I don't know what my new address will be. If they have a vacancy back in the Armored Force School I will go to Fort Knox. It is all fixed up here, but they have no room for me at the moment (and they don't know what they are missing back at Louisville or they would make room for me).

If I don't go east I will stay with the company, and I don't know where we will be. So if you have not answered my last letter just hold everything until I get settled somewhere. Then I will let you know where I am. If you have a letter in the mail it should get here before I pull out.

Now that I have exhausted my only plausible excuse for writing, do you mind if I ramble on a bit about the weather and the country?

The weather is beginning to bore me just a trifle. Every day it is the same. In the afternoon the sun comes through the fog and investigates the landscape. Then for a time the Chamber of Commerce truthfully says "sunny California." But first, after retreat, a fog bank climbs over the western rim of the earth. Small wisps of mist venture out of the ocean and hurry along the streets like ghosts. Before sundown the fog thickens and the sun becomes a dim lamp set on the window ledge of the horizon. The hills have moved their shadow shawls snugly around their shoulders and settled down to sleep. Barracks are, by this time, riding at anchor in a misty sea. The lamps powder the streets with damp yellow pollen. The slender palm trees, which in the afternoon were exclamation marks in the poetry of the landscape, are now damp silhouettes of ghosts. The whole earth shivers under a damp, salty blanket of mist.

How am I doin'? You may be a little puzzled by that paragraph, but I have been reading T. S. Eliot and some of the other Imagists and I am experimenting with impressions. Hope you don't mind my trying it out in a letter.

Loyd and I have been working KP today and was it tough! When I get out of the Army I think a little job of washing dishes for half a dozen people or fewer will be a cinch. May I have a date reserved to show you what a good worker I am in the kitchen? If you had been born rich instead of beautiful this would mean nothing to you, but I am hoping it will have some influence in my favor.

Love,
Leland

Maneuvers Mohave Desert
August 14, 1942

My Dearest Letty,

Weather Report: Fair and warmer. Temperature 132 degrees in the shade (no shade).

Arrived yesterday; only six cases of sunstroke so far. I am OK except for blisters on my hands from handling a radio repair kit and cleaning a machinegun, which may help to explain why my writing is even poorer than usual. It is torture to even hold a pen. Will write when I can.

Love,
Leland

Desert Maneuvers
August 18, 1942

Dearest Letty,

If you were to suddenly come up here you would wonder if I was an American soldier or an Arabian desert rat, and you would never know if you had to judge by appearance only. My skin is the color of a five-cent cigar. Part of this is due to the suntan, but most of it is just dirt. I have not shaved in so long that my beard would be definitely Van Dyke if it were properly trimmed, and my hair should be confined to a snood. At the moment I am sitting cross-legged, after the manner of an American Indian, in the most untidy tent in Company A.

You should see our tent. It consists of four Army shelter-halves buttoned together to form a canvas twelve feet long and eight feet wide. This is suspended three feet above the ground from four short posts in a manner that provides the greatest possible shade and, incidentally, the least protection from heat.

This shelters four men with full equipment, and we have to take advantage of every available inch of space. Our blankets are particularly valuable since they serve the dual purpose of rugs and beds. We walk on them, sit on them (as I am doing now) and sleep on them. No matter how often we shake and beat them, they still retain a feeling similar to sandpaper when we lie on them at night.

And does the Army make strange bedfellows? At night the ants creep in looking for food and crawl about over us. Mule-tailed pack rats rummage among our equipment, and one is never surprised if a desert scorpion wakes him with a friendly sting. There are rattlesnakes (we have killed a dozen in our area), but so far none of them has found its way into our tent.

Then there are the sandstorms and dust devils. Dozens of dust devils pass every day, but they only disturb the tents that are in their paths. The sandstorms are not so considerate. They are like the Texas storms, only more furious, and they play no favorites. All the tents go down.

I have been trying to give you a picture of desert maneuvers. Perhaps you have the impression by this time that I detest the place and the job, but I do not. In fact, I enjoy every minute of it. You see, I have always toyed with the idea of spending a few weeks in a place as wild and as remote as the earth had to offer. This is that place, and all my expenses are paid.

All the boys think the sun has affected my brain, and you may think the same thing, but there is a beautiful phase to this life. We feel no obligation to any society except our own group. We loaf around in shorts, sunglasses, helmets and little else. We have an indolent life, as animal as that of the desert rat. Everyone should live like this for a time so that they can really estimate the progress of what we call civilization.

Then, there is the beauty of the desert. It is a wild, free sort of beauty. If the Army trucks and tents were suddenly removed one could easily imagine that he was looking at a planet at the dawn of creation. No vegetation, and no signs of life, only the white-hot rays of the sun beating mercilessly against the sand.

But on the horizon in every direction are strings of wild, bare mountains, decorated in a dozen colors: blue, green, yellow and purple, in an endless combination of patterns. But the patterns vary as the sun changes the position of their shadow rugs, so that one can never memorize their beauty. One moment it can be truthfully said, "The big canyon to the north is purple, the small one is red, and the ridge is a deep yellow." But presently, if you look again, the big canyon is a deep blue and all the other patterns have changed so that one wonders if it is really the same bit of mountain he was seeing before. But I must change the subject or I will use all my paper uselessly.

There is the most wonderful little valley on the Colorado River about forty miles east of where we are. It is just below Parker Dam, and the river is really beautiful there. It is as clear as glass, and it fairly races along. There is a picturesque little village of small adobe huts in an old Spanish design, but you would have to see it to appreciate it.

I have often thought I would like to spend a few weeks there when the war is over, just living in the sun, talking lazily to a special person, and not expecting an Army whistle to call me to go to work. Does it sound interesting?

Love,
Leland

Desert Maneuvers
Sept. 8, 1942

Dearest Letty:

Had your good letter yesterday and have been wondering ever since I read the poem how you managed to find anything so fitting. I have let a few of the boys who have been in the hospital read it, and they all got a big kick out of it.

Gosh! Wish I could make some of the afternoon hikes you wrote about. I have seen some of the more beautiful spots in your mountains, but doubtless I have missed most of them. Now, don't think I will forget that you promised to show them to me. And you promised to let me show you the Army way to wash dishes. Memory is my long suit, and you must keep that in mind and not make any rash promises that you can't keep. Just remember, you have been telling me you are a good little girl and good girls keep all their vows.

Have just come in from a three-day military problem. Of course, it was not three days for us. Our company never lasts that long. This time, we were knocked out the second morning, which was something of a record for us.

You see, we move out in front of the division as scouts to find the enemy. That is the job of reconnaissance. So when we find him we are always outnumbered. If we get away, it is our job to slip on through his lines and cut telephone wires and that sort of thing. It is nice here, but I don't know how long we will last when we start playing for keeps.

Getting bumped off here is a lot of fun. All we have to do is put up a black flag and come back behind the lines and wait until the problem is over. Of course, we have to do our own cooking while the problem is on, but that is not hard. Most of the stuff they give us is easy to prepare. The coffee, for example, is powdered. All we have to do is heat water to the temperature we want the coffee, put a spoonful of the powdered mixture into the cup, pour in the water, and you have the best coffee you ever tasted. If I should ever get married, I would not use any other brand. It would reduce the time required for breakfast by several minutes, and those before-breakfast fights are supposed to be the most serious.

Just had a short stretch in the hospital dispensary. It was not at all serious and was the result of a ride in an Army jeep. We were cowboy driving across country (we never drive on the road) and the car hit a big ditch. I was knocked out like a prizefighter. My back is still a bit sore.

It looks like the jeeps are going to get me yet. I may have written you that one almost ran over me a few weeks ago. I was sleeping by a scout car and a lieutenant came by in a jeep. He was driving blacked out and it was dark, so he didn't see me. When I woke up, the bumper was against my knees and I was being pushed across the sand. Somehow I managed to get out of that jam without being hurt. How is that for luck?

Love,
Leland

Dearest Letty

Desert Maneuvers
Sept. 29, 1942

My Dearest Letty:

I don't know what the day is, but I think it is Friday. It should give you an idea of how we live. Holidays, Sundays and birthdays go by, and we never notice them. The only days that have any special meaning are those on which we are due to get letters. So you can have some idea of how important your letters can be to a desert rat.

Since you are the only gal in the whole country who writes to me you can see that my special days are pretty far apart.

Have just finished your letter and a quart (yes, I said a quart) of ice cream. Now, please don't accuse me of being a glutton. We had been out on a problem and have lived on Army field rations for a week, so a quart of ice cream is not as unreasonable as it sounds. At that, I enjoyed the letter even more than the cream.

Wish I could serve you a dinner or breakfast from these field rations. So far, we have tried the A, B, C and K rations. I would like to feed you on the K rations, that is, if you are not so old that your teeth have failed you. In that case, you would have to skip them, for they are definitely not made for people with store-bought teeth.

The breakfast menu includes one small tin of concentrated orange juice, one can of mixed meat (It is so mixed that one can never guess what kind it is. It could be goat meat, mutton or horsemeat and you would not know the difference.) and enough powdered coffee for one cup. From here on, you need better teeth than I think you have.

Then there are eight malted milk tablets and four dextrose tablets, half a dozen pieces of hard candy and six blocks of an unidentified substance marked "Compressed Graham Biscuits." Believe me, they are compressed. At that, I guess they are a lot like the biscuits Mother used to make—that is, if you go back to the days when she was a little girl and made mud biscuits.

A K ration also includes six cigarettes and two sticks of chewing gum.

But the stuff must be pretty wholesome at that, for I have gained a couple of pounds since I came out here. That proves that my teeth are still a lot better than I believe yours to be.

The picture was wonderful. Remember when I used to call you Funny Face? (That line is from the "Chattanooga Choo Choo" but it

All's Fair

19

fits anyway.) Well, I'll take it all back now if you will tell me the secret of getting beautiful in your old age. I never thought you would grow to look like that.

You seem to think I just get in the way of jeeps so that I can go to the hospital. You are wrong as usual, and if you could see the desert hospitals we have, you would understand. There are no beautiful nurses out here. The only attendants are rusty-necked privates, and they are none too gentle while handling bruised muscles and lame shoulders.

I went to Los Angeles on a pass last week. Had a nice time, of course, since it was the first time I had seen a town in several weeks. The people in L.A. go out of their way to be nice to a soldier. I had supper in a private home both nights I was there, and I mean it was a wonderful feed. One evening they served Southern fried chicken and the next night we had Virginia-style baked ham.

We had free passes to the wrestling matches, visited the nightclubs without a cover charge, and did all the town on little money. But I really think I enjoyed the beds more than any other one thing on the whole trip. It was my one luxury since my buddy and I stayed in the best hotel in town. Of course, we had to send the bellboy out for a couple of rocks and a bucket of sand to put into the bed before we could go to sleep.

This letter is getting so long that Uncle Sam may not take it free, so I am going to have to stop somewhere.

Oh yes! I had intended to set you straight on your poor guessing since you were acting so innocent and naïve about the whole thing. The beautiful lady's name is —— (To Be Continued)

(Editor's Note: All good writing must contain the element of surprise. That is one of the cardinal rules. If the author cannot create it with his writing he simply writes, "To Be Continued" So—

Who is this mysterious lady whom the soldier is crazy about? Is the Desert Rat going to reveal her name? Be sure to read the next thrilling episode, which appears in the next issue.)

Love,
Leland

Dearest Letty

Desert Dreams
(Continued from Last Week)
SYNOPSIS

In the preceding chapters we learned that the Desert Rat (also known as The Sap) admitted that he was more than a little in love with a girl whose identity is as yet a mystery. The saucy young lady to whom the admission was made (Letty) tantalized the Desert Rat with absurd guesses and clever suggestions until, in the last chapter, he is on the point of revealing her name when his supply of paper is exhausted. Now, to continue the story.

The Sap chewed thoughtfully on the stem of a cold pipe and ran his fingers through what was left of his hair. His scalp was tight and gritty and he remembered that he had not had a shampoo since the last sandstorm. He remembered when that would have been unendurable, but now he didn't seem to mind. That, he told himself, was what the desert did to a man. And he wondered how he would fit into the pattern of civilization if he ever got back to it.

That brought him to the big question he was trying to decide. How did a man say the things he wanted to say? Did he have a right to say them at all? Here he was, a private in the Army, and the Army had a big job ahead of it that must be finished before he could think of doing anything else. What kind of a man would he be when it was over if he lasted that long? Would he be the person they expected to see when he came home?

He had seen other people who were away for a long time. When they returned they seemed more like intruders or visitors than individuals who had once been part of the life pattern. Of course, they were glad to see you when you came back, and they asked where you had been and what you had seen.

You told them about the marvelous color of the desert mountains and how the moon, when it was just clearing the crag, looked for a brief moment like a great snowball that was about to roll down the hill. Or you told them how the Spanish history of California still influenced the architecture. Or you explained how the people of Australia pronounced their A's as if they were I's so that when they said "day" it sounded as if they were saying "die."

But, in spite of all this, there was not quite room for your chair at the table. The reason was that when you went away they adjusted their lives a little so that they got along quite well without you. Usually, after a few hours or a few days, people readjusted their habits to make room for you. Then you were really home.

But he wondered if his old friends (and especially THE girl) could ever quite find room for a roughneck who didn't worry about the fact that there was sand in his ears, and he hadn't been under a shower in a week. . . .

Darn it, Letty, it's no use. Here I waste five pages of perfectly good paper trying to convince myself that I shouldn't say, "I'm crazy about you."

Now I've said it and I'm glad I did. But, of course, you had already guessed it. Clever girls are supposed to know when men are in love with them, even when the men first begin to try to work up the courage to say it.

Surely you can't object to a fellow being in love with you, even if he is a roughneck, so long as he is purely platonic about it and doesn't try to put you under any obligation. So no matter what happens, just remember that I LOVE YOU.

Leland

Desert Maneuvers
Oct. 6, 1942

My Dearest Letty:

I may have time to finish this before we move out, but we only have a few minutes. So please don't be disappointed when you have finished this, for it won't be much of a letter. If you wonder why it is so poor, do this:

Wait until it is dark, hunt for a big sand bed, cover a flashlight with green cellophane so that the light barely filters through, and you are ready to start. Now stretch flat on the sand, try to hold the light and paper while you write, and write fast, as if you had only a few minutes to finish the letter, and you will have a pretty good idea of how I am doing this. Believe me, it is no cinch.

Just had your letter. I mean the one where you were thanking me for the picture. No, I am not in it. In fact, it is not a picture of the 85th Reconnaissance, but our present camp is just where that picture was taken. That is, we are at Desert Center now.

We move many of the same kinds of vehicles you see in the picture, but our tents are different. Those are six-man tents and are high enough for a man to stand erect under. We use four-man tents. They are stretched flat and are about 2½ feet high so that we have to crawl into them.

You also wanted to know where we were. When this problem is over we will be at Blythe. We have covered a lot of the Mojave Desert. If you have a map of the state and can find the towns Needles, Rose, Rice, Parker (Arizona), Blythe, Fenner or Indio, you can know that we are in that part of the country somewhere. But we never stay in one place more than three or four days. I mailed the card from the Barclay Hotel in Los Angeles.

You also offered an apology for writing, but I say, "Thanks a million." No matter how often you write, it will not be often enough, for I am crazy about your letters (and you, too).

So you are picking cotton? How much can you pick?

How is the carnival? Wish I had been there to ride the merry-go-round with you. Who did? Now you can tell me that it is none of my affair who rode it with you, and you would be perfectly right. I was just curious, and maybe a little jealous, too.

I would love to take you to a carnival. We would try all the gyps just for the heck of it and take all the rides, but I doubt if I would get the old thrill from the ride itself. After a fellow has dived into the canyons and raced across the desert without lights, a roller coaster loses much of its thrill.

Love Always,
Leland

Desert Maneuvers
Oct. 12, 1942

My Dearest Letty:

Had your letter yesterday but didn't have time to even read it until last night. You can see that I was really working. It was raining and we had to hustle to keep our equipment from getting soaked. Then when it quit raining we had an order to pack up.

And was it cold last night! A lot of people who think it is always hot in the desert should try to stay warm with a couple of blankets spread on the wet ground after an October rain.

Guess we will be out here an extra thirty days after maneuvers are over. They say we will get a month of combat firing. If we stay, we will get six-man tents, like the ones in the picture you have. That will help a lot.

I'm still wondering who took you to the carnival and who your present heart throb is. Now don't give me that "continued" stuff. Of course, you have a perfect right to say that it is none of my affair.

Yes, I wish you would see our congressman about our mail service. We never get any mail while we are on a problem, and sometimes a problem lasts almost a week. When we pitch camp we are supposed to get our mail every day, but the service is not so good. I can't complain as long as the clerk brings your letters. I am a peaceful man, but if they stopped I might take the place apart. Am forced to close and start the battle.

Love Always,
Leland

Desert Maneuvers
Oct. 18, 1942

My Dearest Letty:

Your wonderful letter came yesterday. Can you imagine me being so busy that I didn't have time to answer it the minute it came? Believe it or not, I was.

Maneuvers are over, and they have stationed us here just four miles south of Needles, Calif. We have six-man tents similar to those in the pic-

Dearest Letty

ture I sent you. We were putting them up yesterday—that's why I was so busy—and it is no easy job for a guy who has never been with a circus or carnival. I don't believe the officers knew any more about it than we did. At any rate, we put them up and took them down until we almost wore them out before we got them up straight enough to suit the Old Man.

Wish you could see this place. It is in the heart of California's most beautiful natural scenery. All around us are walls of the most rugged and most beautiful mountains you ever saw. Since I read that, it seems that I overworked the adverb "most," but there is no other that I can think of. In speaking of them, you simply have to use superlatives. These are not the gentle, wooded mountains that we have back home. They are bare of all living trees or shrubs. The walls rise sheer for a hundred feet or more in a single cliff only to be topped by a higher cliff, and end in a jagged sawtooth silhouette. A few of the spires at the top are a hundred feet and sharp as a church tower.

And the picturesque names: Sawtooth Range, Turtle Mountain, Old Woman Mountain.

But why should I write of trees, mountains and rivers after the letter I had from you. Maybe it's because the letter made me see a new beauty in the mountains.

The Army chaplain is supposed to be a combination preacher and big brother to the men. The soldiers tell him their troubles. But when I got your letter I had no troubles, so I went over and let the chaplain tell me his troubles. Poor chap. You don't know how worried he was because some churches sang "Jesus, Hold My Hand" and other songs written in the past twenty years instead of the Fanny L. Crosby and John Wesley songs of a century or so ago. Even if I couldn't agree with him (I didn't argue and he thought I was agreeing) you should have seen the poor fellow's relief at being able to tell his troubles instead of listening to those of someone else.

But please don't think of me as "fine" or "noble." I am NOT and you will only be disappointed. Just remember that I am just a guy called Joe, as are a few million other guys. If you flatter me like that, I might even get delusions of grandeur and begin to think I was really important. You surely wouldn't want that to happen.

Too, your act of pretending you didn't know I was crazy about you was a good act but it fooled no one. You knew it all along. But remember,

All's Fair

I was more than a little surprised at your letter. I had not even hoped for a letter as wonderful as yours. I only wanted to love you silently until we get this mess over. Then, young lady, I will talk plenty fast. I am giving you a fair warning now so that you can have your mind made up.

Love Always,
Leland

P.S. I stumbled across a little poem recently and had intended to send you a copy in this letter. But it is too late to write it now so it will have to wait. The title is "Lost Valley" and there is a little valley down the river here where the author must have stood when he wrote it. Hope you like it when you get it. At any rate, it will give me an excuse to write you again in a couple of days. So don't be surprised if you get two or three letters a week from me if I find time to write.

Desert Maneuvers
Oct. 24, 1942

My Dearest Letty:

I am expecting a letter from you today or tomorrow. Guess I should wait until I get it before writing this. At least that is what Emily Post decrees. But why should I have to listen to Emily Post? After all, this is the only chance I ever get to talk to you.

I am even doing this in pencil. Hope you don't mind that either. I brought a full bottle of ink with me, but it is gone now and I haven't written that much either. Other guys helped me but most of it evaporated in this dry climate.

The purpose of this letter is to give you a copy of the poem "Lost Valley." As I wrote before, the guy who dreamed it up could have been nowhere except in a little valley about fifty miles down the river from here. The valley breaks away from the canyon of the Colorado River and could easily be "Lost Valley." Perhaps not more than a dozen people have seen it, but here is the poem, which describes it better than any prose could.

"Lost Valley"

I found it on a morning when the wings
Of songbirds rose with music in the sun—
A small green valley gemmed with mountain springs
And filled with sounds of brooks that through it run.
Its trees looked as if stars had nested there
With birds whose notes came forth in starry song
And fragrance of wild flowers filled the air,
And morning lingered long.
There from leaf shadows came a dappled fawn
To drink at that clear spring where I had stood;
A thrush shook dew upon me and was gone
On rapture, drifting through a singing wood.
Trout arched their sudden rainbows in the pools
And circles spread their silver at my feet—
Each time I think of it some magic cools
My throat, the air grows sweet.
I will not find my way to it again
But something of that valley still I keep.
I hear its music as I heard it then
Its fragrance sometimes lingers in my sleep.
It still is there—I have but lost the way
And not the valley that I wandered through
While I can feel it near, and while I may
Share some of it with you.

I hope you liked the little verse as much as I did. But you would like it more if you could see the place. Sometimes I think it should have begun:

I found it when the sun was like a lamp
Set out upon the windowsill of dawn—
And peopled by two thrushes and a fawn

All's Fair

27

There must have been some other wild folk there.

Whoever saw a fawn who dwelt alone?

Or two small birds that could monopolize

A hundred treetops

And three walls of stone.

Etc. etc.

And it could have ended by remarking on the strangeness of seeing war cars and battlewagons invading that peaceful garden. And with the hope that in such places a picture of peace could be retained so that people would not forget what it was like to know normal living. I think I like it better when it doesn't even mention war.

But this was supposed to be a letter and not a discussion of poetry. Will try to follow the formula more closely next time. Gosh! I hope I get a letter from you this afternoon.

Love Always,
Leland

Desert Maneuvers
Oct. 25, 1942

My Dearest Letty:

They say that when a guy starts writing a gal every day it is a sure sign he is in love. I wrote you yesterday, your letter came today, and here I am writing again. Go on, draw your own conclusions. Suppose the guy is in love. Who is to blame him?

Of course, all he can do about it now is to write letters that read like valentines, complete with pink ribbons and lace paper. But maybe it will not always be like that. A lot of men from this company are leaving on furlough today. They say we will all get a chance at them in the next few weeks or months. So if they don't change the order before my turn comes you may have to endure one of my visits sooner than you think. Now I am not sure I will get off. One never knows those things in the Army, and I should know better than to even make tentative plans. But I am hoping.

Just remember that the Bible says, "Blessed am de man who expects nothing for he shall not be disappointed," or maybe it was Shakespeare, or one of the Chinese philosophers who said that. Anyway, it applies to the Army.

One lesson in my recruit days was enough to teach me to expect nothing, and also not to volunteer for anything. It happened like this:

About a week after I came to the Army the sergeant had us in formation and called out, "I want six men who love good music." I had visions of a free ticket, so I was one of the first to step out. I was wondering what kind of a concert it was going to be when I noticed that he was picking out the huskiest and strongest-looking men from the group.

"Now," he said when he had picked us out, "you six men will carry the piano from the service club over to the day room." That finished my volunteering.

Have just had a pretty nice swim in the Colorado River. We came in about sundown. Of course, the water is a little cool. It fairly tumbles out of the Rockies, where it is plenty cold. The current is so swift that it is a lot of fun to swim downstream. But that was the only way we could swim.

By the way, I am writing this by candlelight. It is the only light we have out here, which goes to show you how primitive we really are out here. If you want to know how your great-grandmother lived, just ask me when I come home. I might also give you a couple of pointers on patching clothes the way she did it. I have a pair of trousers that I will have to patch when I finish this letter.

Love Always,
Leland

Desert Maneuvers
Oct. 31, 1942

My Dearest Letty:

Well, young lady, it develops that I waste paper when I write to you. Now don't go jumping at the conclusion that you are stopping my letters just because you are clever enough to guess what I am going to write, even before I write it. My letters are a lot more prescient than that.

Here is what I mean. Last week I wrote that I might get a furlough. It is sort of a warning, you understand, and I thought you would at least be surprised. But before you have time to get the letter you come back telling me: "A bird has been telling me that you may come home before long. I will save up a nice big stack of dishes and put you on K.P. as soon as you get here."

Now, I ask you, why should I write to a girl who already knows what is in my letters even while they are in the mail? It's a waste of good clean paper, but I go on doing it anyway.

Yes, I knew all along that I had no business talking like a February valentine. I even argued it to myself but it was no good. My reason was not that I was too young to know what I was saying. Rather, it was because a guy in the armored force cavalry has two strikes on him when he goes to bat. It simply isn't the sporting thing to do. I tried to be frank about it and make it clear that I was not even asking anything of you except all the letters you could find time to write.

We will let it go at that, but I refuse to take back anything I have said. I promise not to say it again, at least not until I know you better. The bugler has just blown "Lights Out," so this will have to wait until tomorrow.

"Sunday Morning"

Well, the Fifth Armored Division is a year old today. We have not been at it that long, but it was formed a year ago today. They are staging quite a celebration this afternoon. There is a track meet, a bunch of fire-cracker speeches and a pie-eating contest. Tonight, Kay Kayser and his Orchestra give us a show. That, at least, will be good. Wish you were here to help me listen to it.

Lazy girl. You won't even get up and get another blanket when you get cold at night. I can see why you want me to help wash your dishes. When a chap gets cold here, it's not quite so simple as that. Last night my feet were like ice, but there was nothing to do but wait for the sun to come up. We have two blankets and a shelter half. These have to serve as both bed and cover. It gets pretty cold at night.

Making a bed here is quite an art. The first step is to spread the shelter-half flat on the ground. Next, a blanket is folded lengthwise and placed in the middle of the shelter-half. The last blanket is spread over

Dearest Letty

the folded one and tucked under. Then the edges of the shelter-half are brought together over the whole bedroll and laced with a tent rope. To get into bed, we simply lift one fold of the bottom blanket and, starting at the head, work our feet into the roll. When morning comes, we crawl out like a butterfly coming out of its cocoon. If it gets cold, there is no way we can remedy the situation, for we have only the two blankets.

Now, young lady, I have one more little secret and I dare you to guess it. Of course, it may never develop, but I am trying to keep it under cover until I am sure of it. So go ahead and if you guess it, I give up.

Love Always,
Leland

Desert Maneuvers
Nov. 7, 1942

My Dearest Letty:

If this letter doesn't come up to my usual standards, please try to remember that it is created under difficult conditions. This is not exactly the environment a guy would choose to write to a gal who goes to church regularly and is embarrassed when her dog Skipper goes with her to the young people's meeting.

Here is why I am having trouble writing this. The old candle is sputtering and dancing so that at times I can hardly see whether the pen is feeding or not. In fact, it is not even a candle. We had candles for a time, but they are all gone now. All that we have now is the leftover tallow. We have melted this and poured it into an inkbottle. It is not much of a light.

On the other side of the light, the boys are having a blackjack game. Don't know what blackjack is, do you? Well, don't take time to learn. It is an old Army game. It costs some of the boys a lot of money. Personally, it bothers me only because it is such a noisy game. Seems to require a lot of loud talk, which makes it difficult to write. Behind me the radio is going full blast on the Grand Ole Opry.

By the time you get around to answering this I guess I will be back in Camp Cooke. We are supposed to start back on the 16th. Most of the boys are excited over the prospect of getting back into camp. Personally, it makes little difference to me where I am. Of course, the warm showers and heated barracks will be nice. Have just had a nice cold swim in the river. I will miss the swims.

Probably you will wonder if the water is as cold here as it is back there. Well, it is plenty cold. I was swimming down the river and came alongside a catfish whose tail was frozen so stiff he couldn't swim. His teeth were chattering so much that he seemed to have St. Vitus Dance, so I didn't pick him up.

How many times do I have to tell you that fine, heroic and noble stuff is out in this man's war? Don't waste your radio battery listening for me or anyone else to become a hero. That stuff is for home consumption. This is just a grim dirty job where the guy with the most skill and the most luck will live the longest. Mostly, it is a matter of luck.

Hope I can write a better epistle next time.

Love Always,
Leland

Desert Maneuvers
Nov. 15, 1942

My Dearest Letty:

Do you mind if I keep the first few paragraphs of this letter perfectly serious and on the level?

Please, please forgive me if I hurt or puzzled you. That is the disadvantage of having to write instead of talk. In writing one cannot insert a smile or a lift of the eyebrow to show when he is only kidding. That is hard to remember.

But, honest, I was only kidding. In the Army we get a habit of pretending that we are skimming lightly over the serious things. It is the only way to retain our equilibrium. It is a standard Army joke to pretend that we don't think we are getting an even break when all the time we know that we are getting the best of it by far. We get the best food available, our uniform is better than any other in the world, and our pay is the highest. We get the best equipment they know how to make and the tops in entertainment. The people back home treat us as if we were the world's noblest creatures.

How does this concern you? I am trying to explain the mental attitude we drop into that makes us kid about serious things. It remained for you to hit upon the happy solution. The paragraph where you agree to be my "best girl" seems to solve the whole problem. It is much more than I asked and a lot better than I had dared to hope. From this end of the line you are my only girl. I hope this makes things clear. Now am I free to go on with this letter?

You must be an uncanny character indeed. How do you manage to learn so much? Such as, for example, my last name, that I am the oldest boy, and that Dad is a swell guy.

It must have been him that you saw in town. He is rather stout (weighs about 200), red complected, light-brown hair that is slightly graying. And he talks a lot.

Guess I might as well break down and confess my age. You keep hounding me about it. I was born June 19, 1911. Figure it out for yourself if you are not too rusty in your mathematics. But I may be sticking my neck out in letting you in on it. You may lose all interest when you have figured it out. But it is a chance I had to take sometime. Now, confess yours to even the score. Don't try to pull a fast one about being 18. It won't work.

You wanted to know what I had been reading. Frankly, there is little to read. We get a few books, and I have found *The Moon Is Down* (John Steinbeck) and *Lost Horizon* (James Hilton) to be pretty good. They were expendables by an officer who was on Bataan Peninsula. One of the best books I have read was an anthology of poetry collected by Louis Untermeyer. A sergeant in Headquarters Co. loaned it to me. But he went to O.C.S. (Officers Candidate School) and I can't get any more books from that source.

I also got a good little booklet from an interesting gentleman back in the Ozarks. You see, he is a retired Texas schoolteacher who publishes a small paper of Ozark poetry called *The War Eagle Clarion*. He used one of my verses in the *Clarion* and sent me a copy of "Echoes." I am enclosing a copy of his letter. May send the verse along later if you care to see it.

I'd better go to bed now. How else can I dream of you?

Love,
Leland

Camp Cooke, Calif.
Nov. 26, 1942

My Dearest Letty:

Had two letters from you when we got back from the desert Tuesday. Did they make me happy! Some of my mail had been forwarded to Needles, but yours had stayed here, so I was wondering if you had forgotten to write. Funny how a chap can imagine all sorts of things even when he knows different.

Your cookies came yesterday. I have never appreciated anything quite so much. I must confess that I was a little surprised to learn that you could cook, too, in addition to your other qualities.

I was not the only one who enjoyed your cookies. When a fellow gets a package that looks like home-cooked food, all the men in the barracks swarm around to see what is in it. My package was no exception so they all sampled the cakes and made all sorts of complimentary remarks. Then they wanted to know who made them, and I showed them your picture. (Hope you didn't mind, but I was so darn proud of it that I couldn't resist.) One chap said, "If I had a girl who looked like that and could make cookies like these I would marry her in a minute." Another guy chimed in "Why the heck would you fool around and waste so much time?" So you see, you are quite a sensation here at Camp Cooke, even if you never saw the place.

Had a nice trip coming back from the desert. It was more than 400 miles, so we used a couple of days on the road. People in all the little towns turned out to watch us go by, and they showed that everyone is behind us. Air-raid wardens in little tin hats stood at corners and halted the traffic. Most of them were dignified gentlemen with clipped moustaches who looked as if they had seen service in the First World War. I was car commander so I had a chance to stand up and see what was going on. The other guys had to sit down so they missed some of it.

The wardens saluted me as they did the officers who commanded most of the other cars and gave us all a big smile. Rank made no difference to them. They were all doing their part to get the whole mess over. Their job is as much a part of this chain as is the job of General MacArthur.

But this is not supposed to be an analysis of the war.

Yes, I must confess that it was good to get back into hot showers and clean beds. We came in about six o'clock and I rushed to the shower cabinet and missed chow because the hot water felt so good.

34   *Dearest Letty*

The bed was the crowning feature. The clean sheets were so smooth that I felt as if I might fall out of the bed. I am not kidding. I hardly knew how to sleep in a bed. There are some things I miss from the desert. Nowhere else in the world can you find sunrises and sunsets with such gorgeous variety of color. There is no use trying to describe it to you. Wish I could show it to you sometime. There are so many pictures of little towns that offer everything from mountain climbing to swimming. Of course, we had little chance to do either last summer as we had other work to do. But I did swim until we left, when we went down to the river to wash the cars. I filed it all away in my memory for future use.

It is time for the lights to go out so I must say I love you and good night.

Leland

Camp Cooke, Calif.
Dec. 2, 1942

My Dearest Letty:

Surprised? I know I could surprise you once, even if it was only by writing when you didn't expect it. Really though, I do owe you a letter. I had two when we came up from the desert and I have only written you once. So I am only paying my honest debts.

By the time you read this you will probably have missed the only opportunity you will ever have to hear me on the radio. If you should have accidentally tuned in Kay Kayser tomorrow night you will have heard me. Of course, you won't recognize me even if you happen to hear the program. I will be sitting in the balcony (192 feet from the mike) and will be one of the 6,285 guys who yell "Hi, Kay" when the show starts. I will also do a bit of cheering when Judy Conway sings, but it will be even harder to recognize my handclaps among the 12,570 other hands. But I'll be there.

Saw a long list of the boys who were to be inducted into the Army and Navy from home. I know a lot of them, of course, and some were good friends of mine. Wish I could get into a company with some of them. It would be a lot of fun to see them go through their rookie hazing. Some of them will be plenty serious for a few days. Pete Burris, who is an old fishing pal of mine, would provide plenty of comedy. I could even wish to be a corporal just to give him his recruit drill.

I guess every guy who ever went to the Army got sore at the officers or non-coms at one time or another. But I thought I had it all figured out. I even bragged that I had a shell and a temper like a terrapin and nothing they could do would get under my skin. But I had to confess that they got me a couple of times.

A corporal did it effectively. He lived in a private room at the end of the barracks. It was a Friday night and we were cleaning house to be ready for inspection. Just as we finished he called me and another goof into his room.

"Here," he said, "clean up my room. I'm going to town."

I thought then that a corporal held the power of life and death so I couldn't say anything. But I didn't clean the room.

Hope all this personal piffle hasn't been tiring, but it was all I had

Dearest Letty

on tap at the moment and I simply had to write you. I couldn't content myself with a dream.

Love Always,
Leland

Camp Cooke, Calif.
Dec. 7, 1942

Dearest Letty,

Had your letter last night. I had written you twice since we came back to camp, but I guess the letters hadn't had time to reach you. I must make a confession. I was a little bit glad things were slow, because I learned that you really did enjoy getting my letters. That, young lady, is a lot more important than you think.

Of course, I was sure of that, but now I am positive and the result was that I walked around all day with my head in the few clouds we have around here.

Well, I didn't get the furlough. I wanted to leave here with the bunch that leaves the 14th. It would have been so nice to be home Christmas, and you don't know how much I wanted to see you. A lot of other guys wanted the same furlough so I, being a lowly private, was simply included out. Guess I will get into one of the January groups.

But I am sending a spy in to see how you are behaving. You had better be careful. Loyd is on the list, so be careful of your behavior or he might report you. Drittler will probably be there, too. I don't know for sure as I haven't talked to him since we came from the desert, but I am afraid he won't be any good as a spy anyway. In fact, I would hardly trust him on a mission of that kind.

Had an alert the other night so I missed my sleep. Alerts are pretty common occurrences, but that one cost us a whole night of sleep.

The story got out that a convoy of [Japanese] ships was heading this way. We mounted the guns and waited. But it was all a mistake. What bothered us was that we had postponed our breakfast. In waiting for air raids you don't huddle in crowds. We had to eat in groups of five. My crew ate at eleven and I followed them down at 11:15. But I had beaten

All's Fair

other cars on one point. We had moved out of camp, of course, and I had a can of coffee in my field bag and our crew at least had coffee.

It is time for the lights to go out.

Love Always,
Leland

Camp Cooke, Calif.
Dec. 9, 1942

Dearest Letty:

Am I lucky? Had another letter from you today, which is a lot better than I dared hope and much more than I deserve. As long as I get them regularly you have a happy private on your hands—and I do mean private.

Funny, you never seem the least disappointed when I remain a private month after month. I sometimes wonder if you don't think: "What's wrong with the guy? Hasn't he any ambition or ability?"

Guess you might be right if you did wonder. It looks like they are going to have to create a special prefix for my name. They have a rating PFC for Private First Class, but they would have to call my rating PFE, meaning Private Forever.

I didn't get my furlough, as you know if you have my last letter. I wanted to be there for Christmas. Then there is always the chance that we will be in Australia or Morocco by next month. That is the way things go in the Army. One never knows where he will be in a couple of months. It should teach a chap to never make plans.

But it has a special appeal to a lot of us. There is a lot of fun in living from day to day and letting the future take care of itself. It saves the mental effort of trying to live by a pattern, which is nice for a lazy man.

Have been trying to figure out a way to visit my brothers who are at San Diego. They are about 350 miles from me. They are allowed to take three-day passes but are not allowed to go more than 150 miles from their base. I cannot get a pass. They give us a few six-hour passes, which gives us only a short time in the nearest towns (Lompoc and Santa Maria). There are a few overnight passes, but they usually go to the guys who are married and whose wives live in town. Haven't seen the boys since they were inducted last February.

Love Always,
Leland

Camp Cooke, Calif.
Dec. 14, 1942

Dearest Letty,

Hope you don't mind my writing you every time I have a few spare minutes. And I have some time today. I probably owe you a letter anyway, but I haven't had my mail in a couple of days.

Now get ready to laugh. I AM IN THE HOSPITAL AGAIN. Go ahead, laugh!

It is not serious. Only influenza. But I expect you to have different ideas. You could easily say I was goldbricking. Well, maybe I am now, for I could easily work today. But they won't let a guy out just because he says he could go back to duty. There are some pitiable cases here, and some comical ones. One guy who sleeps next to me is an odd chap. There seems to be nothing wrong that causes him any pain, but he just lies and stares at the ceiling all the time and twists a handkerchief in his hands. Always the same handkerchief, and it is shreds now. Sometimes he cries a little but he never talks to anyone.

Our night nurse is one of those breezy characters who have a joke and a clever answer for everyone, but this guy has her puzzled. She can think of no way to cheer him in the least. By the way, the nurse read the poem you sent, the one about Army nurses.

A few of the boys left for home yesterday. Loyd was on the list, and I guess he will be home before you get this letter. Of course, I don't know that he, or any of the boys, got away. One is never sure in the Army. He asked me what I wanted to tell you. I told him to just say I would be home when I get a chance.

They have a pretty nice library here at the Red Cross building, which is quite near my ward. I have been reading more than a book a day besides the papers (I get two, sometimes three papers a day). Have found some good books. If you get a chance to read *I Was a Share-Cropper* by Harry Harrison Kroll, don't miss it. It is one of the greatest books that ever came out of the South. It is an autobiography and most of them are dull, but this one reads like a novel. It could be the biography of a million people except that they never achieved the second phase of the life from which Kroll looks back and analyzes the first phase. The book is so realistic it makes one homesick.

I had better stop this letter before I start writing a book review. The mail will leave in just three minutes so I must get an envelope addressed.

Love Always,
Leland

Camp Cooke, Calif.
Dec. 20, 1942

Dearest Letty:

Hope you won't become bored by my writing so often, but I am wondering just what is happening. Haven't had a letter from you in more than a week, so I am wondering if someone has kidnapped you.

I am still in the hospital, even though I am perfectly healthy now. Don't know why they keep all of us healthy guys here. I asked the lieutenant if they kept us around to do the work, and he only smiled. Gossip has it that they are trying to get all the wards full so the brass will assign more nurses to the hospital.

We do have a lot of fun. I sleep between a former circus clown and a Montana horse wrangler. The clown was billed with Ringling Bros. as the tallest and funniest in the business, and Montana is so bowlegged from riding horses you could sail a ten-gallon hat between his knees without touching them.

In the corner is a tall serious-minded chap from Texas (called "Tex" of course). Montana likes to tell glowing stories of the horse roundup and how they killed colts for meat. Texas swears he wouldn't touch a bite of horsemeat for the world. Then, of course, when they serve us a dry lean roast Montana and I start discussing corned-willie roasts, corned willie being Army slang for horsemeat, and Tex misses his dinner. Sometimes I

Dearest Letty

am not sure that I am eating beef. But in the Army it is never safe to inquire too closely into what one is eating.

We have a good library and I read a book and three newspapers every day, which gives me a pretty full day. There is a show every night. Altogether, they make things pretty pleasant.

Hope my little attempt to say Merry Christmas has reached you by now. Perhaps I should apologize. The gift is not appropriate. I only hope you will bear in mind that my choices were limited. I could only select from what they had at the P.X., which was not much. They had some jewelry, but my taste is so poor that I wouldn't trust myself. So I am afraid you will have to imagine the spirit of the thing.

Love,
Leland

Camp Cooke, Calif.
Dec. 30, 1942

Dearest Letty:

Just got out of the hospital and was grateful when I found your three letters. They were wonderful. Don't know how I manage to enjoy each successive letter I get from you more than I enjoyed the preceding letter, but I do.

Loyd is here. (He is my spy, you know.) But I haven't had a chance to check up with him yet. He was on KP today, which eliminates the opportunity to talk. But I will see him tomorrow. Perhaps I should have waited until then to write this. Then I could have used the information he gave me to incriminate you. But there must always be material for another letter, so don't be surprised if I write again tomorrow.

No, I am still not sure when (or if) I will get a furlough. It is an old Army custom to hold all information from a private.

But why, I ask, shouldn't I tell you the minute I learn whether I am getting to come home. After all, I expect to see you as soon as possible after I get there.

Which reminds me that you wondered about my brothers. Here is the list:

Ardis is 26 years old, 6 ft. 3 in. high, weighs about 200 and is a bit shy of girls. He is in San Diego with the Coast Artillery.

Harold is at home. He is 24, 6 ft. high and weighs 170. He is also a shade bashful. But they both manage to get by without the girls learning how shy they really are.

Aaron is 22. He is the one who is married. He is my height, 5 ft. 11 in., and weighs 170. He was known as The Babe in baseball. Possibly you have seen him, as he was around quite a bit. But family history must be a bore so I must close.

Love,
Leland

Camp Cooke, Calif.
Jan. 1, 1943

Dearest Letty:

I do it almost every day now: Write you. Another letter from you just drifted in, the one with your picture. Of course, I was agreeably surprised. It was a wonderful picture. Say, I never quite realized just how beautiful . . . but there I go. It just tries to say itself. Anyway, thanks a million.

By the way, you wanted a copy of our Thanksgiving-dinner menu. But I neglected to send it until I forgot what we had. But I promise to do better with the Christmas dinner menu. I will send a copy as soon as I find time to go to the postoffice and get some stamps. It is a small booklet and I cannot mail it in the free class.

Had a pretty nice dinner today, too. The main course was goose. Getting the neck seems to prove that I am not a good hustler, for they had me working in the dining room today and I should have hustled a better serving.

Imagine spending New Year's Day as a dining-room orderly. I am on tomorrow for table waiter, which is only a part-time job, but I will have to make the eighteen-mile march with the boys in addition to waiting on tables. I suppose I will be on KP Sunday, all of which should help me get the new year off to a flying start.

How many times do I have to straighten you out on Euless? She is a good friend of mine, but . . . I haven't had a date with her in almost two years. So why should I keep on telling you? Oh, what's the use?

If you don't quit torturing me I will have to use my information I just had from my spy and, boy, is it good. Imagine a girl who is so mean to her poor dog that she won't even let the little chap go to church. But that is not what he tells me. His story is even more sinister.

Speaking of dogs, I have just learned that my old dog is dead.

I must get some sleep, as I have 18 long miles ahead of me tomorrow.

Love,
Leland

Camp Cooke, Calif.
Jan. 3, 1943

Dearest Letty:

It seems a little strange that I am able to write today. You see, we did 20 miles on the road yesterday and it is a wonder that I am not in the hospital again, or in bed at least. I said we were on the road but, in fact, we were going cross-country most of the time through purple sage and deep sand, which made the going pretty tough.

I had some doubt about being able to do 20 miles, for I was pretty soft. One is not supposed to train for those hikes at a checkerboard or by sitting in a library reading room dressed in a corduroy robe and reading Huxley. And that was the training I had been taking for the past three weeks. But I managed to come in under my own power, which was more than some of the guys could do. They had to send a car back for the stragglers. But we had a lot of fun. There were plenty of blisters and aching feet (howling dogs to the Army), but most of the boys are able to be around today.

I am having plenty of trouble writing coherently. You see, I am sitting at a table with a lieutenant, a sergeant and a couple of privates who are discussing their ancestry, their fights and their former jobs. It is quite an uproar. Sometimes the argument gets pretty violent. One of the boys is from Florida, one from Michigan and one from Washington while the lieutenant is from New York. Now the discussion has turned to marriage and they have all sorts of theories.

Monday night

I finally had to give up last night and join the argument. It was too much temptation, so I am finishing tonight.

Just had your letter saying you had received the belated Christmas gift, if it could be called that. So glad you liked it. Think I explained that I was in the hospital and my choices were limited. They had a small stock, and it cramped a fellow's Christmas shopping.

We were on a combat problem today. We went out at 1:30 this morning and finished at 9 o'clock tonight, which is a pretty nice day's work. We will have to do the same thing tomorrow.

The problem is combat firing of all the guns in such a way that the bullets and shells fall pretty close to us. The idea is to make us accustomed to the sound of bullets passing over and around us. Must sign off for now as it is getting late and the lights will go out before long.

Love,
Leland

Camp Cooke, Calif.

Jan. 8, 1943

Dearest Letty:

Don't have the faintest idea what I am going to write since absolutely nothing has happened that would interest you. But I didn't write last night and your letter came today.

Anyway, when I finish work and the lights go out in the barracks (nine o'clock) I find myself with my case of stationery under my arm on the way to the day room. I keep telling myself that too many letters might prove boring and that I am taking that chance. But I always write something. Now you figure it out.

So you are trying to find out who writes to me? You said you kept writing and when you learned that I got eight other letters besides yours you were puzzled. What is puzzling about the fact that I know eight people who can write (in addition to the ones I know who can't write)? In fact, I carry on a steady correspondence with about 15 or 20 people in addition to spasmodic letters to a couple of dozen others. I'll give you a complete list when I come home. To prove that I'm on the beam as a letter writer, I may let you censor some sample letters.

Dearest Letty

We had a Christmas tree at the Red Cross building at the hospital. We set up a small tree in the ward, a miniature beauty. We took up a collection and bought silver bars for the doctor, gold bars for the nurses, and cigarettes for the ward men. Must close for now as I have some more writing to do.

Love,
Leland

Camp Cooke, Calif.
Jan. 12, 1943

Dearest Letty:

I am plenty mad tonight, but there is no one individual to be sore at. If there was someone a fellow could pick out and feel sore, possibly poke him in the eye, it might relieve the pressure, but as it is I have to work off the steam by writing to you. I don't suppose you like being used like that but I have to tell you anyway.

My furlough has been postponed again. I had hoped to be on the train by this time. I didn't learn until this afternoon that I wouldn't be seeing you this weekend. A tie-up developed in the railroads and that's that. Now I don't know when I'll be able to get away. I have paid for my ticket and can't get it. Neither can I get a refund.

Don't dare go out and get a job just yet. Maybe I'm being selfish but I'm asking you to please wait a little while. My visit home would be a little empty if I was carrying a telegram from you saying you had gone to Galveston or some other place to work. Perhaps you were only kidding when you said you were thinking of going job hunting.

I should have closed this long ago. It couldn't interest you to learn why my furlough was delayed. I should have simply said, "Furlough delayed. See you when I can." But I had to tell my troubles to someone. I feel better now. My delay seems unimportant now, so you have done your good deed for the day by reading this and helping get my blood pressure down. I will go to bed.

Love Always,
Leland

Moreland, Ark.
Jan. 19, 1943

Dearest Letty

Hold everything. If circumstances will permit, will try to be up there just after noon Wednesday. Circumstances will have to be plenty tough to stop me.

Love,
Leland

Moreland, Ark.
Jan. 24, 1943

Dearest Letty:

I only hope you were not as disappointed last night as I was. That is, I hope you were not quite as bad as I was. But maybe you don't know what it is all about yet. In case Earlene hasn't told you, here is the story.

I saw her in town yesterday and we made tentative plans for a little party last night. A friend of mine from Little Rock was in town and he was to round out the foursome. He is a nice chap in spite of the fact that he is one of my numerous cousins. After he finished business college he kicked around the country quite a bit and has a pretty interesting background. He still retains a slow, pleasant Southern drawl that a trip to Spokane failed to destroy. I am sure she would have liked him.

But the tires and gas beat us. He was sure his brother's car was in good condition but he had no gas. The car that is here in the yard had a full gas tank but only three tires. We hoped a siphon hose would solve the problem, but it was not as simple as that. He found that one of the tires on his brother's car had expired and he had only three. So there we sat with a Plymouth and three 16-inch tires, a Chevrolet and three 17-inch tires, and one tank of gas. We tried to work out a combination that would work, but it was no good. Chevrolet and Plymouth wheels simply aren't interchangeable. I only hope we will have better luck when we try again. You can tell her he was almost as disappointed as I was and that is saying a lot.

The cousins, uncles, etc., have dropped in today and the place is a maelstrom. There is absolutely no chance to get away. May have a chance to see you again before I leave Tuesday. When you get this, I will be in Little Rock so there was really no point in telling you that I would see you again if I had a chance. You knew that anyway.

Love Always,
Leland

Moreland, Ark.
Jan. 25, 1943

Dearest Letty:

It has been twenty-four hours since I wrote you, and a day can be such a long time. Three days can be an age, for it has been that long since I saw you. But that was not what I intended to say when I started this little note.

Gosh, it's cold tonight and snowing, too. I wonder how I will be able to get to town tomorrow, but I'll be there if I have to walk. The chances are I won't have to walk even if the bus doesn't run. We have bus service every day except Tuesday and that is the day I will need it. Our taxi service, too, is poor. There is only one car in this whole village that will run and can be hired by me. I am hoping it will run tomorrow.

This car belongs to a special friend and he will take me anywhere he can. In fact, he has been driving me around all day. I had a number of obligation visits to make so I finished as many of them as I could. Of course, I didn't get to all of the places I wanted to go, but it is always like that when one is on a short visit.

You may wonder why it is so important that I get back on time. If you remember, I promised to make private first class for you, and I couldn't do it if I were late. But the promise still stands. I'll go to work when I get to camp and I might even make corporal. But corporal is little to offer a girl who should marry a captain, or at least a lieutenant.

Love Always,
Leland

Little Rock, Ark.
Jan. 27, 1943

Dearest Letty

Ten minutes to train time, which is plenty long enough for me to say I'm still crazy about you.

Leland

Camp Cooke, Calif.
Jan. 31, 1943

Dearest Letty:

Had your letter today just as I was preparing to write you, and it was the most wonderful letter I ever had. All of which goes to prove that I won at least one argument from you, even if I should lose them to you for the rest of my life. I can afford to lose some of the others, if you will only let me gloat a little over winning this one.

Do you remember some time ago when I wrote, quite impersonally, that I was crazy about you? You said, "Oh no, big boy, you don't know what you're saying." Now you have confessed that I did.

But I wonder if I should not have kept it a secret. You know why and I can't help thinking that it was not quite fair to you. Now that you know how I feel there is no use discussing the fairness of it any more. The damage is done.

Had a nice trip coming back. Got into Los Angeles Friday night, but since I didn't have to come to camp until Saturday I stayed there.

Guess I'm crazy to keep sending you all the foolish little things like a café menu or a felt pennant from Juarez. We stopped for a little while and I rushed out to buy something to help you remember that I had passed through here. (Juarez is just across the border.) Then I wanted to eat at the Fred Harvey. It is one of those places with an atmosphere. Before they could get around to me the conductor yelled "Board" and all I got was the menu.

But it was a clever menu and I wanted you to see the kind of stripe I would have on my arm when I made a good private. I'll start working on the job tomorrow. So long as I have a girl who deserves a captain the least I can do is to be a good private for her sake.

The little shoes I am including were my selection from the "Art" of the Yumanian Indian. The Yumanian tribe is around Yuma, Ariz., and has the reputation of being the laziest people on earth. Don't know how they manage to do the beadwork on items like this. Maybe they don't. But the old fat woman sits around the station and sells this sort of stuff to gullible travelers. They may buy it from F. W. Woolworth or Kress. I wouldn't know the difference.

You never pass there and find fewer than half a dozen old women sitting flat on the ground with their feet straight out in front of them. Try sitting that way for an hour sometime and you will wonder how they do it all day. On a blanket beside them are a variety of beadwork and that sort of stuff. There is a price card by each group, and the women never say a word. I have tried a couple of times to induce them to talk but have never been able to get one word out of them.

I might as well try to break the news as gently as possible. Brace yourself and remember that this hurts me more than it does you.

A few weeks ago I was quite sure I was in love with you and I recklessly confessed. Events have changed all that and I hope you will forgive me if I caused you any pain. Now I am *very* positive.

Love,
Leland

Camp Cooke, Calif.
Feb. 3, 1943

My Dearest Letty:

Well, here I go again, hoping to find something just a little interesting to write. Now, a guy with any ability to reason things out would say: "Why the heck don't you wait about writing until something has had time to happen?"

That, of course, would be logical, but who wants to be logical? All I want to do is sit around and write letters to you that are all lavender and old lace, and at my age I should know better.

Say, I wish you could see a part of the road between here and Los Angeles. When I see a beautiful bit of landscape I suddenly wish I could see it with you. It would be no use. If you were here I'd probably spend my time looking at you rather than at the seawall or the mountains.

As I was saying, there is a nice strip of road just down the coast. The railroad and highway run along the coast almost all the way, but the most striking part of the road is just below Santa Barbara. From Santa Barbara to Ventura the roads are atop a seawall almost all the way. The waves roll in tirelessly, crashing against the wall and flying up in a cold, salty spray. It is an endless battle and apparently the wall wins every contest. But one cannot help thinking that the wall is constantly being worn away, a chip of stone here, a grain of sand there, and one day the waves will win and the wall will have to be rebuilt or the railroad and highway will crash into the sea.

All along the rail at the top of the wall, the gulls sit and preen their feathers. There are thousands of them and they are gentle. They sit in a row, spaced with such mathematical precision that one wonders how they manage to know how many feet and inches they are from their neighbor. But they seem to know, for they never seem to change the distance. They are so gentle that they never seem to see the cars that almost brush them from their perches. Even halted cars fail to draw their attention. Once we stopped and they allowed us to almost touch them before they would move.

On the opposite side of the road the mountain rises so sheer that one cannot see the top from a train window in some places. But for all its grandeur, it is not quite so beautiful as Crow Mountain. No place is that nice, even if you do seem to get a little bored with living there.

Love Always,
Leland

Camp Cooke, Calif.
Feb. 5, 1943

My Dearest Letty:

By this time you have learned to expect a letter from me every time the mailman goes by. But the heck of it is I have no way of knowing whether you are pleased or not. It may be that my letters are spoiling whatever chance I ever had with you.

What I am trying to say is I have had only one letter from you since I came back to camp and all my later writing may be wasted. I have written no less than ten letters, which is a lot of paper. Please tell me if I am writing too much and I will write only every other day.

They tell me I will start teaching some kind of school next week, but I have been unable to find out what it is. I hope they tell me in time for me to get something organized. In fact, I don't even know if I will be able to handle the job, for I can't find out what I am supposed to teach.

Guess you wonder why I keep writing in pencil. I lost my fountain pen and they have none at this P.X. When I get time I will try to get a new one and go back to ink. Will try to tell you something more interesting next time I write. Meanwhile, just remember that I LOVE YOU.

Leland

Camp Cooke, Calif.
Feb. 7, 1943

My Dearest Letty:

Had your good letter yesterday and, incidentally, yesterday was the first day I had failed to write you since I came back to camp. Sometimes I wonder if I can possibly interest you with letters every day. All I want to do, when I have time, is write to you and think how wonderful you are. And wonder how I, of all people, could have been so lucky.

You write of the pillow and those things and say I am thoughtful, but I hardly remember what the pillow was like. I shall always remember that it was a beautiful frame for the soft picture of your head against it. And I shall always remember how you looked when you smiled from against the silk of it. That is the picture I shall always carry.

You have, by making me love you, disturbed my even, lazy pattern of living, and I suddenly find myself ambitious and even egotistical for the first time in my life. It takes hard work to try to live up to the things you expect of me. And there would be no fun in achieving things if I didn't tell you about it. So please try not to condemn me for telling you the things I am doing. I am only trying to justify your faith in me.

Believe it or not, I am working. We have classes after supper for non-commissioned officers and officers of the 85th Recon. Bn. At the last test last Friday night, I turned in the only 100% paper in A Co. The test dealt with message writing and communication, and some of the boys had a little trouble. The communication sergeant scored 49%. See how you have made me go to work?

I will start teaching a school tomorrow. It is a division school and I don't know how well I will make out. I do know there will be plenty of paperwork. I may not have time to write as often as I have been writing. That is why I failed to write yesterday. They gave me a whole bale of papers concerning the school and I am supposed to be familiar with them by Monday. I still have a lot of work to do on them. This, in addition to the night classes I attend, will give me little time to write.

Love Always,
Leland

Camp Cooke, Calif.
Feb. 8, 1943

My Dearest Letty:

It has been so long since I wrote you that you must wonder if I have forgotten you. In fact, it has been almost twenty-three hours and thirty minutes since I sat at this desk, but, if you will believe me, I have thought of you many times. Such silly thoughts, too.

"Soldier," I said, "she's much too beautiful and pure for you," or "quit dreaming because those dreams are for teenage youngsters with stars in their eyes. You are supposed to be old enough to be a realist." But the dreams simply refused to stop.

The most disturbing thought of all was, "You are giving her such a tough break. She should never have been permitted to fall in love with you in the first place."

Maybe all this is a bit absurd, but I do think those things. I hope you can believe me now when I say I have been more than a little in love with you longer than you could guess. But sometimes I think I should have waited and not mentioned it until all this was over. Or I should have been more inquisitive some years ago. If I had just exercised a bit of self-restraint when I was in Santa Barbara you would not have been—But what's the use? I was quite sure I was in love with you then. But time has changed all that. I am positive now, and if you choose to follow the brave and waiting road there is nothing for me to do but congratulate myself.

Dearest Letty

I started my school today. There are about six chaplains and as many enlisted men on the teaching staff, with a major in charge. The student body consists of two Chinese, sixty Mexicans and about a hundred natives. The Mexicans and Chinese speak poor English and have a lot of trouble reading or writing. The others had little or no formal school.

I believe this would have been a good idea if they had started it last spring, when we had a year to work. But now the time is so short that by the time we get them classified and organized, we will have to move out and our effort will be wasted.

Love Always,
Leland

Camp Cooke, Calif.
Feb. 9, 1943

My Dearest Letty:

I guess you have begun to wonder if I ever do anything but write to you. Well, I do, but you could be arrested for sabotage and undermining the war effort, not to mention interfering with a soldier in discharging his duties. Perhaps I should—But I am powerless, and there is nothing to be done.

Funny how little we are able to control our own destiny. We sail along tranquilly and say, "I am the master of my fate, the captain of my soul." That used to sound so inspiring, but we sail tranquilly only because there are no waves or crosswinds. When the waves come, we lose the tranquility and poise. It is only then that we begin to question the truth of that line.

Take us as an example. Nothing nicer could happen to anyone than our romance, but we had nothing to do with it. It simply happened. I believe we could have picked a more appropriate time. Certainly you could have had a better specimen if you had been governed by logic. So, with all my argument, I have merely proved that we are not permitted to choose in those matters but must accept what fate has to offer.

Now that I have wasted a couple of pages on trite philosophy dealing with love and have proved nothing, am I permitted to come back to earth?

Our school got under way today since we finished a lot of the organization yesterday. A few of the boys are quite sincere and work hard. A few are cold and resentful, of course, but that was to be expected. The percentage is much lower than I had expected. If the school had time it would accomplish a lot, but time is the limiting factor. I wonder why they didn't think of the idea last spring when they had time to accomplish something.

I had only about 20 minutes to do this, so my time is about up. Hope I find time tomorrow to write and say:

I Love You,
Leland

Camp Cooke, Calif.,
Feb. 10, 1943

My Dearest Letty:

Here is another sample of my stationery, but that is about all I can promise in this letter. Writing every night certainly limits the scope of the letters. All it leaves a guy to say is, "I'm still crazy about you."

Of course, one can always think of new and ingenious ways of saying it. Sometimes it takes fourteen lines. If they happen to be iambic pentameter, it is a sonnet.

If it begins, "How do I love thee? Let me count the ways . . ." then it is a good sonnet. Mrs. Browning wrote it, if you remember. If you should read it sometime, try to remember that I only wish I could say it as beautifully. Instead, I must use the simplest prose. After all, that cannot give but the one meaning and it is not easily misunderstood.

People have always said it that way, but I often wonder if it had quite the same meaning to the others as it has to me. I never quite knew it could mean so much, and I am quite old.

El Paso is an interesting town, and it has the most amusing station I have ever seen. I can have more fun watching nervous passengers there than seeing a good ballgame. Most people who pass through know nothing of the habits of the officials.

If you get off the train there you must go through a high iron gate and into the station lobby. As soon as all the passengers are in, the gate is closed and locked. It is purely a one-way gate. As soon as they see the gate close, the passengers begin to look for a way to get back to the train. Doors marked "Exit" lead from the lobby. Going through these, they find themselves in a large glass-enclosed patio. Apparently there are no doors leading out of here. Really, the doors are sections of the glass enclosure, but one must look closely to see that they are doors. So the mob assumes they have been tricked and the signs are false, so they mill back into the lobby like cattle when a storm is brewing.

They find no way to get back to the train, for the doors of the patio are never opened until about five minutes before the train leaves. By this time, most of the passengers are hysterical. They are positive the train will leave without them. It is really a good show. Must hurry before the lights go out.

Love Always,
Leland

Camp Cooke, Calif.
Feb. 12, 1943

Dearest Letty:

Have only a few minutes to say, "I'm crazy about you." Monotonous, isn't it? Every night the same thing! But I want to say it every night. Always. And I don't want you to tire of hearing me say it.

I have just been studying a highly technical book called *Military Intelligence*. All the time I have is spent on things like that. No literature or pleasure reading worth mentioning. I have really developed an ambition, but it may not get me very far.

Yes, Loyd is in the hospital, but I haven't had time to go up and see him. I was not here when he got hurt. It seems that he was in the kitchen and the door was open. He started to shut it when a gust of wind caught and slammed it. His hand was extended so it crashed through the glass. His wrist must have been cut pretty badly because he has been up there for quite a while. I won't have a chance to see him Sunday either since we are restricted. One of the boys took mumps today so we are under quarantine. Lucky for me I had the mumps a little more than a year ago, but that means nothing to the medical officer. They don't take a man's word for anything.

Love Always,
Leland

Camp Cooke, Calif.
Feb. 14, 1943

My Dearest Letty:

I must say you are a disturbing person. "How," you will ask, "could I possibly disturb you, since we are a couple of thousand miles apart?"

Now that I have anticipated your question I shall proceed to answer it.

Since we could not leave the company area and it was Sunday, hence no work, I resolved to do some of the serious reading I had postponed so long. So I selected Col. Edwin E. Schwein's *Combat Intelligence* and started. I did fine for a couple of chapters. But I suddenly found myself wondering, "What is Letty doing?"

"About now, she is coming home from Sunday school" or "I wonder who she is thinking of now?"

And every time I turned a page there was your picture floating an inch above the paper and smiling up at me. I tried to cut it out (I really needed to do the reading, you understand) by concentrating on a single line, but there it was in miniature, the same face, only more mischievous and more disturbing. But I did manage to do a few chapters in spite of you.

This is my last sheet of paper, and I don't know if I will be able to get more from the P.X. tomorrow. So if I fail to write tomorrow you will know it is because I have no paper.

Love Always,
Leland

Camp Cooke, Calif.
Feb. 17, 1943

Dearest Letty:

I was just wondering if you noticed
I was smoking a new brand of tobacco.
You came last night, you know
And stood beside me as I sat upon the grass
Smoking my old briar pipe
And the palm tree let through light enough

To make you visible.
We were silent. There was no need for words.
The warm breeze and starlight was so nice
But someone snapped a light on.
And I turned to look at you with better light
But you were gone.
And there was nothing there but palm trees
And a gentle breeze
And a warm night
And starlight
Made faint by a glaring bulb. Then I
Remembered you were miles and miles away
But just the same
I knew you came
And stood beside me while I sat
Upon the grass and smoked my old briar pipe.

Love Always,
Leland

Camp Cooke, Calif.
Feb. 20, 1943

My Dearest Letty:

Hope you don't mind if I use this paper for a letter. We are still under quarantine. I can't get to the P.X. regularly so I am all out of paper. I pulled this out of another guy's package. It was all he had so I had no choice. Guess it will serve as well as the best linen to say, "I love you."

We will have to go to the combat firing range tomorrow, and it a Sunday, too. Most of the boys are griping. They claim Sunday should be an off day. Can't see why they think so, but they do. We will get to sleep until 7 o'clock, which is an extra hour. That will help a lot.

By the way, I wish you could meet our company mascot. You would like him a lot. He is really a swell guy. His name is Furlough, which is one of the reasons everyone likes him so well. He is friendly, too.

If I hadn't mentioned it before, he is a dog. A little bigger than your dog Martin, or whatever his name is. Oh, yes, I remember now. It is

Skipper. Furlough has a questionable family tree, but he must have a cross of Boston terrier (for his color) and wire-haired terrier (from the stiff bristles around the mouth). He seems to know he belongs in A Company. He comes out every time the whistle blows but pays no attention to the whistles in the other companies. He always goes with us when we take the cars out. He really likes to ride. Will try to get a picture of him sometime.

Love Always,
Leland

Camp Cooke, Calif.
Feb. 23, 1943

My Dearest Letty:

Hold your hat, folks, here we go again. Right this way, ladies and gentlemen, and see the greatest mystery man of all time. A dogface who finds time to write his girl every night! A man who combines the qualities of Romeo, Napoleon, Elmer and Joe. The great soldier, the brilliant writer and the great lover. Only a dime, ten cents, the tenth of a dollar, to see the one and only man, living or dead, who combines all these qualities.

That's how your letters make me feel. You keep saying I'm all those things and you make me want to be all the things you say I am. And you nearly work my fingers to the bone in the process.

Wish I could see you putting out onion plants. Would I laugh at you, all dirty and grimy with your hair down in your eyes, but still beautiful in a pastoral sort of way. I am afraid I won't have the pleasure of seeing that, even though I could give an argument to the company commander.

He is a married man, though, and probably wouldn't understand. A lot of people do grow matter-of-fact after they have been married a few years, you know. I wonder if we would.

I can hardly imagine not feeling a certain thrill that defies description when I see you. It has been that way longer than you could guess, and I don't think it could ever be any other way.

Of all the names for calves! I swear I wouldn't burden a calf like that. Imagine having to go through life with a name like Joe Bob. Now Elsie—

that's much better. All of which shows you could have been more generous with the other.

All of this is pure drivel, and I must close it off some way. Like this—

Love Always,
Leland

P.S. Have just heard that Bob Hope will broadcast his show from here next Tuesday night. Hope we are out from under restriction by then. He puts on a good show.

Camp Cooke, Calif.
Feb. 24, 1943

My Dearest Letty:

Your cookies came this afternoon and they went a lot faster than they came. Yes, they are all gone. You should see a bunch of soldiers go for a box of homemade cookies, especially the kind you sent.

I just wonder if you made them or if you wheedled your mother into the job. I shouldn't ask questions. I enjoyed them too much. Thanks, but you shouldn't do things like that. With sugar ration being as it is, I am sure you had to disfurnish yourself to do it. I wouldn't want you to be without the things you need.

Say, you should have seen us today. I mean early this morning. We had lessons on creeping up on the enemy. It was done this way:

A couple of machineguns were placed in the bushes and set so that they would fire just over the ground, high enough that there was no danger, of course. We were a couple of hundred yards in front of the guns. We were to creep up on the guns while they fired live tracer ammunition over us. Tracer bullets look like streaks of fire, and they look much closer than they really are. The gun sound is a dull thud, but the bullets crack sharply in the air as they pass. It sounds odd to hear the crack, then the thud and know what is behind it all. Believe me, you will really crawl close to the ground, even when you know there is no danger. It is good training.

This sort of thing may not interest you in the least. It has just occurred to me that I know little of just what does interest you, consequently some parts of my letters may be boring. Guess I should have spent all my time I had with you learning just what you liked. But you were so wonderful I simply spent my time looking at you and selfishly wishing I could go on doing it always. It was wonderful while it lasted, and if I had another furlough I might forget to see a lot of people whom I should see and spend the time I saved with you: watching you plant lettuce or carry in wood. I could spend the whole time just doing that.

But I must write Mother, so

Love Always
Leland

Camp Cooke, Calif.
Feb. 25, 1943

My Dearest Letty:

I am still managing to find time to write, which is more than I may be able to say sometime. I did see something of interest today, though, which will help me to fill up this letter, even if it was something that would not interest you.

Joe Louis was in camp today, and I got into a Warner Brothers picture.

They were making scenes for the picture "This is the Army" and Joe is in the picture. They made the fight scene here, and I was in the crowd. I heard a camera grinding and looked around to see a camera taking shots of the crowd. I was right in front of the lens. Of course, they may cut out that part of the picture, but if they don't I am officially in pictures.

If you should see the picture "This is the Army" when it is released and the part comes on where Joe and a guy are boxing and a voice comes over the mike saying: "Sgt. Joe Louis, report to the orderly room just after the bout" then hold your seat. The next scene is a shot at the crowd and I am right there. But they may cut my major part of the picture out completely. Even Warner Bros doesn't always recognize talent when it sees it.

There is one disadvantage to it all. I cannot tell the other guys in the company that I even saw this or the exhibition that followed. I was the only guy in the company who got to see it. We are restricted to the area, you know, so it is not a good idea to tell them I saw it.

Now, Miss Mischief, I don't want you to go writing to the company commander that I have been breaking quarantine. Perhaps I shouldn't have written it to you at all. It will give you something to hold over my head. You can always threaten to tell of my breaking restrictions if I don't do what you want done. But when and if you do I'll still love you.

Always,
Leland

Camp Cooke, Calif.
Feb. 26, 1943

My Dearest Letty:

I'm CQ tonight, but I can always find time for a note, even in duty hours. In case you are wondering what CQ means, it is Charge of Quarters. I usually forget that such things have no meaning to anyone who is not in the Army, so I use abbreviations when I should write the full word.

You may wonder, too, what a CQ has to do. He is the non-com who sleeps in the orderly room and looks after the place. It is his job to turn the lights out at night and wake the company up in the morning. He also has to get up and check it on the book when anyone goes in or out. Of course, he gets little sleep and is on for 24 hours, but the job doesn't come around often. That helps a lot.

If nothing happens, we will be out of quarantine tomorrow. That will be nice. We have a payday coming, too, and most of us are ready for it. Funny how a soldier is always broke. I have an allotment and send $22 per month home. But after I pay for my $10,000 insurance, laundry and that sort of thing I manage to live up to the tradition of a soldier and stay barely above the line.

Why am I writing a financial report when this is supposed to be a love letter? When one is in the hapless state of love I seem to be in there is no accounting for what he does or writes. Then, too, you should file this letter for future reference so that if someday you should find yourself married to a guy who has a habit of being broke you cannot say he was not sporting enough to give you a warning.

That is patting myself on the back. I might as well confess that I wouldn't have written it if I had thought or even dreamed that it would have made the slightest difference to you if I had a million or nothing. Not many girls are like that, and that is a bouquet from me to you.

We were to hear a guy in school who had just come back from the South Pacific. He was at our night school, but I had to miss class, being on the job here. Wish I could have heard him. The boys who did said it was good. He told them stuff that will be handy to know—good tactics in dirty fighting, such as how to twist a knife to make it go between a man's ribs.

A few years ago, I would not have been interested in knowing those things, and no one could have convinced you that you would be in love with a roughneck who did want to know them. Funny what circumstances can do to people.

But circumstances cannot alter the fact that one of those roughnecks is in love with you and will be

Always,
Leland

Camp Cooke, Calif.
March 1, 1943

My Dearest Letty:

I am beginning this just as a new day is born on the West Coast. It is one minute after midnight. I will probably have to finish it much later since my guard relief will be due in a few minutes. I was lucky enough to get the first relief tonight. It is decided by a toss of the coin, and I won the toss. For once, luck was with me.

At this minute—eight minutes past 12—I like to think that you are quite sound asleep. It is nine minutes past 2 there and you and all good girls should have been in bed quite some time ago.

I like to wonder just how you look when you are asleep and all the mischief of your eyes is hidden. It is one of my pet curiosities. I'm willing to bet a month's pay that a trace of the same mischief lingers around the corners of your mouth. Sleep cannot take it away. Or I like to think it cannot. I would be disappointed to know that Morpheus could succeed when my kiss had failed.

It is beautiful here tonight, and I did look at the same stars you saw earlier in the evening. Polaris, Ursa Major, Ursa Minor and Cassiopeia are north of me just as they are north of you. And if I were in Africa, they would still be north of you and me simultaneously. That makes us seem closer together, doesn't it?

To think that she sees the same star I am seeing, she knows the same loneliness, she thinks of the same thing makes you seem near. Sometimes it almost seems that I could reach out and touch you. I tried to say that once before but failed miserably. You said the same thing so much more beautifully. (Will finish later. It is time for me to get some sleep.)

8:30 p.m. Back on the job after a day of work and a night of school. That is, I taught school today and went to school tonight. Guess I learned a little and I hope I was able to teach something.

But I did not learn the mystery of your eyes. They haunt me. They peer at me from the twinkle of the stars and the dancing of the California poppies and from a thousand corners. I see them everywhere, which is why I always find myself saying, "Would Letty approve the way I am doing this?"

Love Always,
Leland

Camp Cooke, Calif.
March 2, 1943

My Dearest Letty:

Please don't expect much of a letter from me today. I am off to the Bob Hope show so I don't have much time. I had to work until 6 o'clock this evening, which makes me a little late. I usually get off at 5. Then, too, I had to rustle a ticket. There were only a few tickets for the company. I got a ticket for the Gracie McDonald Show Saturday night. Well, I couldn't afford to try to get a ticket to two shows in succession when a lot of the boys had missed, so I gave up hope of seeing Hope. But I happened to be lucky. One of the teachers at school was in a company that was going on alert tonight, so he couldn't use his tickets. I got one from him. Lucky!

Well, I am wondering whom you are writing to except me. I am a master at deduction and have a memory like an elephant. So I happened to remember that you promised to write me two letters for every one that you wrote to the other guys. Now (happy day) you have begun to write me almost every day. Who is the other lucky stiff who gets the other letters?

Boy, do I wish I could have seen you dropping the potatoes. Oh, your poor hands. If I could only have held them for a moment when they were all black and dirty. But think nothing of it. I will have plenty of chances to see them dirty. I am a good gardener, in case you didn't know, and here is the way I like to do it:

To garden properly, one needs a well-broken-in briar pipe and plenty of good tobacco. The garden, with proper selection of site and position, is close to a large tree. This is of no value when the planting is being done, but it comes in handy when the wife is hoeing the garden in July. But as I started to say, the proper way to garden is by proxy. Just sit in the shade of the tree and tell the wife which part of the garden to work next.

(Must go to the show.)

The show was good, as you know if you heard it. The Langford gal is some singer. She sang "You'd Be So Nice to Come Home To," which was appropriate. But as I was about to say when the show so rudely interrupted my dissertation on the art of gardening:

Gardening can best be done by two people. I play one part of the team, and I am glad to learn that you are good at the other. I am capable of the part that requires making the plans and smoking the pipe. You, of course, don't smoke pipes so you are no good in that spot. I don't look good in a wide straw hat so, of course, I'll have to stay in the shade. You look good in anything so nature has decreed the jobs each of us shall do. Who are we to contradict nature?

I must add that I am crazy about you.

Always,
Leland

Dearest Letty

Camp Cooke, Calif.
March 6, 1943

My Dearest Letty:

It would have to happen tonight, Saturday: A boy is playing the piano, and his tune at the moment is the same waltz you played for me. I can't remember the name of it, but I shall ask him later. Perhaps he doesn't know, for he plays a lot from memory.

He plays rather well and there is a haunting air about this particular tune, because I heard it first when you played it. Sometime you will have to play it again for me. Meanwhile, I must be content to listen to his playing.

Now he has changed to "Beautiful Dreamer." That, too, would remind me of you, even if I were not thinking of you already. For I would say to myself, "There is the Stephen Foster tune 'Beautiful Dreamer': It is 10 o'clock here. That means 12 back home and Letty must be asleep; hence, Beautiful Dreamer. Wonder what she is dreaming about?"

That is part of the price one has to pay for being in love. No matter what happens it always directs our thoughts into the same channels. I said it was part of the price, but it is a very pleasant price.

For a change, we had the afternoon off. That is, we went on a sort of a picnic just out from camp and stayed all afternoon. They brought our supper out to us. That is, they brought out cheese-and-ham sandwiches, hard-boiled eggs, celery, olives, green onions, shoestring potatoes, cakes and orangeade.

We must go on a picnic like that sometime. But I don't want a company of dogfaces along. Nor anyone else. Just you and me. Is it a date? (You bring the lunch.)

The piano has stopped now and there is silence save for the click of dominos at another table, a radio in "B" Company's day room, the low hum of the furnace fan, and the scratch of my pen as I try to tell you that I am still in love with you. Realizing that you are a dumb girl (by your own admission), I just have to keep reminding you of the fact else you might forget how I felt and start shopping for some other guy. Since you are so nice and so easy to look at, you might be lost to me long before

All's Fair

65

I have time to come back and convince you thoroughly of the fact. You
see, I have a good reason for reminding you every day that—

I Love You,
Leland

Camp Cooke, Calif.
March 7, 1943

My Dearest Letty:

Just bought a new pipe and am busy breaking it in. Didn't know a
pipe had to be broken in, did you? Well, it does, and you might as well
learn it now, for I am a confirmed pipe smoker.

Perhaps you don't like the smell of pipes. Some people don't, you
know. But you can always open a window, for I usually have about half
a dozen pipes lying all over the place.

You would be amused at this new pipe. It has a large amber-colored
transparent stem with a black mouthpiece. The stem has a large cavity
designed to cool the smoke. Puffing lazily, as all good pipe smokers should
puff, causes the smoke to curl slowly through the stem, weaving all sorts
of curious patterns. All the springtime patterns of the Arkansas storm
clouds are recreated in amber miniature in the stem of my new pipe.

The bowl is of briar and seems almost detached from the stem, so
slender is the connecting portion. It is not at the end of the stem, as is
the bowl of the conventional pipe, but screws into the top of the stem
half an inch from the end. So precarious is the balance that one expects
it to topple off every time the pipe is tilted. One always has the feeling
that he is a juggler, balancing a golf ball on a broomstick.

(You must think this is a terrific waste of paper, three whole pages
about a pipe, and you don't even smoke one.)

Went up to the hospital today and saw Loyd and some other guys
who are up there. He is getting along OK, but is terribly bored with the
place.

His condition is quite tragic. What I meant was his hand gives him
no pain. This is confidential, as he may not want his family to know that
he suffered quite a cut. I'm sure I wouldn't write anything about it if I
were hurt. But two fingers are quite useless and have no feeling. He was

holding a cigarette in those fingers yesterday and it burned back to the flesh. He could not feel the fire, and it burned quite a large blister on one of his fingers.

I am sure you will remember that he may not have written this to his family and will not discuss it with them. He should have a medical discharge from the Army, but they are not so easy to get. Of course, he can't go along with the rest of us when we leave here. So he will miss all the fun.

A whole letter and I have not once said "I love you." But you must know that I would not write such crazy letters unless I did.

Love Always,
Leland

Camp Cooke, Calif.
March 8, 1943

My Dearest Letty:

I had thought I was not getting a letter from you today. We only get mail at noon, you know, except that we get packages in the afternoon. So I was writing away at 5 o'clock, wishing it were time to quit, when the mail clerk came by and tossed your latest letter on my desk. I couldn't read it then for the captain and three or four lieutenants were there, but I did rush my pen and finish the job early.

And it was worth the added effort. Your letters always are. If the captain happened to be around while I was rushing to finish a job and read every one of your letters, he would be convinced that I was one of his hardest workers when I am really one of his most ingenious goldbricks. You should be ashamed of yourself, cheating on the old man like that or, rather, causing me to fool him that way.

By the way, my school is closed. Too bad it couldn't go on, as it was just beginning to show some good results. (Circumstances that you will later understand forced it to close.) Some of the boys made rapid progress. Others who were slow learners had just begun to get an idea of what it was all about.

I am sorry Joe Bob the calf was so insulted, but he should have been more insulted when you gave him the name. But I suppose he was quite young in those days and was not able to defend himself. You are like that, taking advantage of poor, helpless young creatures who are unable to defend themselves and weaving them into a net from which they are later unable to extract themselves.

For example, look at what you did to me. Years ago, when I was young and vulnerable to your charms, you added me to your victims list. Of course, you kept me dangling around for quite a while, hopelessly thinking it was no use. Then I learned it might not be so hopeless and by that time I was completely lost. Another example: Look at what you do to the poor high school boys, letting them think you are merely 16 until they go desperate, then disillusioning them. I only hope the rest of your victims are as happy about the whole thing as I am. But I don't want them to be happy for the same reason that I am.

But I must write Mother and Marie. Marie Leavell, by the way, is a cousin of mine. She is a high school kid who writes me all the home news. Maybe I should explain about her, as you might go getting ideas.

Love Always,
Leland

Camp Cooke, Calif.
March 9, 1943

My Dearest Letty:

Another day, another note, or, if you choose to call it that, another letter.

Boy, am I tired! Worked in the supply this morning and had it pretty easy. All paperwork, but they had a big parade this afternoon and I couldn't get out of it. And was it tough! We started at 1:30. It was streaming rain and all the camp was a sop. We wore our best uniforms, of course, and a raincoat, which was entirely too hot. At 2 we were waiting for the old general (that is the one who was commanding here) to come and tell us "goodbye."

At 4:15 he came, but meanwhile we had stood in the rain a couple of hours in formation.

Of course, there was a band to cheer us up. I have been to two country fairs and a crib raining back home, and I have never heard so much brass in all my life. My ears still ring with such stirring tunes as "Bring the Broadax, Mother, There is a Fly on Baby's Chin," "Looking Through the Knothole in Grandpa's Wooden Leg" or some such stirring tunes. Anyway, I am tired, but I am still able to write.

Perhaps it is tiring because I never did like to take part in parades. Fanfares and parades mean little to me as morale boosters. Of course, they play a big part in the Army plan, and most of the guys go in for it in a big way.

My morale seldom needs boosting. I simply figure there is a job to do. But if I begin to forget that it must be done, one of your letters is all I need. I take one look at the envelope and remember: My morale is at the top.

But this is not like letters should be written. They should be all interestingly informative and descriptive without discussing military subjects. Then, no letter from me to you would be complete without a bit of "Lavender and Old Lace" or the "I love you" phrase. Regardless of how I fail on other parts of the letter, that part always creeps in.

Leland

Camp Cooke, Calif.
March 10, 1943

My Dearest Letty:

I have a dozen letters that should be written tonight, but I am starting on yours. The others can come later.

Even Mother's letter can be postponed until I finish this. She doesn't expect a letter from me every day, so if something should happen and I didn't get a letter she would only think I didn't have time to write to anyone. Anyway, she knows that I will write to both her and you anytime I do get a chance.

Another of your letters came today. I was wondering if you got the division insignia or shoulder patch. You now belong to the 5th Armored Division, and there is no necessity for you to think of joining the WAACs. Anyway, there is an Army regulation against a soldier marrying a WAAC, and for that reason alone (I hope) you would not want to get in.

Don't tell anyone but you have a regular GI (government-issue) patch. That, too, is against AR (Army Regulations) but I am safe. You see, I bought some of them before they issued them, and I have bought quite a few. So I have more left than I am charged with. In this, the GIs are better than any you can buy, so I sent you the best. I wish you had been near enough to sew them on all my clothes for me.

I was never any good at sewing (this will do to remember) so it will do no good to try to wangle me into doing it sometime later.

Mother always was amused at my mending jobs, which I did on my clothes when I was away from home. She wondered how I mended the knee of work pants on a sewing machine until she discovered that I had ripped the seam of the leg and resewed it.

It seems that this letter has been concerned a lot with my mother, but I think you will like her a lot when you get to know her. Perhaps all people think that of their mothers, but I am trying to be impersonal. I believe you would like her even if she were someone else's mother. She is a gentle, even-tempered person who cannot knowingly hurt anyone. Hope I am not being sentimental.

If I can get the stamps I promise to mail you seven letters tomorrow. I figured if I mailed you seven letters in one day it would not be necessary to write you for a whole week if I became so employed that I couldn't write.

Love,
Leland

Oakland, Calif.
March 11, 1943

My Dearest Letty:

Two days ago I wrote the date you see above, March 11, but I was interrupted and this is the first chance I have had to continue the letter. This is Saturday the 13th and I woke up in a new world this morning. We are moving and I am on the train. The heck of it is I don't know where I am.

We boarded the train about 9 o'clock last night, after standing by the railroad a couple of hours waiting for the train. I drew an upper berth, which is desirable on a GI train. I went to bed immediately and was asleep before the train started. But I had no idea whether we were going by the northern or southern route.

It was an eerie feeling to awaken and not know where I was. It was the sort of feeling one must have had when they took a ride on the Magic Carpet.

We must have traveled north. The low-hanging clouds hide the sun and my compass is not with me. But there seems to be a chain of mountains to my right and to the left a series of silver-barrage balloons blending with the fog so that they are almost invisible, which seems to indicate the coastline.

The landscape tells us little. It is typically California and that is all. The towns we have passed were all small. El Dorado, Santa Rea and San Clara were villages I have never heard of. However, the country—what we can see of it—is beautiful. At the moment, we are passing through a marsh. Ducks, geese and a hundred species of waterfowl that I cannot identify swarm over the tiny lakes and ponds. The train disturbs them not at all and they will sit under the small bridges while the wheels pass only a few feet above them. On two occasions I have seen cock pheasants strut across an island only a few yards away. If they were aware of the thoughts of all the would-be hunters who are peering at them they might not feel so secure. But I am thankful that they do not know all this for they are beautiful, so beautiful that I cannot imagine how anyone could call it a healthful sport to kill them.

We are coming into another town now, but I have seen no sign that tells me what it is. We seem to be in a factory district. On my left is the Morton Salt Works. On my right the R. A. Young wire factory and now the Clorox Chemical Co. But no town name. Ah, there it is: East Oakland. I was right. We are going north. I thought I was sufficiently familiar with Southern California to recognize some landmark if we were in that part of the country.

This letter is about as large as I can write now. My envelopes are small, but I may write another today. It is hard for me to write a legible hand on a moving train, and you may have trouble reading this. However, it is the best I can do under the circumstances, and if you have ever tried to write under these circumstances you know how it is.

I can't mail this until we get to our destination, so don't be surprised if you get about a dozen letters in the same mail. It is an order that we mail no letters, but there is no law against writing.

Oh, yes. Our destination is Camp Forrest, Tenn., and my address will be the same except for the change from Camp Cooke to Camp Forrest, and you might add: A.P.O. 255. For convenience, I guess I should number these letters with this as No. 1.

Love Always,
Leland

P.S. We are at a siding now in Oakland. A dozen boys and girls, less than 13 years old, have been putting on quite a show of wrestling and boxing in payment for the gum and candy we tossed to them.

On the Troop Train
March 13, 1943

Letty Darling,

Now I am writing twice a day, for I wrote you this morning and now I am writing in an upper, which is no place from which to compose a letter. But I am doing it anyway for I'm still crazy about you and this is the only chance I have to tell you that AGAIN.

Shame on you. Still pretending you are trying to make me fall in love with you. How many times do I have to say something before you believe me? Will I have to always tell you things a thousand times before I can convince you? If so, I am condemned to go through life repeating myself.

Say, you should try writing in a place like this.

The climate has changed a lot since I wrote you this morning. Oakland and the Bay area were nice and warm. Grass was ready to cut and the fruit trees were in full bloom. But when we turned east and climbed into the Rockies it began to grow cold. In a few hours we began to see snow and a little later the tracks had been cleared by snowplows. Drifts were piled to the eaves of the houses, and it was cold. But now we are down in more level country and there are only occasional patches of snow.

We passed by the famous Golden Gate just after I finished my letter this morning. It was nice but so foggy one could hardly see Alcatraz Prison. It looked pretty rugged.

The mountains are beautiful with their magnificent canyons and their stately pines. We were not supposed to lift the windows, but I did just to get a whiff of the pine perfume. It smelled so good that I left it up. We have just passed Reno, Nevada. That is, we passed just before I went to bed. Don't know what we are passing now. But I was genuinely sorry to see it grow dark. There was so much to see and so little time in which to see it.

The track is rough, and it is impossible to write. Must postpone this until tomorrow.

Sunday morning, and we are still in Nevada. The town is Montello, but I must confess that I never heard of it. We took water there and are just pulling out. Montello is smaller than Pottsville. It is on a high mesa as level as a floor, but it is completely surrounded by mountains. It is fewer than ten miles in any direction to snow-covered mountains, but there is no snow here.

9:45. We are now passing over the Great Salt Lake. It is the most beautiful body of water I have ever seen. Actually, it is clear as glass as one can see by looking straight down. But looking toward the horizon one gets all sorts of illusions as the light plays curious tricks. The water becomes blue, green, purple, and even red as it catches the light from different angles. The lake takes on all the colors of the rainbow. The water, they say, is among the saltiest in the world. It is so salty that swimmers find it difficult to sink due to the heaviness of the water. Floating is easy and drowning a rare tragedy. The water churns and bubbles constantly as if it were boiling, and a cover of sheer white foam like a huge lace bedspread covers the shoreline. But the pattern of the lace changes constantly.

The bridge we are now on is 30 miles long, which is quite a bridge, and the lake is about 75 miles from the northern to southern tips.

We never quite lose sight of the mountains. To my right now I can see the silver-capped peaks seeming to rise out of the water like islands. Their lower half is purple or blue, corresponding with the color of the water and blending so perfectly that it is hard to see just where the water ends and land begins. But the top is snow and reflects the sunlight like a huge silver shield.

We are off the bridge now, and this will more than fill this No. 2 envelope.

Love Always,
Leland

On the Troop Train
March 13, 1943

My Dearest Letty:

Now we are somewhere in old Wyoming, but I don't know where. It all looks alike to me: barren mountains, mesas and tableland, sheer cliffs, rocks and snow. No towns of any size, and only a few isolated houses.

It was impossible to tell when we left Utah, for it was much the same kind of country after we got away from the salt flats. We have just pulled into a village. Its name is Green River and it is a typical cow town— mostly bars and cafes with one general store. The signs advertise such places as Green River Bar, U. P. Hotel, Shanghai Cafe and Jenkins General Store. If I listed half a dozen more bars, cafes and hotels you would have a complete city directory of Green River. Very boring, I'd say, but one of the boys claims the town has historical value and that Wild Bill Hickok was killed here. Since I am not informed on the history of the Wild West, I couldn't say about those things.

But we just missed Salt Lake City, for which I was genuinely sorry. The town has always fascinated me, I guess because of its history. I have always thought that someday a great American novel would be built around the history of the place, and I am still looking for it.

The harassed moves of the early Mormons should provide plenty of material. Persecuted religions always offer good material for historical novels, and the Mormon persecution was especially rich.

There was the incident of the seagulls, for example, that would be good for at least one chapter in such a novel. After the Mormons were settled around Salt Lake, they planted crops of wheat and other small grain, but the grasshoppers invaded and threatened to destroy all their crops. But Brigham Young, who was leader of the church, prayed for divine providence to deliver them from the grasshoppers. A short time

Dearest Letty

later, flocks of seagulls swarmed in and gobbled up the insects. So was the religious faith of the doubters renewed. It is an interesting bit of American history, and someone will make use of it sometime.

It is snowing hard now and the wind is blowing from the west like fury. It must be very cold outside. My other envelopes have been too full, so I will stop this on four pages.

Love Always,
Leland

On the Troop Train
March 15, 1943

My Dearest Letty:

Today it is cold as blue blazes, if that metaphor means anything. All morning we have been in what these natives call a "mild blizzard," but we would call it pretty severe. It must be about like the weather that got your poor garden.

The ground seems to be frozen hard and tiny towers of ice have spewed up from the banks along the road. An occasional squall of snow pulls a lazy curtain across the windows as if the country was jealous of its icy beauty or being shy of its wintry nakedness. The last reason seems the more logical, for the country is naked. All grass has been clipped away either by the mowing machine or the white-faced cattle. Great stacks of hay dot the landscape and surprisingly fat and contented-looking cows huddle in the lea of the stacks.

Frost is everywhere. It paints the fence posts so that they seem to be covered by a light coat of whitewash. Telephone wires are like overgrown cobwebs, and farmhouses are like ships riding at anchor in a sea of frost. But there is no human in sight. One can imagine that they have learned to do their chores with maximum efficiency and spend most of their time inside.

But I write of the country when all the while I am thinking how much I will miss your letters until you have time to get my new address. Too bad I couldn't write that we were moving. You will miss only a couple of days, then be flooded with all these letters in one bunch. I would hate to have to face your letter carrier when he has to deliver them all. Or when you try to read this stuff. But I could explain that it was written on a moving train and that I am crazy about you and you might forgive me.

Love Always,
Leland

Camp Forrest, Tenn.
March 18, 1943

My Dearest Letty:

Just have one sheet of paper and can't get more today but here goes this one. We arrived last night about 9 o'clock and are in pup tents in an old pea patch. The mud is not over eight inches deep in the bad spots, and where I am it is not more than half that thick.

Had a little train wreck on the way out. Guess you have seen pictures of the Toonerville Trolley [a popular newspaper cartoon] jumping the track. That happened to my car. I was asleep in the upper berth and it was hard to stay up there while the car bounced along the ties and jumped into the ditch. A couple of trainmen were killed, but none of the soldiers was hurt, except for a few bruises. Both engines turned over and one of the crewmen was still under an engine when we left. They had only found one of his feet and were cutting the engine with torches trying to find the rest of the body. It was a pretty nasty wreck. Must close.

Love Always,
Leland

Camp Forrest, Tenn.
March 21, 1943

My Dearest Letty:

If I were not sure you understood why I had not written to you I would begin this by explaining the situation. Perhaps I should explain anyway. But please don't think I am complaining, for the Army is like this and you can understand that this is part of our job.

We are bivouacked in the biggest mudhole between Nashville and Chattanooga and are in pup tents. This gives us little room, and there is neither light nor heat. We work as long as it is light, then the only thing

Dearest Letty

one can do is go to bed since that is the only way to stay warm. (Even that is no guarantee.)

We came in with a blizzard that followed a big rain. The next morning ice covered the place. Then it turned warm. Then came a storm and another blizzard, and today it snowed all day—hard.

I am on guard tonight, which explains how I find time to write. Also, I was sent to town yesterday and found time to pick up some paper and a dozen candles. But a dozen was all they had and stationery is hard to get. Hope you don't mind my writing on both sides of the paper.

You wanted to know if I sat back and watched while the boys cleaned the barracks and did the other jobs. Yes, young lady, that is exactly what I do. In fact, that is what I am supposed to do. It is my job to tell them what to do, and how to do it. So, you see what you are letting yourself in for. By that time, I will be in a habit of telling people what to do (if I am not busted before then) so I can tell you exactly how to plow the garden.

One o'clock in the morning

Boy, am I hitting hard luck. One of the guards just sprained a knee, and I opened my big mouth at the wrong time. So now I have to walk his post. Corporals of the guard are supposed to sit in the guardhouse and only go out to take new guards to the posts. But with one guard out, the other guards had to do extra time. So I let myself into the extra job. Now don't start looking hopeful. You won't be able to appeal to my sympathy like that.

Say, I lost all my pipes in the train wreck. Our car was so badly tilted that they ordered us out of it and told us to leave our equipment. They would get it out later. They did get everything except my pipes and tobacco. I lost that. They even got the pack of letters I had written to you. I guess you got about six in one bunch. Five of them were in the wreck.

My fingers are so cold that I can hardly hold a pen. Wonder if I'll ever write you without apologizing for my penmanship. But I can't write, even when I have no excuse, and I sometimes wonder that you are able to make out what I am trying to say. There are three words I should print: "I LOVE YOU" so that there can be no mistake. I hope you never have to guess when I write that.

Love Always,
Leland

Camp Forrest, Tenn.
March 23, 1943

My Dearest Letty,

Finally, I find time for another note. Hope you don't mind my not writing often, but I am sure you understand that I write every time I get a chance. It's just that I don't have time to write.

Have written you a couple of times, home twice, and one letter to an uncle who writes me regularly. Not much for a guy who had a habit of writing two or three letters a day.

You were wondering in your last letter just what I was doing on the Sunday before you wrote, but I guess you have my Sunday letter so now you know. But last Sunday was a different story. I didn't read *Alice in Wonderland.* In fact, I didn't read anything, for I have no time to read and there are few books—only a few Army manuals, a couple of technical books on tactics, and a copy of "The Rubaiyat of Omar Khayyam." I don't have time to read them. I do like "Alice" though and the other Lewis Carroll stuff such as:

"Beware the Jabberwock, my son!
The jaws that bite, the claws that catch!
Beware the Jubjub bird, and shun
The frumious Bandersnatch!"

Or:

"The time has come," the Walrus said,
"To talk of many things:
Of shoes—and ships—and sealing wax.
Of cabbages—and kings—
And why the sea is boiling hot—
And whether pigs have wings."

Then the walrus and the carpenter sit down and eat the oysters. (By the way, I had oysters for supper.)

But how did I get into this when I was trying to get around to some ingenious way of saying I am still crazy about you and was sorry I couldn't write you more often?

Was it cold last night! My feet froze. I have ordered a new sleeping bag, and I wish it would hurry and get here. It will by the time it gets warm enough that I won't need it anymore.

Have been getting wood today. That is, I took out a crew of boys and let them do the work. Then we fixed up a stage for an open-air theater. Hope we have some shows out here, but so far we have had no entertainment of any kind.

Hope to find time to write again in a couple of days. We are about to get the place straightened out and drained. Please remember that I love you.

Leland

Camp Forrest, Tenn.
March 25, 1943

My Dearest Letty:

I won't have time to finish this, but I am at least demonstrating an honest desire to write. (Oops, I knew it. There's the chow whistle.)

Just finished dinner, and it is raining. One of those cold spring rains. One finds it hard to remember that yesterday the sun was shining and it was so warm we didn't need a coat, and tomorrow the sun may shine again.

It seems funny to be in a pup tent with the rain hammering down just six inches above your face.

It is night now, and everywhere there is darkness, everywhere except the tiny pools of light in the tents whose owners are fortunate enough to possess candles. If I didn't have one I couldn't be writing this. It is the thick, inky blackness that comes with a steady downpour of rain. The drops hammer on the tight canvas like tiny fists beating a huge drum. But they play a sleep-inducing bit of soft music.

It is really quite cozy inside the tents as we have them now. The regulation pup tent is a two-man tent with one closed end and one open. That arrangement is not so good when it rains for the obvious reason that the rain might come from the wrong direction. But we have solved the problem quite neatly by pitching two tents with the open ends together. So instead of the tents looking like this:

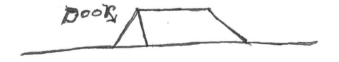

They look like this:

And they hold four men instead of two. (See how the two are buttoned in the middle?) Of course, we have to button up the ends when we get inside, which is a bit inconvenient, but that is the only way to stay dry. Then, too, it is a little crowded for the floor space is limited. But two people could practically set up housekeeping in it.

Living like this would be fun if one did it when he wanted to. When I get out of the Army I shall try to get four shelter-halves. When we grow bored with the luxury of chairs, beds and tables, we can go camping. We must pick rainy nights like tonight or we wouldn't appreciate the shelter, and I want you to hear the rain just above your face.

You must promise not to touch the canvas. Rubbing the underside of the tent causes it to start leaking, as one of my tent partners learned last week. Then, too, we must have a candle. No light is quite as romantic as candlelight. It is no good for writing letters, but we will have no need to write letters then anyway.

My candle is almost burned out, and I have not said, in so many words, "I love you," but the whole letter has been an attempt to say that.

Love Always,
Leland

Camp Forrest, Tenn.
April 4, 1943

My Dearest Letty:

Sunday and nothing to do so far, but I am keeping my fingers crossed. The whistle could blow any time.

Am I lazy today! It is the first day I have had in quite some time when I could read, write, listen to the wind whip the tent flaps, or think of you and wonder what we would be doing together.

When we first came out we had to swim in the creek, which was a little cool. We could go to town for showers but the places were all crowded, and the water there was quite cold. So we used the old ingenuity of the American soldier and rigged up an old boiler down at the creek. Now we have hot showers any day. Of course, it's in the open and a little cool when we come out, but it's still quite nice.

You seemed to think I was kidding about it being fun to live in a tent for a short time. Guess I'll have to show you that it really is, but I don't mean for a decade—only a couple of days at a time. And, I hope you don't choose to eat any worms. It won't be necessary, really, if you are planning to do it only after I have stopped loving you.

The Army has issued us a booklet, which says that many worms are quite edible. The purpose of the book is a guide on what to eat if we are stranded or lost. It contains some interesting recipes for such delicacies as fillet of rattlesnake, toasted grasshoppers and monkey steak. Snake, it says, tastes like fried chicken, and the recipe for cooking grasshopper instructs: "Pick off wings and legs. Toast body over live coals by suspending on sharp stick."

I hereby veto your idea of the garden. It is no good at all. You can take the snuff if you wish, but, after all, that only requires a minute, and you can continue working while you chew it. But any pipe smoker of experience knows that a pipe was designed as an aid to relaxation and rest. Look at Sitting Bull and Richard the Restful and a host of others. All were pipe smokers and all members of the Sons of Rest. Then there was Henry VIII, Captain John Smith, et al., who were men of great energy and partakers of snuff. So I hold to my theory.

Must close and repair my tent. The wind is wrecking it.

Love Always,
Leland

Camp Forrest, Tenn.
April 10, 1943

My Dearest Letty:

I intend to write you a letter tomorrow if I have time, but I can get off a note tonight. Have been so busy this week that I had little time to write anyone until tonight. I have written all that before. But I always repeat myself when I say I love you and you don't seem to mind this admission of age.

Say, I wish you could stop by and have dinner with us some day. No, on second thought, you'd better not. Too many soldiers are around. But it would be fun to see you try to eat from an Army mess kit.

Did you ever see one? They are like a small frying pan with a flat lid or cover and a folding handle. When not in use, the knife, fork, and spoon are placed inside, the cover is pushed into place and the handle is folded over and snapped down. The trick in eating from one is to be able to hold the mess kit and lid in one hand without spilling anything. The meat, beans, potatoes and everything goes into the mess kit together. The dessert goes on the lid. It is a pretty good juggling act to be able to carry each in one hand without spilling it. The other hand is employed with the cup and silverware. It is quite easy when you master it, but hard at first.

We have a show every night now, but I seldom go. Many times I am too tired and at other times I am too busy. Then it is no fun to see an ordinary picture alone. I like to see them through twice without caring how they come out, and then go to the hut for a cup of coffee.

The farmers around here take full advantage of the free shows and come out every night. They come out with a week's growth of beard, a slouch hat and a kid under each arm and laugh lustily when Lou Costello gets smacked in the face with a soft pie or tumbles down a flight of stairs.

They and their boys are quite shrewd, too. They soon learn that the average soldier pays no attention to prices and will buy anything. So they sell everything from last month's magazines to ham and eggs, and at fancy prices.

This is all the paper that will fit into my envelope.

Love Always,
Leland

Camp Forrest, Tenn.
April 20, 1943

My Dearest Letty:

By this time, you either think I have deserted completely or have been shipped. Neither is true, so don't get your "V" stationery out, and don't start looking for some other guy. I did have a reason for not writing for more than a week.

I have been out on one of the Army's famous Secret Missions. Way down in Georgia.

They jerked us away on the Sunday I had planned to write to you, and we could neither write nor talk to anyone. So, no letters.

We camped in a pine forest near Warm Springs and isolated ourselves from everyone. No civilian was allowed near the area and we could not leave. Even the guy who owned the land came down to see what it was all about and we chased him out. The only time we got near a town was when we were actually on guard. Then, of course, we could talk to no one.

All the time I was missing your letters so much that I may not have been a good soldier. And wondering if you were missing mine, too. Now, since I have learned that you take cod-liver oil when I don't write I am wondering if I could make a deal with your druggist. If I'll agree not to write, he will split the profits from his sales with me. Who is your druggist? I'll approach him on the matter.

I read in the paper about Lora's wedding, but they did not even mention all the disrupted plans and cold supper. Funny how the society editor can cover things up. But a wedding should, like everything else in life, be unplanned. An elopement, if you please. Plans can get screwed up easily, so when people marry they should do it suddenly and impulsively. If they cannot find a preacher for thirty minutes, they are the only ones who are disappointed. Then they can go to the hut where the coffee is always hot and no pretty girl will have to fuss about the dinner and make up jokes to keep everyone in good spirits. It is much simpler.

We can't escape plans entirely, even when we are in the Army, and know they are no good. Sunday night, for example, we camped in Cedartown, Georgia. I had planned, with Jimmie Modlin, to go into town and eat a thick steak. Both of us were quite sure we could get a pass, so we ate none of the goose liver and cheese for supper. But the colonel said, "Give 20 percent of the men passes," and they gave them to the driver. So Jimmie and I could not get away. Then they said they would bring candy, drinks and ice cream out to camp on a truck. So we sweated a line for 30 minutes, by my watch, and when we got to the truck the SSO said, "Sorry men, we are all sold out." Then, just to make things perfect, it started raining. I decided I didn't like Army life.

All day yesterday it streamed rain. When we pulled into camp last night the field was ankle-deep in mud, and not a dry place in sight to pitch a tent. I must confess that my bed was pretty soggy last night, and the water that seeped up through the blankets was none too warm. But today the sun shone and I dried my clothes. So the Army is not so bad after all (if I escape a cold).

Better not trade for the mule just yet. I am afraid of your judgment. You might get one you couldn't plow at all. If you intend that I become tax assessor, how do you expect me to do it? By the way, where did you get that idea anyway? I'll probably be a hobo when this is over, and who ever heard of a hobo being elected tax assessor? Or owning a mule? I have no idea how you got the notion, but that is out. A politician could not leisurely visit Mexico, Palm Springs, Rock City and Salt Lake, or swim in the Colorado River, or the Gulf as he chose. Only a genuine hobo can do that without money. So dig up an old pair of overalls.

But I do love you and I am not sure you couldn't make me change my mind—to anything but politics.

Love Always,
Leland

Camp Forrest, Tenn.
April 22, 1943

My Dearest Letty:

Have just had another piece of your cake, which reminded me to write you. (I was going to write you anyway.) Jimmie and I have about finished it, so with nothing to remind me to write, you may not get any letters.

I almost forgot. There is still something to remind me to keep the mailman busy. It is the fact that I am much in love with you, and that I could not forget how beautiful you are, even if I tried.

No, I am not in Poland, even if the weather is much the same. It is cold as the North Pole tonight—and raining. In spite of this, I will stay warm and dry.

I have decided that if you get it pitched on dry ground this pup tent is the thing in a storm. The night before we went to Georgia it came quite a storm. Lightning was quite close, the rain came down in torrents, and the wind blew down quite a few trees, but we stayed dry. We did have one damp spot. A Frenchman, who was one of my tentmates, rescued a puppy and brought him into the tent. The pup was not housebroken and we had quite a comedy at the expense of the Italian prizefighter who was also a tent partner. Will tell you about it sometime.

I have a new sleeping bag now. I had been trying to buy one for quite a while, but they are hard to get. However, they are worth the $20 and all the effort it takes to get them.

Ever sleep in one? You must try it sometime. They are quite cozy. Mine is a wool-filled comforter with waterproofed canvas fastened to one side. It is folded in half so that the canvas is on the outside. A zipper closes the foot and the sides, which are folded together so that it is almost like a cotton sack, only larger, and almost airtight. Two people could sleep in it quite comfortably. I don't know why the Army doesn't issue sleeping bags instead of blankets.

(Time out while I finish my cake.)

You asked about my brothers in one of your letters. I have just had a letter from Ardis and he has been moved to Camp Tyson here in Tennessee about 175 miles from here. I don't know if I will be able to get over to see him. They are tight with passes. Aaron is still in San Diego, but I don't guess he will be there long.

It would be a hard job to name a calf I have never seen. Calves are like people, you know. They have distinctive personalities, and the name should fit the individual. You wouldn't, for example, call a robust, manly boy Cuthbert or Reginald. So I wouldn't dare suggest Minnie or Ethel when she should be called Mitzi or Tilda. I am afraid you will have to name her yourself.

Love Always,
Leland

Camp Forrest, Tenn.
April 30, 1943

My Dearest Letty:

By all Army rules I am a dead soldier, and dead soldiers are not supposed to write. But I am writing anyway. I was "killed" in the problem, you see, and it happened so easily.

I had left the crew with the car and gone to report my position to the officer in charge. While I was gone two of the enemy ambushed the crew, and when I got back it was easy enough for them to get me. But that is not new to me. I was knocked out on most of the problems on the other maneuvers.

No, I have not been to the Grand Ole Opry, but we are only about 40 miles from Nashville.

Wish I could get to go and talk to the girl who interviews soldiers. I like to talk to pretty girls. You see, she always asks if there is a girl back home. Then I could say, "Yes, there will always be one." Then I would have a chance to tell everyone what a wonderful girl I have. They might not be interested, but that would be because they don't know you.

Easter was pretty dull. The only bright thing about it was your Easter card. On Easter Sunday, we were camped in a hog pasture in Cannon County. Guess you have heard Uncle Dave Macon sing about the Cannon County hills. Well, that is where we were. We could not get out of the hog pasture, so things were rather dull.

So you want to let the cows graze the lawn so that you won't have to mow it? It is a brilliant idea. I should have thought of it myself. But I like flowers too much for that. Believe it or not, I grew flowers as a hobby back home. Nothing that ever won a prize, you understand, but they were beautiful, and I once gave Mother a rose garden for a Christmas present. I bought and planted fifty two-year-old roses for her, and she thought more of them than anything else she got that year. The freeze last winter killed some of them, but she wrote that they would be pretty nice this year. (They were planted in 1936 and she still writes me about how her roses are doing.) But if you can teach the cows to eat only the grass we may try your idea sometime.

This is my last sheet of paper and there is no place to buy any tonight.

Love Always,
Leland

Camp Forrest, Tenn.
May 2, 1943

My Dearest Letty:

This is the last time I will have a chance to write for three or four days, maybe longer, and I only have a short time now. That should be enough to tell you I am still crazy about you.

I do hope you will understand that I am really rushed for writing time. When we are out, there is absolutely no time to write, no stationery, and no way to mail letters. When we come in for a rest period there is so much to do that we have practically no time for writing. So please don't think all the impossible things when I fail to write. And don't worry your pretty head about a dogface. We are not worth it.

I guess you are at church this morning. I can imagine just how you look with your bright spring dress and your hair flying in the wind. All the 4Fs and 16-year-olds are trying to flirt with you, but you shake your saucy head and tell them all "No."

I tried to get a pass to see my brother last night. He is at Paris, which is about 150 miles from us. But that is too far. The only way we can get a pass of more than six hours is to prove that we have a relative within 60 miles of our camp. So I took a six-hour pass and went to Murfreesboro. There, my bunny, is some town. It would be OK if there were not so many soldiers. There are about six soldiers to one civilian, and you can imagine what milling and crowding is going on all the time. It is worse than a bunch of hogs. There is not enough of anything to go around. I tried to find something to eat in the best cafe in town, but all they had were ham-and-cheese sandwiches.

Our next problem starts in the morning, and I am wondering if we will do as well as we did on the last. We pushed the Red Army around quite a bit, so much, in fact, that the general staff gave them a lot more strength for this problem.

Say, I almost got bitten by a dog on the last problem. We were scouting a road and I saw a Red hidden behind a smokehouse. I jumped out with my tommy gun to capture him, and a big shepherd dog belonging in the farmhouse attacked me. While I was fighting off the dog, my enemy got away.

The chow whistle just blew.

Love Always,
Leland

Camp Forrest, Tenn.
May 6, 1943

My Dearest Letty:

Well, I am a dead soldier again, but this time I have three sheets of paper. Can't mail my letter until I get back to the company, but I can have one written.

Somehow I always get bumped off in every problem, but our car did well. They had my car in the front of the column. The lieutenant was there in the first problem and only lasted 30 minutes. We lasted two days and knocked out two other scout cars and two jeeps. The car that went up after we were knocked out didn't get over the first hill.

Getting knocked out in mock wars is quite a snap. I slept until eight this morning and then all afternoon. I dreamed I was crazy about a girl with her hair all piled up on her head. She was cute and quite nice.

Boy! What would I give to have dinner with you tonight? We would have lettuce, green onions and radishes. I have lived on C rations for a week and am hungry for fresh vegetables.

I am learning the art of being a hobo. At our last rest stop I talked an old farmer out of a swell dinner. (We were camped in his pasture and he invited me up.) Then two days ago we camped on a farmer's lawn. His daughter, an old maid of 28 or 30, quite frankly told us she didn't like soldiers. I finally aroused her sympathy until she agreed to sell me some eggs. When we cooked them I found that she had given me half a dozen extra. How's that for being a hobo? Looks like we will be able to get along OK.

But I am out of paper.

I Love You Always,
Leland

Dearest Letty

Camp Forrest, Tenn.
May 7, 1943

My Dearest Letty:

Just had a bunch of your letters and are they morale builders! I was tired, sleepy and hungry when I got them, for we had been driving for quite a long way. I almost missed the first hot meal I have had a chance at for a week just to read them. Now I am writing you when I could be sleeping.

Yes, it has been almost a year since I wrote you my first card. That, my sweet, took a lot of courage. I didn't know that you wouldn't throw it back in my face, for Miss Post says that sort of thing simply isn't done. And I knew you were a conventional person.

But I was pretty lucky, for you must have been in a rare good humor when you got it, so it was the beginning of a beautiful romance. Of course, it could have been more beautiful under different circumstances, but it has been nice from where I stand. You must be satisfied, too, or you wouldn't sit on the lawn and play William Tremble Toe, of all games. It could be that you play it because only 4Fs and schoolboys are around, but I prefer to think differently.

Oh, say, what's wrong with your life, aside from being an old maid who thinks she is in love with a hobo soldier? If you had a dozen younger brothers and sisters they couldn't change that. You could have nothing to do with the number of younger brothers you have, no matter how many times you lived your life over, but surely you could have avoided being an old maid.

You mentioned Norman Dickey. Yes, I know Norman quite well. He is one of my favorite bores.

Have just been swimming in Stone River. It is quite beautiful. We swam just above an old milldam. The dam, they said, is 150 years old, but it is still in perfect shape. The millrace is still there and would turn the water wheel if someone cared to restore the mill. Ask your mother about the old water mill. She can tell you how they worked.

I have decided that you and I should live here at one of these old milldams. There are many of them in this country. We could bum down south in the winter and spend the summer paddling around in the clean, cool river. I could teach you to fish (obviously, it would take a lot of teaching), and then you could get the fish for dinner if I wasn't in the mood to fish for the sport. Tobacco for the pipe would be easy, for they grow it here.

Here are nine pages and the ninth says:

> I Love You,
> Leland

Camp Forrest, Tenn.
May 8, 1943

My Dearest Letty:

Don't think I have time for a long letter since I am supposed to get a little sleep. But I can tell you:

(1) It's raining.

(2) I could have gone to town and didn't.

(3) We are camped on Cripple Creek.

(4)

(5) I love you.

Now to elaborate and fill out the outline I just laid out.

(1) It came quite a storm tonight, but I was expecting that. All day it had been cloudy. I did not pitch a tent last night for it was quite clear when I went to bed. But this morning I was awakened by rain in my face and half an hour before first call, too.

Then tonight the storm broke. Lightning cut weird jagged gashes in the sky just above the trees. Thunder rumbled like a regiment of General Grant tanks passing in review, and the wind rode the cedars to the earth, or almost to the earth, like a troop of boys playing Cowboys and Broncos. The rain came in torrents, drenching the trees and washing the foliage clean of all the dirt and dust the spring winds had deposited upon it. Tomorrow, the sun will shine and the trees will hang out their emerald leaves to dry just as Mrs. Jones hangs out the family wash. But my tent stood up well and I am perfectly dry, as is my sleeping bag.

(2) I could have gone to Nashville tonight but the pass was only for eight hours and it is about 50 miles up there. Since I had to be back in camp by 10 o'clock I did not think it worth my time. Now I am glad I decided not to go.

(3) I suppose you have heard the hillbilly song "Crippled Creek." Well, we are camped on Cripple Creek tonight, and it is the creek from which the song takes its name, believe it or not.

(4) This is the paragraph I could have written and didn't. When I do, it will please you, I hope.

(5) There is no point in writing a paragraph here. Less than a book would be incomplete, and more than "I Love You" would be superfluous.

Love,
Leland

Camp Forrest, Tenn.
May 16, 1943

My Dearest Letty:

Even though I won't get to mail this until tomorrow, I can write it today. Have been out all the week and we are not allowed to write while the problem is on.

Had a pretty nice time on this problem even if it did rain three times. Last night, we had a flood. There was more electricity in the air than I had ever seen. Lightning was constantly jumping off a big transformer in front of the church where I was sleeping.

Yes, I slept in a church in spite of the Army order that no one is to enter any building while a problem is on. But my car was so far away from the command post that they could not check on me. I told the boys to find a dry place if they could, and I found a church. It was a nice church with rugs on the floor. I really slept well.

I had to sleep out in the other rains, but they were not so bad. I simply draped my shelter half over a fence and rolled my sleeping bag under it.

Yes, I wait for your letters just as you said I should. Every sentence is just as interesting as you laughingly suggested. Maybe you think I don't care who came to see you or what happened at Sunday school, but I do. A lot of the people you write about are friends of mine and this is the only way I ever hear about them. Anything you choose to write is interesting, just because you write it, if for no other reason.

You wondered if my staying in a hog pasture would cause me to pick up any of the habits of the swine. I am not so sure that I can escape. It is pretty hard to behave like a civilized human when we live in hog lots and eat when we can. If you expect me to behave like Miss Post's blue book when I get home you may be sadly disappointed. I am sure I will not know which fork to use when I come in to sample your garden peas, or whatever you may have. Hope you will overlook those little things, but I am not sure you will be able to do that.

Love Always,
Leland

Camp Forrest, Tenn.
May 18, 1943

My Dearest Letty:

I am writing this between bites of cookies, so don't be surprised if crumbs are in the letter. In other words, it could easily be crumby. I am eating the kind of cookies they sell at the P.X., and they are pretty good. That is because they are quite large and I go in for quantity rather than quality in the food we get here. If there is plenty of it, I can eat beans or vegetable stew for breakfast and like it. I dare you to ever offer me a bean for breakfast.

Had to work most of the day at such jobs as repairing a truck top and washing scout cars down at the river. The best man in my crew was on KP today so the car washing was tougher than usual.

One of the boys in the company has a pet fox and I wish you could see it. It is no bigger than an ordinary cat and is quite amusing. It will follow like a dog and tries to play with Furlough, the company mascot, but Furlough is afraid of it.

Its name is Herman, but it could just as well be Ethel or Pearl.

So you got the souvenir of Rock City? I was not sure whether it would get there safely, as it looked pretty fragile. The matches are for your boyfriends to light their cigarettes with, not you. I will send you a lighter sometime when I find one that suits me.

I was thinking what a tragedy it would be if your boyfriends happened to come and you had no matches for them to light their smokes. An ashtray is no good without matches, you know. But I warn you that the matches are loaded and will blow up in their face, so don't let it happen to you. Let each guy who comes around use one of the matches and that will take care of him.

You spoke of Loyd being at home. I had been wondering about him. Yes, I always liked Loyd so you didn't lie to him. I intend to write him a letter when I get time. Quite a few things have happened in the company that he would like to hear—stuff about getting a new company commander and a new first sergeant. He hated the sergeant we now have, but he did not like the old one either, and he would laugh to learn that the boys ducked him in the creek to sober him up.

After saying I'm crazy about you I'll have to sign off and write Mother.

Love Always,
Leland

Camp Forrest, Tenn.
May 23, 1943

My Dearest Letty:

I finally got around to writing the letter I promised to write yesterday. Didn't even have time to comb my hair yesterday. I couldn't have combed it if I had found the time, for at the moment I don't have a comb. Why? The hogs carried it off along with all my other toilet articles. It's no joke.

We moved into a hog pasture, as usual. The next morning I dug out my shaving case and proceeded to get some of the dirt and grime out of my hair. I carried all of my equipment in a small zipper case. When I had finished one of the boys wanted to use my soap. So I left it on the ground. Five minutes later, the hogs had carried it all off. Now I have no razor, toothbrush, comb or anything. I have had no chance to replace them. I told the guy who owned the hogs if any of them turned up with a clean shave just remember that he had used my razor.

I liked your last letter immensely. Now every time I hear a whippoorwill I know just how you must have been feeling when you wrote it. The whippoorwills are quite numerous here, and tame. Or it may be that late at night they forget that men are sleeping under every tree. Last night, one came in so close to my sleeping bag that he awakened me. I lay still and could hear the clucking sound he made between calls, and I wondered if you had ever been near enough to one to hear his chuckle.

Had an easy time during most of the last problem, but I may have told you all about it in an earlier letter. Can't ever remember just what I have written to you except I vaguely recall writing that I was more than a little in love with you. I may not have said those exact words (more than a hundred times) but that was the general idea anyway.

We were held in reserve for a time on the last problem and then sent out at cyclone speed. That night the lieutenant tried to take us up a road that was dug from the side of a hill, and it was not wide enough for a farm wagon, let alone a scout car. For two miles we felt our way along without lights. On the left was a bank of dirt six feet high. On the right was a drop-off as much as 20 feet. We almost made it, but the scout car in the front of the column broke a bridge and the car in the rear slid a wheel over the bank. So the column was stuck for the night. The jeeps had crossed the bridge so the lieutenant and the sergeants climbed in them and took off, leaving me with a platoon all bogged down. We had to tie the scout car to a tree to keep it from turning over, then went to sleep.

Next morning, we decided we couldn't do the job on the carrots and beans in the Army C ration, so we scouted around and located a farmer who sold us some ham, eggs and honey. Boy, was that a swell breakfast! You should have eaten some of my cooking. Then we went to work, built a bridge and lowered the scout car into the gully, then towed it out. All in a day's work.

We do all sorts of weird things such as floating cars across the river on rafts and lowering jeeps over mountain drops, which are too steep for them to negotiate, by using ropes. It is all a lot of fun, in a way.

Guess I won't get a chance to write again for a few days, but I will be thinking of you and wishing I could have one of your letters.

Hope you got to go see the river as they say it is wild.

Mother was writing about a little girl back home who went with her parents to see the river. When she came back, Mother asked her what the river was like. She said there was so much water they couldn't get close enough to see the river. Hope you didn't have the same trouble.

Love Always,
Leland

Dearest Letty

My Dearest Letty:

Didn't have time to write you after we came into camp last night. It was rather late and a whole day's work simply had to be done before we could go to bed. We didn't get it all done, but when we got off it was too late to write.

My letters may be less frequent now, for we have to work at least a day longer than we did in the early part of the maneuver. But I always try to write as soon as we come in. I have said that so many times I guess you are tired of hearing it. I also keep saying I love you and you never complain about that, so I have concluded that you are not an easy victim of monotony. When you begin to tear your hair and go into tantrums from my repeating things I will try to be more original.

Had three letters from you in the mail last night, and they were wonderful. Even in the paragraph about the boys bringing you home I only wish you had omitted the request that I refrain from teasing you. I could think up some spicy remarks on that score.

I still think the poor saps must have been blind or they were trying to flatter you on your age. Perhaps they were so swept off their feet when you smiled at them that they forgot to look closely for the signs of age. Maybe they were just hungry.

Yes, I know Lonnie, but I don't know the other boys. You didn't know his full name is Lonnie Lotion. He is the second guy I ever knew with Lotion for a name.

We had a lot of rain this week and a couple of nights were pretty uncomfortable, but the rest of the time was pleasant enough. Monday, we crossed the Cumberland River, using rowboats and amphibious cars, and left our scout cars on the south side. My sleeping bag and raincoat were in my car and that night it rained. We all got soaked and pretty cold since we could not build a fire. Tuesday night, it was clear but colder and we still had no sleeping bag. The engineers finished the bridge about two in the morning and our cars got across. By three, we were in Gallatin, which is about the size of Russellville, and my car was knocked out on the Main Street of the city. I unrolled my bag and went to sleep on the curb at the edge of the street. When I woke up it was nine o'clock. The boys had hidden my revolver, stuffed paper in my shoes and carried off my watch. People stared curiously at me. They seemed surprised that a guy could sleep in the middle of all the traffic of their fair city, especially since two companies of 28-ton tanks had passed a few feet from me without disturbing me in the least.

When I woke up, the first thing I saw was a big sign across the street that said: "Free showers to service men." I was simply caked with mud, and the hot shower really felt good.

Guess you are in the cotton patch today if the sun is shining there as it is here. At least if you are in the field working I can be reasonably sure you are not in any mischief. If you are at Sunday school, I can't be quite so sure. Girls can do such naughty things behind a Sunday school book, such as whisper too loud and make faces at the teacher.

Have just put out my weekly wash. It is hanging on the fence, all nice and clean. Well, not exactly clean, but I boiled most of the sweat and mud out of it. If I ever get out of the Army, I promise to never wash another pair of coveralls. But I have a lot of work to do, so I must say "I Love You" and run along.

Love Always,
Leland

Camp Forrest, Tenn.
June 3, 1943

My Dearest Letty:

But for a little luck I would not be writing you today. At least not with this pen. I lost it this morning over in a little village called Walter Hill. Or rather I was writing a report over there when they yelled "Move out!" and I left it on the ground. Missed it when I started to finish my report, so I got a jeep and went back. Another guy had found it and his outfit was ready to move, so I barely got it back. Don't know if I could train another fountain pen to write "I love you" as naturally as this one does. It is pretty well broken in, so that when I start writing you that is all it wants to write.

You say you haven't seen anything but bugs and worms. There you have an interesting subject. I should know. I live and sleep with them, and sometimes I suspect that I have eaten them. When I swallow a bit of creamed potatoes and feel something scratch my throat it could easily be a grasshopper, and when I get to sleep and something crawls around in the sleeping bag I think nothing of it. Mosquitoes with a wingspread of less than six inches mean nothing. Only big ones bother.

I keep learning about you, too. Now I learn that in addition to the other sweet things you can do you can make 'lasses candy. Or are you just baiting me and leading me to believe all sorts of sweet things about you? Sometime I hope to learn the truth about all this stuff. The heck of it is you will probably learn the whole truth about me, too, and I am afraid you will learn enough to balance the scales against me. But after you begin learning it, it will be too late to do anything about it. The fact that I am a hobo and a chain smoker (lots of other things, too) can't alter the fact that you are mine.

Love Always,
Leland

Camp Forrest, Tenn.
June 4, 1943

My Dearest Letty:

The last letter I wrote only went off today but I am writing again. If you get two letters from me in the same mail don't let yourself be surprised.

Have just come in from the river and my clothes are all wet. I only have one pair of coveralls with me and they get pretty dirty, so I washed them and they have not had time to dry.

We swam at an old milldam, but this one still has a mill in operation. I had seen several old dams and had passed a number of them that still operated. But this was the first one I had found time to inspect. It proved pretty interesting. You could watch the wheat go into the top and the flour, shorts and bran come out at the bottom. Your mother may remember the old water mills.

We had a pretty good comedy yesterday. When the problem was over, we assembled in a pasture. A sign at the gate said, "Beware, Dangerous Bull." Some of the boys who knew nothing of such things went out to see just how bad it was. It was a nice race but the bull lost by a full two yards. However, he finished with a rush and if the race had been longer all the fans agreed that it would have been closer. No official time has been announced on the race, but I am sure it was near the record for the dash.

The fans loved it and half of them were cheering for the bull while the other half was equally enthusiastic in their support of the GI. Oh, well, things like that help to relieve the monotony.

You seemed to be worried for fear I would try the hero stuff. Well, you can ease your mind on that. I never had any desire to be a hero, at any time, and especially not in the Army. Then, too, the modern Army is not built with heroes. It is a job just like the chap who drives a truck or works in a factory. The soldier seldom thinks there is glamour in the job any more than the truck driver does. And if one does get an idea like that, the other guys and the officers soon take the wind out of his sails and straighten him out.

All the glamour of the job of crawling in mud and eating beans for breakfast exists in the newspaper stories, and most of the heroes are just like a few hundred thousand other guys. But the reporters happened to pick them out. Must say I love you and get to bed.

Love Always,
Leland

Camp Forrest, Tenn.
June 11, 1943

My Dearest Letty:

Guess I'll only have time for one letter this week, for they are giving us quite a rush. We came in here last night, but it was pretty late and I had a mild case of ptomaine poisoning (if it comes in a mild form), so I did no writing. No sleeping either.

Today was clean-up day and even though I let the boys do the work there was no chance to write you and Mother. We start out again tomorrow night so now I hope you understand why this is the only letter you will get this week. You always understand those things, or pretend you do, which is one of the many reasons you are so wonderful.

Dearest Letty

Remember the O. Henry characterization in which different types of people were compared to different parts of the anatomy? In that table you, too, would have to be a shoulder. If I know you or have judged correctly, people instinctively lean on you, as the kids do—and as I do. If they have troubles, that must be told to someone. They tell Letty. She is always willing to listen. And if they must cry, they cry to you. Crying doesn't help if you can't cry on a shoulder. And you are always around for them to unload on.

Oh, by the way, I had a nice thrill this week, but it was shocking. Hope you don't mind my telling you a shocking story. It happened like this:

It was raining in torrents and the night was black as ink. We were driving without lights across a pasture. The car in front of mine ran upon a stump, and we had to tow him off. Just as I was rewinding the towing cable a bolt of lightning struck quite close to us. The electricity bounced around all over the place, and most of it must have come down the cable through me. It burned my hands and almost knocked me down. It was strong enough that the lights on the car flared up almost as if the light switch had been snapped on. Quite thrilling, don't you think? I will try to avoid holding a steel cable attached to a scout car when the next electrical storm comes.

Too bad you had to go back into the cotton patch. But you should not mind that seeing that you will have to go on doing it the rest of your life—or something just as tough.

I must get some sleep tonight. May not have a chance tomorrow night, and I missed last night. I do love you.

Always,
Leland

Camp Forrest, Tenn.
June 18, 1943

My Dearest Letty:

You are probably thinking of suing me for breach of promise or something by now, thinking that I had deserted you. But that is not true and I could prove it in any court. If any man can do the things we have done this week and still find time to write, well, he's a genius. But I still love you in spite of the fact that I have not written in a week.

Believe it or not, we set some kind of a record for going without sleep. Here is our record:

Saturday night, we stayed up all night getting ready to move out, which we did sometime after midnight Sunday night. We guarded the river until midnight, then moved across, floating our cars on rubber boats. Monday night at 2 o'clock I unrolled my bedroll for the first time since Friday night. We caught up with our sleep then and started out again to repeat the performance. But we ended up here at 5 o'clock yesterday morning.

It may not sound reasonable, but I actually went to sleep standing up in the front of a scout car, not once but a dozen times. More than once I was awakened by small twigs slapping me in the face as we passed under trees. Luckily, there were no large limbs or I would have been beheaded. Once I actually dreamed about you. Thought I was on furlough and on my way up to see you. It was quite disappointing to have a twig smack me sharply across the cheek and find myself climbing a Tennessee mountain instead of an Arkansas mountain.

But it was a good problem, and great training. We did everything we would do in actual war. We had a cage of carrier pigeons, which we used to send back a message, and we had a bunch of troops jump from planes in parachutes to help us out. Wish you could have seen them even if it had meant taking a chance on losing you to one of them.

Then there were the troops who came down in gliders, which are huge planes with no engines. They tow them behind planes just as one car pulls another. When they get over a meadow or a corn patch they cut loose and soar down. Most of them crash, of course, but there are surprisingly few injuries, even if they do carry 15 men. They are made from light stuff so they come down easy, and if they hit a tree or run through a fence no one cares. I brought in a piece of one of them and will send it along sometime if I have not lost it so that you can see how light they really are.

They have names painted on them, just as we have on our cars. Such names as "Hitler's Hearse," "Hitchhiker," etc.

Don't let yourself get excited over a GI convoy. Don't want to lose you to another dogface, you know, and it could happen if you go about thinking of them as glamorous. But they all have dirty ears and sand in their hair.

You know about their dirty ears. You are always advising me to wash mine, which makes me suspicious. I must write Mother a couple of pages tonight.

Love Always,
Leland

Camp Forrest, Tenn.
June 19, 1943

My Dearest Letty:

I have time for a short letter today. All I can think to do in celebration of my birthday anniversary is to write you a letter and say "I Love You." But a celebration is not a celebration if you do it every night. Of course, I don't do it every night, but do it every chance I get.

You seem excited over the fact that I made sergeant. It is really not so important as all that. It only means a little more pay and a little more responsibility. I have been doing the job most of the time since we were on the desert, so it is just an increase in pay. I don't even know how much of an increase it is. Never looked up the scale and never asked anyone. I'll find out when I get paid the first of July.

I think it's around $78 per month. A corporal gets $66 and I think it is a $12 raise. It won't be enough to make a heck of a lot of difference. Can't see that I have any more money than I did when I was a private. I don't suppose $12 will change that.

Guess we'll have to depend on you to save the money by not buying more than one hat a season. Then you can save a penny now and then by not weighing on the penny scales to see if I still love you. It is such a waste of money, you know.

Say, I wish you could see the light I have just lit. Boy, it is a honey. I had four candles lying on a tobacco pack and the sun melted them and welded them to the cardboard. Now I merely bury the box edgewise and light all four candles. It makes such a swell light. But I am afraid the heat will melt the candles again and I will have to hunt for a new candlestick, which is just what is happening now. Time out while I fix my light.

All's Fair

I can afford to be generous with my candles now. Last spring when I was going to need them for such a long time and they were so hard to get, I only used one at a time. Now I have a whole box, so I use as many as I wish to make a good light.

Hope you don't mind if I make this short, as I must write all my brothers tonight.

Love Always,
Leland

Camp Forrest, Tenn.
June 20, 1943

My Dearest Letty:

Nothing has happened today that could be called interesting by any stretch of the imagination, but I am writing you again.

Guess you are at the young people's meeting, playing the piano, about now. It is almost nine o'clock so you should be, anyway. Wish I could sneak up to the window, but you would be making eyes at some poor boy who was too young to know he was wasting his time falling in love with an old maid.

Boys are like that. I remember my first serious affair. I was fully 14 and the girl was no less than 18. Did she have me snowed! Although she later denied leading me along deliberately, I always thought she did. She was a girl named Annie Taylor, and she is now in Tulsa or Oklahoma City. I was terribly shocked when she married. My 15-year-old pride could hardly stand the shock.

The last paragraph was for your information, as I knew you would go to asking questions.

Now, to even the score, how about telling me about your first serious affair? Now don't pick one of the later ones since I probably know the story behind them as thoroughly as you would dare tell me.

Say, you should have been in one of the little towns along the highway north of the river the night the problem ended last week. You have seen Western towns shot up in the movies, but never anything to compare with what we did to Red Boiling Springs, Silodam and a few more. It was a sort of celebration as the last problem of the maneuver was over.

We had two .30-caliber machineguns on my car and about a thousand rounds of blank ammunition. We didn't want to turn it in so I told the boys on the guns to use it up to celebrate.

Our car was the last in the convoy, so everyone in the towns had plenty of time to get out and see us. When we would get even with a crowd the boys would turn both guns loose. Two machineguns, each firing seven times per second, can make a lot of racket. You should have seen people take cover. I don't think they were too sure we were firing blanks.

Since this is all the paper I have, I must cut this short. But I still love you.

Love Always,
Leland

Camp Forrest, Tenn.
June 22, 1943

My Dearest Letty:

One day I am sitting around thinking of this and that, but mostly I am thinking of how hot it is and of a certain doll back home, which is what most dogfaces generally do. Only they don't always think of a doll back home but maybe it is one they met at the Crocus Club or some other place the guys go when they are lucky enough to get a pass, and sometimes they are thinking of the crap game or the poker party they are having after supper.

Me: I never play the games of chance, for I figure too many men in this man's Army are already too good for a man to learn the game by playing with them.

But the odds are 8 to 6 that if the guys are thinking of a crap game way back in their minds they are only hoping to make some potatoes so they can go out with the doll they met at the Crocus Club, or send a chunk of ice to the doll back home.

Like I said before, I am sitting around thinking of the doll back home, for I am not meeting any other dolls at any of the clubs, and she is the only doll there is for me to think about. It occurs to me that I am not writing her yet today, so I out with my old scratcher and find that I have no paper but this stuff.

Just about this time a guy at the kitchen yells "Mail Call" like a foghorn out from Ventura Point in California is sounding off. About half the guys in the company start crashing through the bushes in the general direction of the kitchen, hoping they have a letter from their ever-loving doll. The other half are yelling "Bring my mail, Joe," this half being too lazy to crash through the bushes or else figuring their ever-loving doll didn't write them anyway.

Me: I stroll down figuring there is no hurry since the first few minutes is used in getting rid of the papers, and I have no papers anyway. But I am pretty sure I have a letter from my ever-loving doll as it is about time for her to write.

When the mail clerk, who is the guy with the voice like the foghorn out at Ventura Point, calls my name first it is only a birthday card from an old guy and his ever-loving wife. How it comes in so late I don't know. Finally, as I am beginning to think my ever-loving doll didn't have time to write me after all, being busy with this and that and one thing or another, he calls my name again and there it is. It is a wonderful letter indeed, for it says my ever-loving doll still loves me and she is wondering why I don't write to her for such a long time. But there are plenty of gamblers who will lay you 8 to 5 that it has not been more than four days since she had a letter.

Which makes me happy indeed, for if four or five days between letters seems like such a long time the chances are she is still in love.

I am also glad indeed when I remember she is not like the dolls you are apt to meet in the clubs along the broadway. While they may pretend to be ever loving, they always tell the other guys the same story they are telling you. Which is why I don't care to meet them in the first place.

I am hoping you are not minding my Runyonesque letter. I am reading his yarns today and copying his style. Also, I am saying I love you more than somewhat, which is all I have paper to say.

Leland

Pine Camp, N.Y.
June 26, 1943

My Dearest Letty:

Just have time to say I love you two days more than I did when I wrote last, or is it three?

Arrived this morning and they are rushing us around more than somewhat. Haven't had time to look around, but it seems like a nice place. Hope to have time to write tomorrow.

Love Always,
Leland

Pine Camp, N.Y.
June 27, 1943

My Dearest Letty,

Have been thinking of you all day, and there is only one thing to do in a case like that. A long, boring letter is the only remedy.

I don't know how long it will be before your letters begin catching up with me, but if it is tomorrow that will be too long. Haven't had a letter from anyone since we left Tennessee, but that was to be expected, for no one knew I was coming up here. That makes it a little tough about getting mail, but it is the Army way and is the best for all concerned.

We had a nice trip up. Came by Cincinnati, Cleveland, Rochester, etc. Trips on a GI train are always interesting, for even if we know where we are going we never know which route we will take or which town we are going through next.

If a newspaperman were writing an account of a troop train trip he might say:

"Rocketing through the small towns and switch points, a long train hurries through the night. Aboard it, boys and men in khaki lounge in their berths. They are American—the grocery clerk, the farm boy, the banker's son, and the alley rat, all surprisingly alike now, all going some place in a hurry.

"The drama of the rushing troop train is the drama of America in 1943. Civilians wait on platforms as the long train hurries by. The train has no listing on the timetable except train 'to Berlin,' or 'Rome' or 'Tokio.'

"The trains rattle through the yards at Lexington, Lincoln, or Chicago. They send their headlights searching into the night through the Cumberland Mountain passes or startle the dogs to barking in an Ohio farmyard with their long drawn-out whistles at the crossings.

"The atmosphere of the troop train is the atmosphere of a nation at war. The wheels click off the miles carrying a whole unit with their guns and cars down the track."

Some guy from Ohio wonders if we will pass through his hometown. Someone else wonders when we will get there.

There is the usual Army routine for some of the men: cleanup squads, KP (I once peeled potatoes all the way from Fort Worth to Ranger). But the rest of the men are left to amuse themselves. Some sleep, some read, some play games, some talk or argue, others watch the panorama of America through a Pullman window. But few are bored.

We travel in great style. The porter makes our bed. The USO tosses up magazines if we stop long enough, and there is clean linen every night. And it is all free, except what we choose to buy at the stops (and we are seldom permitted to get off for anything). We must have someone bring it to us. On this trip I traveled from Cookeville, Tenn., to Watertown, N.Y., and spent 55 cents: 25 cents for cigars, 25 cents for candy and a paper. The small total, of course, was due to the fact that we had no chance to buy anything.

This is a pretty nice camp, not far from the lakes, and in the middle of the pines, just as the name suggests. Haven't had time to look around but it should be interesting. We are not far from Lake Placid, Lake Ontario, the St. Lawrence River, Canada, Syracuse and only a few hours from New York City. I hope to be able to get down to the city before long, and I also want to go to Canada.

I must sign off and write Mother.

Always,
Leland

Dearest Letty

Pine Camp, N.Y.
July 3, 1943

My Dearest Letty:

Well, your letters have begun to catch up with us now, as have the letters from all the other people who were supposed to write to me. Had eight letters in the mail today and ten yesterday. Was it fun to read all of them, but it won't be so easy to get them answered.

We have so little time to write. Some nights we don't get off until midnight. They even have an indoor firing range so they just turn the lights on and we go ahead with our firing.

You keep telling me how old I am, but you are mistaken there. Old men can't do what we are doing. Show me an old man who can walk through the obstacle course that we ran through. And I'd also like to see an old man who could keep up with the pace on our cross-country runs. You have to be in pretty good shape to do three miles in this sand at the pace we do it. I don't intend that as a boast but it helps explain why I can't write too often.

Poor little girl! Why don't you tell the loving mamas to take care of their own brats? You have more important things to do.

Oh! So it's against your religion to make things happen, is it? Now don't give me that line. Don't I know things always pop when you are around. Like the time you drank up all the wine at the communion and they had to postpone the service while someone went out and got another quart of Amontillado. Or the time you tied the can to the dog's tail and he ran through the church house and threw the Sunday school crowd into a panic. But you're a good little girl!

Just had a letter from Loyd. He was cheerful but I am not sure he doesn't wish he were back in the Army. Yes, he asked me if I wanted him to go up and see you occasionally.

Love Always,
Leland

Pine Camp, N.Y.
July 5, 1943

My Dearest Letty,

Thought I would find time to write you today and here I am at the job. On the company's time, too.

Oh, yes, there is another pillowcase on the way. Monotonous, isn't it? But I am not an original person and when you seemed pleased over the first one I just keep sending them along and hoping they serve to tell you that I still love you. I may be able to find a more original souvenir when I get to town, but until I do this will have to serve. Tell your mother she may have enough to make a large quilt top if my dear uncle keeps moving me around.

Remember when I wrote that I could not get any letters? Well, they have begun to catch up with me now and I have more than I can answer. School kids, farmers, old men, bankers (and I don't owe him either) all wrote me at once. Don't know how I will ever find time to answer them all, but I think I can manage some way. Letters are one of the best ways in the world to retain friendships. In fact, it is the only way left for a soldier. You forget people and they forget you if you don't retain some contact with them.

That last sentence does not apply to you in any way. If I did not hear from you for a decade or a century it would be all the same.

Love Always,
Leland

Pine Camp, N.Y.
July 6, 1943

My Dearest Letty,

It is almost 10 o'clock and I have just come in from school. So I am writing you instead of reading Anatole France. I have a good book that I should have been reading.

But, no! I always find myself getting greater pleasure out of writing to you than from improving the mind. Naughty girl you are to interfere with my education that way.

Just had a letter from you today. Say, did you go poetic in a big way! Frankly, I didn't know you could do it. I loved it.

Things are about the same here. We still have the work to do, but they are always adding to it. Now we get up half an hour earlier than we did last week, which is not so pleasant. When I get out of this Army I won't get up until ten in the morning. It will be so much fun lying in bed and no one to shout "Hit the floor" or "Roll out." No one to blow a whistle or a bugle.

I saw a good show last night. It was one of the Camel Caravan shows, and I just got out of school in time to catch the last performance. They had several pretty good acts, including an exhibition by two of the country's leading ping-pong players.

So you went swimming and picked up a couple of chiggers, and you couldn't take it. I'm a bit surprised at your admitting it, even though I had suspected it all along. A chigger is so small, too. A bug that size couldn't hurt anyone. Why, when we were down in Tennessee we didn't even look at a bug if it didn't have a wingspread of more than six inches.

I would like to know what you think of South America as a place to live. We might go there, you know, as it is nice open country. Maybe I can get a job down there when the war is over. It should be fun doing a geodetic survey of Brazil or some such job.

Your stars would be right if they said I thought of you always.

Love Always,
Leland

Pine Camp, N.Y.
July 7, 1943

My Dearest Letty:

I guess I shouldn't write this tonight as I have neither the time nor the news to construct a readable letter. But neither do I have the will to resist writing, even though this brings the standard average of my letter quality down several points from the already low base.

Even saying "I think of you every day" and "I miss you always" and "I'm crazy about you" doesn't make it a good letter.

Guess you have burned out on the cotton chopping by this time. If you haven't, I am a bit surprised. I didn't think you would last until the first of July with the weather getting hot and the shade getting more inviting all the time. Can't say that I blame you at that. You are not supposed to chop cotton.

Love Always and Always,
Leland

Pine Camp, N.Y.
July 13, 1943

My Dearest Letty:

I may find time to finish this after I come back from school, but I won't get many lines written until the whistle blows. It is almost time.

So you are surprised that I still go to school. Well, there is nothing surprising about that, and don't feel stuck up because you have finished. It only goes to show that you learned it when you went over it, and I still have to study it. Then, being older, you have had more time to cover such subjects as "The Rise of Fascism in Italy," which was the subject of last night's lecture, or "The Possibility of a Russo-Japanese Conflict," which is tonight's subject. The guy last night is a former newspaperman who has spent six years in Italy, so he knew quite a bit about that subject.

Wish they would let me lecture on the subject of "The Soldier and the Girl Back Home" or "Why Dogfaces Fall in Love." I could tell them all about that, having had a wealth of personal experience, what with being in love with you all these years.

But do you think they give me a chance to discuss those subjects? They do not! They say, "You will lecture on 'The Nomenclature and Function of the Browning Machine Gun, Cal. 50m M2' or 'The Ballistics of the U. S. Carbine, Cal. .30. M1.'" I ask you, what chance does that give a guy to express himself?

I am glad you liked the pillowcase. You seem to get enthusiastic over everything I send you, no matter how small it is. The appreciation you express makes a guy want to send you the Brooklyn Bridge and the Empire State Building. The best I can do at the moment is to send my heart.

Love Always,
Leland

Dearest Letty

Pine Camp, N.Y.
July 25, 1943

My Dearest Letty:

You may think by this time that I have forgotten how to write or that I have forgotten to write to you, but neither is true. It happened this way:

Early last week, the day I mailed my last letter to you, they took us out to the lake firing range. They said to take along enough equipment to last one night, which means enough cigarettes, candy, etc. There is no P.X. out there, you know. Well, we stayed until yesterday, so most of the boys were caught off base. The USO did send out cars with cigarettes, etc., for sale. That helped but we had no stationery. If they had told us we were to stay several days I could have taken some paper along, but that is the way they do things, and sometimes Letty doesn't get her letter on account of it.

So the boys from Gum Log are coming (or wanting to come) back again and you seemed to want to know my reaction. It's this way with me, as you probably know:

I am crazy about you but there is nothing I can do about that now. There is a little job to do first, you know. Since I am more or less a victim of circumstances, I can't be fair to you by trying to put you or anyone else under promise or obligation to me. So if you want to have boyfriends there is nothing I could do or say. That has to be decided by you alone.

However, since I have told you a thousand times that I am in love with you, it should be easy to guess which decision would make me happy and which would make me sad indeed. But, as I said before, the problem is yours and I think I know which way you will decide. I am quite sure you will give none of them a serious thought, so I am already happy about the whole thing.

Perhaps this whole paragraph was no good, but I hope to make myself clear. What I was trying to say is, I'm crazy about you and I know you feel the same way. And this is the main point. I trust you fully to go ahead feeling the same way. Full mutual understanding is the only way two people can go on loving one another. If you should feel any other way about the matter, write your opinion and I will give it my consideration and study. No matter what your idea may be, I shall go on loving you just the same.

Love Always,
Leland

Lake Ontario, N.Y.
July 30, 1943

My Dearest Letty:

Don't guess I will get to mail this for a day or two since we are out on Lake Ontario. Have been up here a couple of days and I don't know when we are going back to camp.

This is a wonderful place in summer. Let's come up here sometime and spend a few weeks. We could take a motorboat and explore all the islands and caves, and there are plenty of them. The Thousand Islands are not far east of here, and you can see dozens of islands from here.

Have just been swimming in the lake. The water is clear as glass and cool. It is like swimming in the ocean. The waves get high when the wind blows.

Birds swarm all over the place. A strange variety of birds, few of which I recognize. There is a northern tanager in every tree and several kinds of blackbirds and thousands of gulls, lazy, graceful gulls beating their wings against the sunset. Suddenly they sideslip, dive and plunge into the water. When they emerge, a fish is swinging in their beak.

We are about forty miles from Pine Camp. This place is an old Civilian Conservation Corps camp or National Guard encampment. There are half a dozen barracks, a mess hall, shower room, etc. The targets on the firing range are set along the top of a bluff, and the bullets fall out into the lake.

I sat in the lookout shed all afternoon and watched for boats. It is a little concrete shed between the targets and the water. The job of the lookout is to see that no boats come in the line of fire. It is weird to hear dozens of bullets cracking the air just above your head, but it does not greatly disturb the tranquility of the country. A little white spray flies up where the bullets hit the water, but that is all. The gulls wheel and circle as if nothing was happening, and a pair of Canadian thrush have a nest just outside the lookout shed. They go on feeding their young and paying no attention whatever to the swift death that passes only a few feet from them.

The lights will be out in a few minutes, just enough time to remind you that I'm still in love with you.

Love Always,
Leland

Pine Camp, N.Y.
August 1, 1943

My Dearest Letty:

It is Sunday and I find myself with enough time to say, "I'm still in love with you." Also time to write Mother and some other people, and then read the Sunday paper. After that, I can poke around in a book or loaf about the camp.

Boy, is Sunday a swell day in the Army for a lazy guy. They come around at 7 o'clock and wake the company, but there is no rule that says you have to get up. Chow is at 8, and then everyone is free to do what he chooses. If every day was like that, boy, would I get fat and even lazier than I am.

You wanted to know if my teacher had been able to teach me the alphabet. Shame on you. I learned that last year. I am now at the stage of education that Uncle Slug was at when he learned to write.

He was sitting in the corner scribbling or making crooked lines on a piece of paper. Suddenly he jumped up and yelled to Aunt Peachy, "I've learned to write."

"That's fine, Slug," Aunt Peachy said. "What have you written there?"

"How should I know?" he came back. "I ain't learned to read yet."

How dare you ask if I get tired of your letters. You know I don't. If they came four times as often as they do I would enjoy them four times as much. They are always fresh and breezy, even though you protest that they are dull. You say nothing ever happens to you or anyone else we both know, but I enjoy every sentence of the letters, especially the trivial things that happen to you. I like to know every little thing you do (that is, the things you want me to know) and don't think anything too little or unimportant to write about. Those are the things that make me know I am not losing touch with the normal civilian way of living.

I wish I could come home this summer. We could sit on the bluff and watch the world go by without caring where it went. But this winter or next year will be all the same. The bluff will still be there and we will still be in love just as we are, so why should we hurry?

Love Always,
Leland

Pine Camp, N.Y.
August 2, 1943

My Dearest Letty:

Surprised that I should find time to write on a Monday? I am a little surprised myself. They let us out of school a little early tonight so here I am.

The Army is a funny place. I have to go to school at night, and they gave me an assignment as a teacher. So I teach a couple of hours in the morning. That is, unless we are at Stony Point range. Nothing else interrupts the class.

I may have written before that I am teaching. Have been at it for almost a month now. It is the same kind of school we taught at Cooke, but this one is smaller and only takes in the battalion. But we must be doing OK with it. The major who is battalion commander stopped me this morning and gave the school a compliment. It is the first time he ever hinted that he even knew me. But he has visited the school several times.

In fact, the school is a favorite haunt of the battalion officers. Several times we have had both majors, three or four captains and any number of lieutenants drop by at once.

The staff of the school consists of the chaplain and another first lieutenant, Ed Sherman (I have written about him), and me.

But this could not be of much interest to you. What I want to say is I'm in love with you as much as ever (maybe more), but what sort of letter would that be? I have to fill in with something, and nothing that happens could be of interest to you, or nothing of importance can be written. There are restrictions, you know.

But no one could officially object to my writing about being in love with you.

Love Always,
Leland

Pine Camp, N.Y.
August 7, 1943

My Dearest Letty;

Two of your letters came today, and they were just what I needed to build my sagging nerves. Yes, my nerves took quite a slump this morning. We crawled through the infiltration course.

No, I know you don't know what that is, so I'll try to give you an idea, but I can't properly describe it. It is a course designed as nearly as possible to simulate battle conditions. Fifty men are lined up in a trench about eighteen inches deep. Half a dozen machineguns fire a hundred or so rounds just over the trench. Then they crawl out and inch along the ground toward the guns. Barbed wire is stretched about six inches from the ground, and the crawler must lift that and go under it. As he crawls along, charges of dynamite placed in shallow holes in the ground are exploded on all sides. All the time the machineguns are blazing away, the bullets passing no more than 18 inches above your head. Tracers are fired so that they can be seen. They are a streak of flame like a shooting star, and they look much closer than the 18 inches they are supposed to be. They crack like a Fourth of July firecracker, and the hot wind fans the sweat from the crawler's face.

Realistic looking dummies splashed with red paint hang on the wire entanglements as a grim warning to stay low. But no such warning is necessary. The rim of every man's helmet plows a trench in the mud as he worms along. At the end of fifty grueling yards is another shallow trench, but the guns are still firing and the bullets look even closer, so you don't just dive into the trench. That would put too much of the body above the ground. The proper way to get into the trench is to turn until the body is parallel with it. Then simply roll over and there you are.

It is really not as dangerous as it looks. Only one man was hurt. He happened to be too close to a charge of dynamite when it exploded and the concussion burst one of his eardrums. One charge almost buried me with mud, but I was not jarred much by it.

So now you see why your letters were so necessary. I did need something to settle my nerves, and they were just the thing to do it. When I read them I forgot how tired I was or that the mud was caked in my ears where the dynamite had buried me, and I only remembered how wonderful you are. Now you see what a great service you are doing for this part of Uncle Sam's Army.

Do you mind if I let off some steam about one of my peeves at the Army? You don't like a guy who gripes when he thinks he gets a dirty deal? OK. OK. I'll tell you anyway.

I was supposed to be in New York City this weekend on a three-day pass. By all the rules it was my time to go, and my pass was approved. Then one of the boys in my squad failed to shoot a qualifying (70) score on the machinegun. One of the louies who has never been classed among my favorite people seemed to think I had not given the boy proper instruction, so he took away my pass.

I knew and tried to explain what was wrong but it was no good. The kid is a raw rookie who had never fired a gun bigger than a .22 rifle, and 20 machineguns firing simultaneously make a lot of noise. Naturally, he was nervous, but it cost me a pass anyway.

I did get revenge, in a way. Yesterday the kid came back and shot a neat 94, while the louie who took my pass away barely eked out a passing 73. Boy, did the platoon cheer.

The stories about the privates hating the sergeants and vice versa don't go here. These boys are swell guys, and there is no resentment against any sergeant in the platoon. They were all hotter over the pass than I was. The louie tried to give the pass to every other man in the platoon but none of them would accept it. I insisted that so long as I couldn't have it there was no reason for them to reject it, but it did no good.

Now, you've had to listen to the gripe whether you liked it or not. I'll try to not let it happen again. Must let off steam, you know, and it relieves me more when I tell you than when I tell anyone else.

Love Always,
Leland

Dearest Letty

Syracuse, N.Y.
August 14, 1943

My Dearest Letty:

Haven't reminded you that I am crazy about you for a couple of days, so consider yourself reminded.

Jim Modlin and I finally got a three-day pass so here we are in Syracuse and having a good time. We thought of going to a dozen other places but decided it would use up too much of our time in traveling. Syracuse is not so far from camp and it is a nice town. The population is around 200,000, I guess. It is not like New York City, but a country boy can find plenty of things to keep him busy for three days.

Just came in from the ballgame, which Syracuse won from Buffalo, 2 to 1. It was a pretty good game. We intended to see a doubleheader last night, but it rained a flood so there was no game.

Yes, I suppose you did see my dad all these times you have been writing about him. He is in town every Saturday, but Mother doesn't go that often. So you have been seeing my aunt. She is my father's sister, and she is in town almost every Saturday. You should have talked to her, if you wanted to get lined up. She can talk more than Lois, as you probably learned. This Duvall clan is the talkingest bunch you ever saw, and Mrs. Malone is a contender for the championship. I am also in the running, as you already know, but you will learn all that soon enough.

Love Always,
Leland

Pine Camp, N.Y.
August 21, 1943

My Dearest Letty:

This is the first chance I have had to write to you in two or three days. I could have written last night but we had a show.

It was Gray Gordon's Orchestra along with several good acts. Lola Lane sang a couple of good numbers and Mona Maxwell did a couple of swell dance acts. I had seen her do the same numbers before, but they are still good. Then there were some good acrobatic numbers, but I could not describe them, so I will make no attempt.

Two of the boys just brought in a live porcupine, and there is more excitement than when Frank Buck brought in a cargo of animals from the jungles. They had him here in the barracks for a while, then took him outside and let him climb the fire-escape ladder. Now they have taken him out and let him climb a tree.

I am still crazy about you. Will write again in a few hours.

Love Always,
Leland

Pine Camp, N.Y.
Sept. 9, 1943

My Dearest Letty:

I guess you have begun to wonder just why I had not written you. You always do, you know. But it is the same story from here. All day Tuesday we were out and didn't get back until 2 o'clock Wednesday morning. Then we had to work last night until late and had school tonight. But we got out of school around 9 o'clock so here I am writing you.

So you still love me a little? Fine, sometime I'll see if I can convince you that you should love me more. I believe it could be done.

Had a pleasant weekend at Lake Placid, as you may have gathered. Tried to see everything they had to offer but didn't get around to all of it. Lake Placid is the playground of America. It is like Hot Springs in many ways, but they run to winter sports. Most of the town is along a single street that runs at the foot of the mountain and circles the lake. In winter they ski, race bobsleds and skate, and all the big contests are held there. In summer the big shots spend their vacations there, for it is cool and pleasant and some of the vacationers have plenty of scratch.

Did I tell you about the dinner some guy bought me? If I did, excuse me and I'll repeat myself anyway. Another dogface and I were putting on the dog and eating in the best place the village had to offer. We were each having shrimp cocktail, half a broiled chicken and, well, everything on the menu. The check must have been four or five dollars, but when I asked for it the girl said the gray-haired gentlemen who ate at the next table had taken care of everything. I tried to find him to at least thank him but he was gone. One never knows. I might have been able to fast-talk him out of another feed. Runyon says if you rub up against people with scratch often enough some of it is bound to rub off on you.

Love Always,
Leland

Pine Camp, N.Y.
Sept. 12, 1943

My Dearest Letty:

It is plenty cool up here today, and I am wondering how you would take it if you were here. If you have to sleep under cover down there, you would have plenty of trouble here. But this is only the beginning. It will be plenty cold in a month.

This weather has given me an excuse to wear my new jersey and feel like I am in civilian clothes. It is one I bought and is not GI so I cannot wear it out of the company area. Also, it is drab and baggy and I would not care to wear it even if it were permitted. But it is comfortable and feels like civilian clothes, even if it is olive drab in color and has "U.S. Army, Pine Camp" and the Army insignia on the chest.

Also, I have a plan figured out to beat the wood-chopping racket. It may not work, but here it is: In summer we live on fresh fruit and vegetables that need little cooking. You can break brush for the cookstove. In winter, we take a tip from the birds and go south. In the islands we can live on coconuts and bananas and will still need no fire. Simple, isn't it?

Sorry you didn't get to go to the circus. If I had only been there, we would have seen the elephants and everything.

By the way, there is a guy in our company who was a ticket seller for Ringling Brothers and he can tell some interesting tales. Another boy who goes to my school was a trapeze artist with some of the biggest shows in the world. He was born in Europe and has been everywhere. His only reason for being in school is that he has trouble with English pronunciation. The truth is, I am more the student than the teacher, and I have him telling me things most of the time.

The ball team took a beating last week, 10 to 6. We were playing a regimental team and we are only a company, so they gave us the works. There are a dozen or so companies in a regiment so they have more talent to pick a team from.

They have had me working some this weekend. It is like this: Three guys were A.W.O.L. and were given seven days at hard labor for punishment. It was my time to guard them and see that they worked. So they gave me extra duty when these guys were supposed to be the ones who got the punishment. Believe me, I made them work. They were cracking rocks with hammers.

Love Always,
Leland

Pine Camp, N.Y.
Sept. 20, 1943

My Dearest Letty:

I am waiting for you to blast me for not writing. But if you will look at my new address you will see that we have been busy. They are reorganizing the whole set-up. Everyone is getting moved around from one place to another and we are now a cavalry troop instead of a company.

A lot of guys, including six sergeants, had to leave. I thought I would be on the list since I was among the newest and have practically no seniority. But for some unknown reason they kept me. The heck of it is they made me a platoon sergeant. Now I must look after three squads instead of one. Of course, it is supposed to be a promotion, but since there is no increase in pay you can pardon my dubious laughter.

A new dog has taken up with us, and I would give anything for him. He is really a classy pooch, a mahogany-colored cocker spaniel, which happens to be one of my favorite breeds. He knows all sorts of tricks. If I could only get him—but I can't find the owner, and if I did I am sure he could not be bought.

Yes, it has been a long time since January. But sometimes it seems like only last week. Some of the things that happened stand out so clearly, and I remember the details so vividly that it does not seem possible that they could have happened almost a year ago.

Say, aren't you ashamed to work so hard? Imagine picking 30 pounds of cotton. At that rate, the crop will soon be gone and no one will have anything to do. Be moderate, girl, be moderate. Don't overdo the thing.

I'm afraid I'll have to agree with you when you say I am just something you dreamed up. For I am definitely not all the brave, wonderful, generous creature you keep saying I am. So I am warning you now. Don't expect me to live up to that stuff.

On the other hand, since I am a much better judge of people than you are, I can see just what I am in love with. But I still say I would not have you any other way for the world, and if you were any other way I would probably not love you as much as I do. So don't change, if you want me to go on loving you.

Love Always,
Leland

Pine Camp, N.Y.
Oct. 2, 1943

My Dearest Letty:

Oh, yes, I'm still crazy about you. Might as well get it into the first paragraph since I intend to put it in somewhere.

Hope you don't mind my putting it on this kind of paper since it is all I have at the moment. They have no other kind at the P.X.

Now I suppose I should explain why I have not written in a few days. We have been up on Lake Ontario. It is a nice place but quite isolated. There is no way to get letters out and no way to get mail into the place. Also, there is almost no free time.

We were shooting the carbine, which is a lot of fun. I managed to make a sharpshooter score, and I think I could not have shot that high except for one thing. But I won't bore you with details.

We came back yesterday but had to crawl through the infiltration course last night. Boy, was I a mess. All day it had rained a slow drizzle and the course was a soup. But we had to crawl anyway. You see, there are three machineguns shooting about two or three feet above the ground, and, believe me, a guy does not think of the mud. He doesn't crawl on his hands and knees either. He lies flat on the ground and inches his way along like a snake. At the barbed wire, he has to turn over on his back to get under it (it is only six inches high and must be held up) so you can imagine how muddy I was. Even my face and hair were caked. If you had only seen me then, why you would not have recognized me. I gave a guy sixty cents to wash my clothes clean enough for the laundry to accept them. That's no joke.

And cold! We went through first about six o'clock under a smoke-screen and then stood around in the rain until nine o'clock and went through again. After that, we rode into camp (ten miles) on the back of trucks. It took me an hour to get the mud out of my ears.

Love Always,
Leland

Pine Camp, N.Y.
Oct. 10, 1943

My Dearest Letty:

It is Sunday afternoon and all is quiet. I am taking time out to write you a later letter. Hope you don't mind that it is a little late. I guess you have learned to expect that by now.

We have been up around the St. Lawrence River country part of the week, and it is another place you should see sometime. Wild, yes, but beautiful, especially at this time of the year. The fields are all dun and brown but the trees are a hundred shades of red, yellow, brown and even purple. Every breeze brings a cascade of multi-colored leaves, and the ground is covered with a rug that rivals the Persian rugs sold by fakers on the back streets in Syracuse or Los Angeles.

In the villages the children rake the leaves into piles and roll over in them like kittens playing in the tall grass. Perhaps I should say they are like the squirrels, for squirrels are numerous here. It is not surprising to see three or four playing at one time. They are always hurrying to get some place but never seem to arrive. They scamper along the rail fences or scratch among the leaves like children.

Your last letter seemed to indicate that some things are getting the better of you. We can't have the old chin sagging. This offers you a chance to perk up and get the old smile back.

Winter is just around the corner and I am waiting for the big snows.

Dearest Letty

I'll not have to wait long, for they say there are some nice ones: three to four feet, and fifteen feet in drifts. When that comes I want to go up to Lake Placid and see the skiing and bobsledding. Must sign off.

Love Always,
Leland

Pine Camp, N.Y.
Oct. 17, 1943

My Dearest Letty:

Since it will be impossible for me to write again for two or three days, I am getting a letter off tonight, just to say that I am still a lot in love with you.

It is nice and cool here today, just the kind of day you would like to sit by the fire and eat roasted peanuts. No, it is too cold to sit outside and eat hickory nuts. Besides, it has been raining and snowing all day. Not much snow, just a little mixed with the showers.

The showers have been coming at more or less regular intervals, not the sudden dashing rains of California, nor the steady downpours of the Southern rains that ride in on the gulf storms. Constantly threatening clouds hang heavy in the sky so that the actual rain, when it comes, is no surprise.

Fog hangs a gossamer curtain across the landscape, hiding the shame of the half-naked trees. Two weeks ago the trees stood on the landscape stage in full-dress evening gowns. But like a Gypsy Rose Lee, they have tossed all this aside and are now clad only in lacy undergarments. Some are down to the feather, similar to the most daring Broadway dancers.

But the pines are conservative ladies. Prim and reserved, they remain fully dressed and hold their skirts aside if a brazen birch happens to be standing near. You can even hear them whisper in a not-too-soft aside when the wind sends a shower of leaves down. "Do you see that?" they whisper. "Perfectly shocking, my dear."

But I did not start out to write a three-page weather report. The weather is supposed to be a military secret. I only hope it lets up some by tomorrow. Otherwise, I may get a little cool sleeping on the ground.

The drunk who paid you a visit could not have been Pete Burris.

Pete does not drive a truck and he is allergic to blood, so he never fights. Otherwise it could have been him.

Very likely it was one of his brothers from Oklahoma. They drive trucks and are not averse to an occasional fight. But Pete is in Florida now, so you won't see him. He was discharged from the Army and went to Florida to work. It doesn't seem that many people are around home now. So many have left, for one reason or another.

Love Always,
Leland

Pine Camp, N.Y.
Oct. 28, 1943

My Dearest Letty:

I can just imagine that you are casting all sorts of dire threats in my direction for not writing to you in three or four days, but since I am so far away I can feel quite safe.

Have been out on the range in the rain all day. We had some guys who had some firing to do, so we were trying to clean it all up. The captain sent me out with one group and sent others to the other ranges. They were supposed to come over to my range when they finished their firing at the other places, but they never got around to it, so I had to wait all day. Boy, how it can rain here!

Then I had to come in and go on guard tonight, which is how I happen to have time to do some writing. But being sergeant of a guard is not a bad job. The poor boys who actually walk the guard are the ones who have the tough going, especially when it is raining as it is tonight.

Love Always,
Leland

FLASH: It has been reliably reported to your newsboy that a certain soldier, now stationed at Pine Camp, may get a furlough. See you next Wednesday.

My Dearest Letty:

Well, I am here, not in camp yet, of course, but will go on in after a short rest here. Had a nice trip but missed you terribly. You grow into a habit so easily, you know. It seemed that since I had not seen you for a couple of days it was about time I should see you last night. But instead of going south to your place I was rolling east and north across Indiana, Ohio, Pennsylvania and New York. It didn't seem right.

Left Russellville Saturday morning but stayed in Little Rock until 9:30 that night. Made St. Louis at 7 a.m. Sunday and Syracuse at 4 this morning. Will write a letter when I get to camp.

(Forgot and left my fountain pen at home.)

Love Always,
Leland

Pine Camp, N.Y.
Nov. 16, 1943

My Dearest Letty:

Just have a moment. Maybe I can stretch it to two. So I am writing a note to let you know I still love you and that I got back OK. I may have time to write a letter tomorrow, but this will have to be short.

I had a nice trip up here. In a few hours I had the experience of passing from autumn where the trees were a thousand colors to a winter where they were strung with silver icicles and sparkling snow.

Yes, we have about six inches of snow. It is not cold yet, but the snow is not melting. It does melt on the roofs of the buildings but freezes into immense icicles at the eaves. They are three to four feet long now and grow longer by the hour. Every time I look out I think of the verse I read somewhere.

> When icicles hang by the wall
> And Dick the shepherd blows his nail,
> And Tom bears logs into the hall,
> And milk comes frozen home in pail . . .*

It goes on for several stanzas, like the Pussy Cat song, and I can't remember who wrote it. I think a chap called Shakespeare had a hand in it.

Must sign off as I am busy. You see, I am acting first sergeant while the Top Kick is on furlough. I don't know much about the job, but I will get along. Will write when I get time.

Love Always,
Leland

[*From William Shakespeare, *Love's Labours Lost,* act 5, scene 2.]

Pine Camp, N.Y.
Nov. 19, 1943

My Dearest Letty:

If I did not know that the type of paper I use in writing to you would make no difference I would apologize for my bum stationery. But I will say nothing about it.

Had your wonderful letter today, and I am glad you have at last shown signs of making good as a teacher. It will be so nice to have you successful, so we won't have to worry about money and that sort of thing.

Yes, I'll forgive you for crying. After all, girls always cry when I leave and I constantly have to forgive them. So I can do it gracefully.

No, seriously, it was quite all right. I knew just how you felt. Mother always cries when I leave in spite of all I can say.

But I did have a wonderful time, every minute I was there, and just think, we did not have to go anywhere or do any of the usual things to have a nice time. Guess it will always be like that though.

You can be quite sure Aunt Addie will never forget you or anyone else. She makes it a habit to remember people, as does my father. I only wish I could remember as well as they can. I was not sure you were not terribly bored that day in town. But I had not seen all those people in quite a while, and I simply had to speak to them. But I am not going to preach while

Dearest Letty

you run for assessor. Nor am I going to run. That is just my way of spending a pleasant day, when I had you to show off to everyone.

Love Always,
Leland

Pine Camp, N.Y.
Nov. 21, 1943

My Dearest Letty:

If I can snatch a few minutes time I'll send along a note to let you in on the fact that I'm still in love with you. But time to write is scarce. After I wrote the heading, I had to rush over to the orderly room to straighten out a detail and fill out the sick book. All those things have to be done on Sunday, just as on other days, and it is hard for me to remember everything, for I am not accustomed to the job.

Your beautiful letter came this morning. I thought you would have a note from me by the time your letter was written. I wrote one at Syracuse on my way back and sent it airmail. I suppose you will have had three or four by the time this reaches you. Can't even say how many times I have written.

It is snowing beautifully today. Snow is one of nature's most charming pantomimes. Unlike the storm or the tide there are no sound effects to augment the beauty, but the alteration is greater than that produced by either. Houses are blended into the landscape. Posts are capped by a white hood that resembles the snood of a high-school girl. The trees lose their identity and become silent, white-shrouded ghosts. You cannot say, "Here is a birch, there is a maple." They are all alike.

Yes, I had a wonderful furlough. Don't know when I have had so much fun. Just two weeks ago yesterday, about this time of day, we were having chicken at Woody's. Remember? It was a swell dinner, too, but I would probably have enjoyed tuna fish.

No, there is no point in your eating worms, and don't imagine you can get even with me for making you wait by hiding my pipe. You can't hide them all, you know. On my desk now are eight pipes, not counting the one I am smoking. That may give you the idea that the desk is slightly cluttered. A few other items add to that impression. For example:

Two packs tobacco, one tobacco pouch, one pack cigarettes, one cigarette case, one cigarette holder, three ashtrays, two books matches, one cigarette lighter, six pencils, three fountain pens, five bottles ink (different colors), one pack pipe cleaners, one bottle lighter fluid, eight unanswered letters, one box paper clips, one box thumbtacks, one mirror, one bundle band papers, one S.N.L. for scout car, one training bulletin, one pair snow glasses, two blotters, six rubber bands, one bundle blank envelopes, one nail file.

Now say I am not a neat housekeeper.

Love Always,
Leland

TWO

Waiting for D-day

By early December 1943, planning for the invasion of Normandy was well underway, although the great amphibious assault would not occur for another seven months. The Fifth Armored Division loaded its gear and headed for Indiantown Gap, Pennsylvania, which, although it was 150 miles from the Port of New York, was an embarkation point for the army.

Leland Duvall's Eighty-Fifth Cavalry Reconnaissance Squadron boarded the British ship Athlone Castle in the New York harbor on February 10, 1944, and the convoy threaded its way across the Atlantic, by now largely cleared of German submarines, to southern England. Because of the enormous number of men, vehicles, and supplies on the ships, the soldiers bunked six deep in stifling quarters below deck and ate two sparse meals a day. The Athlone Castle arrived two weeks later in Liverpool.

The men of the Eighty-Fifth Cavalry spent weeks drawing supplies and engaging in small-unit training there and then went by train on April 10 to the southwest tip of England for D-day preparations. The armored division would not be in the first assault on June 6 because it depended upon the installation of artificial harbors at Utah and Omaha beaches to get its heavy equipment on shore, but it helped run the training and marshaling camps for the first invasion force.

Censorship would become more rigid once the men were headed for Europe, and until the final weeks of the war Duvall's letters would not again say where he was or what he had been *doing, with the rare exception of when he was ensconced away from his unit and the censor. The opportunities and materials to write became far more scarce when his cavalry troop was dashing across France, Luxembourg, and Belgium or holed up in outposts distant from the headquarters. No longer could he scribble twelve pages on letterhead stationery either, at least until the Germans were in full retreat, his division went into repose, and he found real stationery. Soldiers were confined instead to the tiny forms of Victory Mail, or V-mail, which allowed you to pen one hundred words if you had a fine hand. V-mail shrank the massive volume of service correspondence and sped mail delivery. V-mail stationery functioned as both a letter and an envelope. Having completed his message in the space of about four square inches, the soldier or his correspondent back in the states wrote his return address and the recipient's at the top and folded it into a self-mailing piece. It was microfilmed and turned into a letter again at a processing center.*

While Duvall could not specify the town, region, or country he was in, his unit's location on any day can be established by the secret action logs kept by the commander and from military maps. Where he does not list it himself, Duvall's approximate location in Europe is shown in brackets.

Indiantown Gap, Pa.
Dec. 12, 1943

My Dearest Letty:

Well, here I am in a new camp. I am full of surprises since I am doing the Army job. The element of surprise wins a lot of battles, you know. Maybe when the war is over and I come home I can come in suddenly and with great surprise so that you will be swept off your feet and marry me before you have time to think it over.

We got here yesterday. That is, I got here yesterday. Most of the troops arrived a day earlier. They came down by cars while I stayed behind with a few men to clean up our area, ship the remainder of our equipment, etc.

Then we came down by train. The trip took 24 hours, but we traveled rather slowly. It is really not so far.

The trip was pleasant enough for me, but it was plenty tough for the poor guys who had to stand guard on the flatcars. It was around zero and you can imagine how that would be. I was sergeant of the guard so I only had to check when the train stopped. At that, it was plenty cold.

To give you an idea of how bad it was, one chap had his goggles adjusted too tightly so that they cut into his nose. When he came off guard, his nose was cut and the front of his clothes was splattered with blood, but he was not aware of it.

This seems to be a pretty pleasant camp. It is two blocks to the service club, theater and bus station, and the P.X. is just across the street.

I have not had time to look around much, but I did go to Hershey, Lebanon and Palmyra last night. They are nice little towns. Hershey is the town where they make all the Hershey chocolate. The whole place belongs to one corporation. It is no larger than Russellville, but the buildings downtown would be a credit to Hollywood or any other town. The park is one of the nicest I have seen.

We went over to see the ice hockey game, and it was worth the trip. The arena is a beautiful building, seating 10,000. The game was rough and exciting. There were half a dozen fights. Think I shall go back again one of these days.

Jim Modlin, Ed Sherman, Joe Horwath and I were together so I had swell company. All sorts of funny things happen when you go into strange towns. I'll tell you one incident just to give you an idea.

We were standing on the corner at Lebanon waiting for a bus and a guy came up to us and asked for a cigarette. He was one of those well-dressed bums you see so often. Of course, he was in the first war (they all were) and he had a son in Italy.

I pulled him aside and told him to please not talk of the war since my friends had just come back from there and were particularly sensitive about it. (They have never been farther east than New York.) Horwath has a lame knee and walks with a slight limp so this gave credence to my story that he had had a machinegun through the leg. Ed and Jim had walked around the corner to save cigarettes, so they became victims of shell shock.

He insisted on talking to Horwath and did he have him on the spot.

Of course, I had to duck when the guys finally got rid of the bore, but he followed them around quite a while.

Oh, well, a guy has to liven things up some way. Must say I love you and write a flock more letters.

Love Always,
Leland

Indiantown Gap, Pa.
Dec. 16, 1943

My Dearest Letty:

Oh, yes, here we go again. With not much to write but a great spirit. That is, next to getting one of your letters, I enjoy writing to you, but there is always the question of what to write that will interest you. (Except to say "I love you as much as ever.")

First, I was out to the hockey game again last night. Had a nice game at a nice town. By the way, I think we should live at Hershey when the war is over. I have already made inquiries about jobs and they think you would make an excellent hand in the candy factory. Then you could bring me a bar of chocolate when you came home from work each day.

If I do not mention the question you asked you will be angry indeed. You asked if I were going across right away. In the first place, a soldier is not supposed to know when or where he is going. In the second place, he is not supposed to discuss those things even if he learns about a move in advance. So you see why I cannot give you an answer.

But why should you get excited if I happen to go across? Then it will be harder for me to check up on you, and you will be freer to do as you please. Then, too, it will offer an opportunity to see the other side at the expense of Uncle Sam. As a last clinching argument in favor of going over, when I come home after the war I would not want to explain to people that I fought only in the Battles of Casmalia (Calif.), Liberty (Tenn.), Sterlingville (New York), Rome (Ga.), etc. What would they think of me as a soldier?

Love Always,
Leland

Dearest Letty

My Dearest Letty:

Well, here I sit listening to Bing Crosby sing "People Will Say We're in Love." Remember the tune? We played it a couple of times on the jukebox when I was home, but I am afraid we did not pay much attention to it. It's one of my favorite tunes, too.

You should get this letter about Christmas, and I do not feel that I have wished you a really personal Merry Christmas. An insignificant gift and a printed card is not enough for that. In fact, in this environment I find it difficult to really get into the Christmas mood.

Christmas, to me, means all the things I remember.

The crisp clear nights with the silver stars hanging above the serried spars of the tall pines, neighbors dropping in to say Merry Christmas and to linger and talk a while, great logs burning cheerily on the wide hearth, the youngsters dreading to go to bed for fear they would miss something on this most important night of the year, the church bell ringing as it rang no other time, and the general feeling of "Peace and Good Will."

But all these are missing here. We are not supposed to feel any peace and good will, and there is little of the Christmas atmosphere. Only the crisp nights and the stars give a vague promise and point the way to the long road back to the things we remember. But they and the positive knowledge that those back home are keeping the real Christmas alive are enough to make it a good season.

So have a merry Christmas for yourself and for me, and keep the tradition alive that we may enjoy it more when the peace and good have returned to the world, and we have traveled the long road back.

Love Always,
Leland

Indiantown Gap, Pa.
Dec. 25, 1943

My Dearest Letty:

It is Christmas day and I am doing nothing to celebrate the day except rest. To me, it seems more like Sunday than anything else.

But we had a special dinner. I am sending you the menu in another envelope. Let me tell you it was just as good as it looks on paper. Of course, I did not sample everything. I couldn't get around to that much, but I did justice to the dinner. I really wish you could have been here just for the dinner. Perhaps I could have kept an eye on you that long, but I still say I could not risk you among all these wolves. Many of them claim they are plenty popular with the girls, and I am afraid they would make you feel too important.

Say, I admire the taste of the fifth grader you wrote about. The lad has possibilities, and he knows a beautiful woman when he sees one. When he grows up he should be a useful citizen, socially. The country needs more like him.

You seem highly concerned over the fact that we moved and you were not informed of the fact. But you must remember that this is war, and even though you may be my general there is still higher authority. It is quite important that all military moves are secret. We cannot tell anyone, not even the girl back home, what we are doing. It is not hard to see why.

Suppose I write you that we are going to Shangri-La or Timbuktu at a certain time. But my letter gets into the wrong hands, and the train or ship becomes another victim of the war. You can see how that could happen. That is the reason I cannot write you what we are doing or when we are to move. Of course, you understand.

But that does not alter the fact that I'm still crazy about you.

Love Always,
Leland

Indiantown Gap, Pa.
Jan. 1, 1944

My Dearest Letty:

Happy New Year! I beat you to that one, and don't start saying you thought of it first. And don't claim you saw the New Year first either, for I know I beat you there, too. The New Year got here an hour before it got there, see. Come to think of it, I am an hour ahead of you on everything. The sun comes up an hour earlier here, lunch is here when it is only 11 o'clock there, and the evening is just a step ahead of your time, lazy bones.

I did see the New Year in, but not in the accepted way. It should be done with tooting horns and ringing bells, but they had us out on a problem. We went out yesterday morning and stayed all day and all night, without the benefit of a fire, too. The temperature was down near zero. Our only chance to keep warm was to wear plenty of clothes. I took advantage of it, too, and I would not want you to see me, bundled up as I was.

There was, first, the long wool underwear, but the GI kind is not red, so they do not fit into the old jokes about red flannel underwear. Then there was a wool sweatshirt, a Red Cross sweater, a pair of coveralls, a field jacket and an overcoat. Then there were three pair of socks, a pair of shoes and a pair of Arctics. For a hat, I wore a Red Cross pullover (just a hole in the front to see from), a knit helmet cap, a plastic helmet liner, and a steel helmet. (Talk about women wearing silly hats!) Then there were gloves and various other items so piled up that I looked like a cocoon that would never disgorge a living animal. (In the cocoon, a butterfly comes out, but that would be stretching the comparison too far.)

Anyway, I was gradually freezing into a well-wrapped cube of ice when the New Year appeared on the eastern horizon.

I am afraid I did not greet the youngster with much enthusiasm. I had hoped to be in New York City when the chap was born. It is supposed to be quite a gala affair in the city. You have read of how they do it there, and I wanted to help.

Think what I missed, too. They say in the papers there were three girls to every man on the street. They must have been a desolate lot, and I could have helped boost their morale.

I was only kidding. I'm afraid I'm too much in love with the picture on the shelf to help much.

Oh, I just made a New Year's resolution. Here it is: "I resolve never to give you another thought." The catch is, I am perfectly happy with the thought I have had for you for a long time.

Love,
Leland

New York City
Jan. 9, 1944

My Dearest Letty:

I wrote you a letter yesterday, so here is a card today. This is a picture of the hotel I am patronizing, and it is a swell place. That is the Empire State Building in the background. I have just been up on it. Also, just saw "For Whom the Bell Tolls." May see Jimmy Dorsey tonight.

Modlin and Sherman just called their wives. I had none to call, as you have no phone.

Love,
Leland

Indiantown Gap, Pa.
Jan. 12, 1944

My Dearest Letty:

Now, don't tell me. I know I didn't write last night as I said I would. Now go ahead and tell me I broke my promise.

First, what you don't know is how I am snowed under with work. Boy, it is a shame. I am trying to do two jobs at once, and it is no fun. My clerking job is supposed to be full time, and since I have been on it I have not put in as much as a half a day at it. I do that job in my off time, which means after supper and during the noon hour. In fact, I have just put the papers aside and it is almost time for the lights to go out. I am ten letters behind with my writing by actual count, and I don't know when I'll be able to catch up. Can't even take out time to read the paper.

But I have written too much of a complaint already, so I'll change the subject. Suppose we talk about you for a time, and we are sure to have a pleasant subject.

How are things going with my girl back home? And does she still love me a little, or is there another man in her life so that she is slowly forgetting me? "Girls are fickle," an old proverb says. Of course, I have never had a chance to learn the truth of it firsthand, but I am quite sure it is all wrong. In fact, I don't think either of us could forget the wonderful times we had. You know, the brief beautiful hours when we did not even know of a thing to do that would be more interesting than sitting by a stove and saying nothing while the fire slowly died and I dreaded the advance of the hour hand on my watch. The passing of time is a ruthless, sinister thing when it is carrying away the minutes that are as wonderful as those were.

We did not want to see a show or go to town or anything. Remember? It was not necessary to talk. You know, we must be in love.

Love Always,
Leland

Indiantown Gap, Pa.
Jan. 15, 1944

My Dearest Letty:

Had you known the snow was coming you would probably have tried to make me carry in coal and kindling when I was there, so I am glad you are unable to forecast the weather.

But I am not so lucky in other ways. For instance, it was unfortunate that my furlough came before Leap Year. With a proposal such as I recently had I might have even gotten married when I was home. Would that not have been something? Since the girl is not in this vicinity, it is not exactly practical.

Maybe the girl thought of all that when she wrote the wonderful letter. But I am taking a rain check on it and I shall probably remind her of it about next leap year. Of course, I am a little bashful myself, but I hope she will repeat. Is it a promise?

We are having quite a snow here tonight. If it keeps up until tomorrow we will be really snowed under.

Winter comes at intervals. You see, we are south of a chain of mountains. The clouds come over the mountains like flocks of blackbirds. Squalls of sleet and snow cover the place. The wind sweeps through the gap as if it were an open door, and our little valley looks like some place in Alaska.

In a couple of days a different kind of wind comes up from the south. It is a gentle wind promising birds and flowers. But it fools no one. Even when the snow melts and the ice is all gone, no one gets optimistic. It is always a gamble to send an overcoat to the cleaners.

Love Always,
Leland

Indiantown Gap, Pa.
Jan. 16, 1944

My Dearest Letty:

I hope you don't mind my using the typewriter on this letter, but I sometimes wonder if you are really able to read the stuff I am always writing in long hand. I got to thinking that you might be missing the main point of all my letters (viz., the part that always says "I love you") for the simple reason that you found them illegible.

So I said to myself: The solution is to type it out so that the gal cannot miss it. And here it is: I LOVE YOU.

Now that the most important part of the letter is done on this machine, I might as well go on until this is finished. But this is not a machine I have been using, and I am not accustomed to it. So if there are more mistakes than you had expected, give a little credit to the machine. But, to tell the truth, I am not so hot at this sort of thing anyway. I use the W.H.I.I. system of typing, and it is not so good as some of the others. (Now, don't ask me what the W.H.I.I. is for; I refuse to tell you.)

Oh yes, I had your letter today, and you were asking me all about New York. Of course, I can tell you little about the place, but since you have not been there at all, I have the perfect opportunity to hand you a great line and you will never know if it is true or not. Well, my trip is like this:

At 4 o'clock in the morning we (the three of us) get off the train at Penn Station and start strolling up Broadway. In fact, we are strolling down Broadway, but we do not know it at this time. We think we should get a hotel room and slumber for a few hours, so we start looking for a place. The only catch is that we are strolling in the wrong direction, but we are unaware of this fact, too, just as we do not know a lot of other things about the place.

Dearest Letty

Well, the chances are we will walk straight into the harbor if we do not become entangled in a maze of buildings. When we do this, we find ourselves walking back up Broadway, only this time we are not on Broadway but Fifth Avenue. Even this makes little difference to us for we do not know where we are going anyway. Finally, after walking about 30 blocks more (we walk 30 going downtown) only to find that we are back where we start, we have a meeting and decide to call a cab and put ourselves in the driver's hands.

The driver looks at us to see if we are drunk, but he soon sees that we are only some rubes who do not know the score. So he says, "There is a very good hotel about a block over that way," which is how we happen to be at the McAlpin Hotel when I write you a couple of cards.

But when we have a chance to go up on the Empire State Building we see that we have wasted a lot of time walking here and there.

Anyway, we spend three good days in the Village and I learn much about the ways of the world, all of which I hope to tell you sometime if you care to listen.

Here I had hoped to tell you all that I did, but I find that it is time to go to bed and I have told you nothing. We only got 60 blocks and into the hotel, and I must begin to close this off.

Love Always,
Leland

Indiantown Gap, Pa.
Jan. 17, 1944

My Dearest Letty:

I guess you think my letters are coming with monotonous regularity. That is part of the price you pay for making me fall in love with you. Now don't you wish you had not gone to all the trouble of making me love you?

Our snow is still with us. I had thought it would be gone by now, but it is not, and now it looks like it might snow again.

Just had a letter from home, and Mother has had pneumonia. They had written that she and dad were sick, but I had no idea she was in that condition. Dad only had flu, but she had pneumonia also. They gave her sulfanilamide and she only had fever a couple of days. She was up part of the time when she wrote, so I hope she will be all right.

Say, would you advise me to take a correspondence course, too? (I am serious now.) I have been toying with the idea, and since you are having a course now you should know something about it. I can get a course from almost any university through the Army Institute and it should help break the monotony. Don't know yet which course I want most, but I think it will be a course in journalism from the University of Arkansas. Guess I'd better sign off.

Love Always,
Leland

Indiantown Gap, Pa.
Jan. 20, 1944

My Dearest Letty:

Thursday night, and I am wondering what you are doing. If I were to ask you, you would probably say you are listening to the radio. This is Bing Crosby's night, you know, and you are probably listening to him.

By the way, give me your honest opinion of Frank Sinatra's singing. Do you swoon when he sings like so many teen-age girls? I'll bet you do, but you won't admit it. He sang in Philadelphia not so long ago, and the girls formed a line at the ticket windows at 7 o'clock in the morning. They stood there all day waiting for the box office to open that night. If you had been there you would probably have been the first in line.

Guess you noticed that I am writing with a different pen in the last few days. You see, I broke mine and had to resurrect an old one. I dropped it and the point stuck into the floor. It didn't damage the point any, but the board cracked.

This is the pen I used while on the desert and the point is not so good. The sand there wore it out so that it is not shaped right. One way it writes a fine line, and if it is turned the other way the line is as broad as your tiny foot.

Say, come up and help me for a few days, for I'm afraid I'll be busy. I am acting first sergeant while Sgt. Redfern is on pass. That is not so bad, but so many of the other key men are gone, too. I don't know if I can keep all departments moving. The motor sergeant, the mess sergeant, supply sergeant, company clerk and personnel clerk are all gone, too. So I shall probably be chasing all over the place trying to get all the jobs done. Do you think I can see that the company is fed, the supplies are issued, the cars are serviced, the papers are filed, the records are kept, the morning report is turned in, and the men are all at work on the proper job?

Say, I think I have spent a lot of time when I should simply have said, "I love you."

Love Always,
Leland

[Camp Kilmer, N.J.]
Feb. 6, 1944

My Dearest Letty:

Just happened to think it is time to remind you that I am still in love with you. Since it is impossible to drive over and tell you personally, it must be done by mail.

Incidentally, letters are handy things. If it were not for them, you would probably forget me entirely, and that would be a disaster, or maybe a catastrophe. I wonder who invented letters, anyway? It would be an interesting question for you to bring before the history class. They could do some research and maybe you could learn something by going through the papers. You could have them write an essay on the days when letters were written on stone tablets.

They would have unlimited possibilities on such a subject. They could deal with the clumsy, bundlesome job of the mailman (contrasted with the V-mail of today) when handling a few bags of stone-letters. It should be worth a couple of paragraphs to cover the corns and bunions of the city letter carrier. Then there would be the advantages of the system such as the enforced brevity of the stone letter.

Few men would be energetic enough to say more than "I love you" if he had to chip the letters out with a hatchet, and that is in favor of the primitive letter. One of the tests of good prose is that it says the essential thing as briefly as possible. But here I am writing as verbosely as Lamb on the "Advisability of Being Brief." Contradictory, isn't it?

Say, I saw Martin today but didn't have a chance to talk with him but a minute. He lives in the next barracks, but he was on KP. We eat in the same mess hall and I was getting early chow when he came by and stopped for a minute. He didn't mention you but he did say he hoped to see me doing KP. Thought I would make the mess sergeant a good kitchen man. Could it be that there was a barb in the remark, or is he capable of such subtlety?

Wish I could have seen the basketball games you were writing about. I have not seen a game this year, and I would like to see a good high school game. The University of Arkansas played a game near here early in the season, but I was on guard and did not get to go. I did not care too much about it anyway since I know nothing of the team they have this year. Have lost contact with all the local sports. In fact, I don't know one man who played for the Travelers last year.

The lights will go out before long.

Love Always,
Leland

[Aboard the *Athlone Castle,* Atlantic Ocean]
Feb. 11, 1944

My Dearest Letty:

This will not be much of a letter, but I'm sure you don't mind that. My stationery doesn't have room for long letters, and they are really not necessary anyway.

In fact, all the best people are writing short letters these days and using this type of stationery (Victory Mail), according to Emily Post. It serves the purpose quite well, too. Really, it should have been invented long ago. At least it has plenty of room to say "I'm still in love with you," which is all that is necessary.

Love Always,
Leland

[Salisbury, England]
Feb. 28, 1944

My Dearest Letty:

By this time I suppose you think I have either forgotten you or forgotten how to write, but neither guess is right. It is simpler than that, for I am as much in love with you as ever.

But I am wondering if you are thinking along the same lines as usual. You see, I have not had a letter from you or from home in quite some time.

Say, you remember Arthur G. Presley, the singer, I am sure. I met his boy a few days ago. He has been around all this time and I never happened to see him. I also discussed that the sergeant major is an old quartet troubadour. He worked with the Stamps-Baxter Quartet before he came to the Army. We had quite a jam session, and I learned quite a bit about some of the old timers. I did not know that J. A. McClung is dead, or who was in charge of the Hartford Company. We may organize some sort of a quartet if we can get hold of a couple of books.

Love Always,
Leland

[Salisbury, England]
Feb. 29, 1944

My Dearest Letty:

Yesterday's letter may reach you at the same time this one does. If so, you can throw one of them away. They both probably say the same thing anyway, viz., I am still in love with you.

I have not had a letter from you or anyone in weeks. It is quite a job to handle Army mail, you know. V-mail has priority and airmail is next. Maybe if you would use some of the V-mail stationery you have been using to your other GIs the letters will get through.

Love Always,
Leland

[Salisbury, England]
March 3, 1944

My Dearest Letty:

I hope this letter has better luck in getting to you than yours are having in getting to me. How else would you know that I am still crazy about you? I have not had a letter from you in so long I have almost forgotten what your writing looks like.

However, I know you are writing and you will go on writing regularly. Please, they will catch up with me sometime, and I can take a day off to read my mail.

Things would be pleasant here if the chow were better, and that is improving. But be ready to cook me a chicken dinner when I come home. I reserve the right to eat as much as I want.

Love Always,
Leland

[Salisbury, England]
March 4, 1944

My Dearest Letty:

Since both the fire and the pipe are going good I can think of nothing better to do than write a note and imply the same things I always say. (See if you can figure that one out.)

It is Saturday night and the only show within reach is one I have already seen, and that is the only possible thing there is to do. There is not even a good book to read.

But being bored does no serious damage, and when I finish writing I shall go out and try to organize a game of bridge, or checkers. There is even a disadvantage to that. The bridge players are all too good for me, and the checkers players are so poor that they offer no competition. The only guy who could play checkers in this troop got a Section VIII discharge long ago.

Love Always,
Leland

Dearest Letty

[Salisbury, England]
March 6, 1944

My Dearest Letty:

Even though I am still waiting for one of your letters, I keep writing, but a letter would help the old morale greatly. The fact that I share a room with the troop mail clerk has absolutely no influence on my letter situation.

And a V-mail sheet cramps my style, too, so my letters are poor. Maybe I should write them in series and number them like installments of a continued story in the *Saturday Evening Post*. Or maybe I should use airmail and hope they reach you before Christmas. Which do you suggest?

Love Always,
Leland

[Salisbury, England]
[Date Censored]

My Dearest Letty:

Now go ahead and say I have been neglecting my writing and should have penned at least four letters since I wrote last, and I will agree with you. I should have. But I have reached a new degree of laziness. It is a state of delicious torpor that you do not dream exists. And I will show you how it works when I see you. It consists of doing nothing all day long except smoking a briar pipe and watching the smoke curl toward the ceiling.

The only thing wrong with the picture is the food has not been too good. I shall expect better food if I am to demonstrate the art of inactivity. I shall write more regularly in the future.

Love Always,
Leland

[Salisbury, England]
March 10, 1944

My Dearest Letty:

Your letters have begun to arrive at last, as have all the other corre-spondents'. So I have quite a nice time reading after each mail call. It is nice, too, believe me. It's wonderful to learn that you have not forgotten me after all these weeks.

By the way, I do remember the argument we had about that partic-ular note, and I still think I am right. You should get the music and see for yourself.

Just came back from a pass to London. Will try to get out an airmail letter this week and will tell you something of the city.

Love Always,
Leland

[Salisbury, England]
March 11, 1944

My Dearest Letty:

After writing V-mail for quite a while I am not sure that I can think of enough material to warrant a full-length letter. The habit of a terse, compressed letter has grown on me. There seems to be so little to say except that I am enjoying life in a dull sort of way, and that I am still in love with the girl back home.

But the censor is generous in the subjects he allows us to discuss. He says:

I. "Discuss the English people." That could require volumes if one cared to go into the subject deeply. It all depends on the degree of discus-sion. The simplest and shortest way to cover this subject is to compare and contrast them with Americans. In many ways we are similar but they differ in so many other ways that most of us find them hard to understand.

There is, for one thing, their different standard of values. We admire size and strength. They point with pride to the old things. We admire the chap who dares blaze a new trail. They look to the guy who does the tra-ditional things. They measure by this standard, and even though I cannot fully appreciate it I have seen enough to admire the yardstick they employ.

There are many little things, too, that would amuse you. For example, the steering wheel of the English car is on the right side of the vehicle, and drivers adhere to the left side of the road. (This makes the streets of towns an unsafe place for me. I invariably look in the wrong direction for approaching traffic.) All buses are double-decked jobs. The driver sits in a glass cage over the right front wheel, and the passengers enter from the rear. Railroad freight cars (known as goods wagons) are about the size of an American truck, and are uninviting to hobos. There is simply no place to ride. But all these things serve the purpose of the English.

"Then," the censor says, "discuss the English beer."

But the stuff they call bitters, brown, stout, etc., does not warrant a paragraph. So we will skip that one.

Next he suggests "English girls," but adds a word of warning: "This is not advised in letters to your wife." So, you, too, probably would not be interested in the subject.

Then there is English money. That, as L'il Abner would say, is confoozin' but not amoozin'. At first I had great trouble with the stuff. The penny, for example, is about the size of a half-dollar. Instead of using two denominations, such as dollars and cents, they use three, viz., pence (pennies), shillings, and pounds. At first, I solved it by holding out a handful of money to the clerks and allowing them to take what they wanted. Since all the other guys did the same, the traders must have found it profitable to deal with us.

But here I have used all my time and most of my paper. Such subjects as architecture, language, and my recent two-day pass in London (as well as many [censored]) are not yet touched. Will try to get around to them when I find time.

Love Always,
Leland

[Salisbury, England]
March 17, 1944

My Dearest Letty:

Spring is almost here and remember what Shakespeare said, "In spring a young man's fancy . . ." Well, I am not exactly a young man, but my fancy still turns in such a manner that one would never guess my age. But this happens when I think of you, which is more often than you might guess.

Have just taken time out for a cup of coffee. I usually do that every evening. You see, we manage to buy coffee around here, and it is quite a habit to sit around at night and sip the stuff. Keep this in mind and get the old boiler out when I come home.

But there are many things you will have to do then, such as—oh, well. I have mentioned many of them already and will tell you more as time goes by. Probably it would be too much of a shock if I listed all of my expectations at once.

Did I get around to telling you about London? We could have had a wonderful time if you had been there. It has a different atmosphere from New York, St. Louis, Los Angeles or any other American city, which makes it all the more interesting.

Modlin, Sherman and I managed to get a pass together, so we saw as much of the place as time and the permanent blackout permitted. This, of course, was not much, for it is a city that cannot be seen in a couple of days.

Many of the streets are narrow and all of them are crooked. Most of the buildings are flats of from three to five stories. The pattern of the streets does not run to square or the checkerboard of the American city. Rather, they branch off from central areas like spokes from the hub of a wheel, which is confusing to me. I stayed lost much of the time, but that is not unusual for me. I have been lost in New York, Los Angeles, St. Louis, Oklahoma City, Pottsville and many other American cities. So it was only natural that I should be lost there.

The taxi is handy on such occasions as are the subways. In this way, one can always pretend he knew where he was going in the first place and no one will ever know he was lost. But we had a lot of fun, and I am willing to repeat the act when my turn for another pass comes around.

You asked me in your last letter what you should do this summer, as if I were capable of telling you. Of course, I do not know and could not tell you if I had ideas on the subject. When school is finished and you find yourself without a job for the summer you will grow restless. That is only natural. But since it is your life (yet) I would be going out on a limb where I have no business being if I made a suggestion. I only ask that you write and tell me what you decide to do.

Love Always,
Leland

P.S. The jerries staged a small air raid while I was in town, but I slept through it.

[Salisbury, England]
March 27, 1944

My Dearest Letty:
Guess I might as well confess that I must be getting old and forgetful and because of that you are getting an airmail letter instead of the regular V-mail job I usually turn out.

You see, I have misplaced my clipboard, on which I usually write, and I can't find it. I may have left it on my desk at the motor park or perhaps some of the other guys are using it. But if this is a sign of dotage I may as well confess that the symptom is pronounced in my case. (Incidentally, I have not forgotten that I am still in love with you.)

Your letters are coming regularly now, which is helpful to the morale. Hope mine are doing as well for you. But no interesting letter could come from here. If one thing sets this village apart from any other it is the sameness with which the days pass. In the evening after chow the guys usually gather in groups and discuss everything from the war to baseball, and one group is always in my room. But the tête-à-tête of a bunch of dogfaces is no good as material for a letter to the girlfriend. If you culled the language and made it admissible to polite society you would take all the color out of it.

Of course, we make coffee on such nights, boiling it in a can over the open fire. Believe it or not, it is good coffee, too, the same kind one has on fishing trips when he makes it over a campfire. But perhaps you never did that. If not, you have definitely missed something. I must show you what it is like sometime.

Then we usually have cakes or some sort of sandwiches, but I must tell you about one bunch of sandwiches we got. They were made on the style of fried apple pies with a beautiful nut-brown crust that promised to be delicious. But when we bit into them we found a filler of raven meat.

Of course, you know what a raven is. It is a crow with a British accent. Poe did more to eulogize the raven than anyone else when he wrote:

Once upon a midnight dreary,
While I pondered weak and weary, etc.

But he arrived at the dismal conclusion "Nevermore," which was the unanimous opinion of everyone who tasted raven pie.

The tech sergeant (Sgt. Davey) had visions of something much more delicious a couple of nights later when the boys took him snipe hunting. You would have to know Sgt. Davey to really appreciate the joke. He is the rugged-individual type who thinks he can do anything and proceeds to demonstrate that it is not an idle boast. So when the boys said they wanted a man to hold the laundry bag who had a steady nerve and could pull the closing string at exactly the right moment, Davey volunteered. He made elaborate preparation for frying the birds in my room, selected a laundry bag with a free-pulling string and the hunt was on.

They stationed him by a log in a nice bit of marshland (the snipe is a semi-waterfowl) and slipped away to make the drive. The gag, of course, was that they came back to the barracks and left him holding the bag. (Incidentally, the phrase "holding the bag" originated with the snipe hunt.)

But he enjoyed the joke immensely, as did everyone else. The monotony of the camp exaggerates the comedy of all jokes, and any bit of humor provides laughter out of proportion to the true value of the gag. But men who laugh too easily are supposed to be the best soldiers.

Guess you are thinking of vacation by now and of your victory garden and your lovely flowers. Have a good garden and I may be home in time to help you eat some of the vegetables—if they are properly canned.

Love Always,
Leland

[Plymouth, England]
April 26, 1944

My Dearest Letty:

If this din doesn't get me down I will do my stint of writing tonight. It is pretty noisy. Our party is larger than usual, and that means the room is full. Coffee is boiling and there are at least half a dozen separate arguments going. These range from baseball to bombs or, "How did the Yanks of 1942 compare with the 1928 squad?" and "Can a country be beaten from the air alone?"

With such intellectual arguments conducted by such learned men it is little wonder that this may sound confused. But it is enlightening, even better than your psychology course.

The only idea in my mind that is clear and unconfused is that I am a bit in love with you.

Always,
Leland

[Plymouth, England]
April 28, 1944

My Dearest Letty:

Since it has been a couple of days since I said "I love you" I had better say it now. Hope to get a pass tonight so I will have no time for any writing. Won't even have a chance to do my evening laundry.

Well, I guess you have about finished your job for the year, and I am wondering what you will be doing next. For all I know you may be in Texas or California by now.

You would get a kick out of these English kids. They are clever little chaps and usually manage to get most of my gum ration each week. But it is worth every stick of it to see them grin.

Love Always,
Leland

[Plymouth, England]
May 2, 1944

My Dearest Letty:

It may get monotonous for you to get one of these every day, but I am sending letters that way anyway. Of course, I suppose letters reach you in bunches just as mine reach me. I have had as many as 22 letters in one mail call. It is like reading a book to get through them, but it is more interesting.

I have been reading more than usual in the past few weeks. At the moment I am reading "U.S. Foreign Policy," by Walter Lippman. It would probably bore you, but it is a good book.

Must say "I love you" and run along to bed.

Love Always,
Leland

[Plymouth, England]
May 7, 1944

My Dearest Letty:

Sunday morning and, believe it or not, I got up at 9 o'clock just to write you a letter. Now, you must remember this so you will know I am in love with you. If I were not, I would have slept until noon. Nothing else could have coaxed me out of bed at this unreasonable hour.

Of course, you may be in Texas by this time as I suppose your school job is finished. But if you are, please remember to not take a job that is too bad or demands too much work. I really mean this. And write me all the news of that part of the country. I have about lost contact with the plains and panhandle country. Most of the people I knew there write infrequently.

Love Always,
Leland

[Plymouth, England]
May 18, 1944

My Dearest Letty:

Well, I suppose you are in the country of the coyotes and cactus by now, but I am writing anyway. Maybe the letter will follow you and eventually you can read that I still love you.

Wish I knew your Texas address. Have not had an excuse to write to Texas for several weeks. The last one I wrote has not been answered. But that is pretty good country. I would not miss a chance to see it again if such an opportunity should come my way.

We staged a small parade yesterday and I saw some pictures of it on display in town last night. May be able to send you a couple if they are offered for sale.

Love Always,
Leland

[Plymouth, England]
May 23, 1944

My Dearest Letty:

The coffee is all made and all the gang is all gathered. You can imagine how they are batting the breeze. Or maybe you can't imagine. You have never heard a bunch of GIs exchanging yarns. At the moment, they are comparing the merits of their respective home states. I never knew Florida, Wisconsin, Texas, Oklahoma or Arkansas were so wonderful. But these guys prove it conclusively, every night.

But they do not have to prove to me that you are wonderful. I know that already.

Love Always,
Leland

[Plymouth, England]
May 25, 1944

My Dearest Letty:

Well, we had a short summer, and here it is winter again. At least it seems like winter if you listen to the rain on the roof and feel the wind stinging your face. But the spring is still with us. By looking closely, you can see her braiding her hair with apple blossoms and weaving an apron of arbutus and soft green grass. And all the time I sit around and wait for the letter from you that will be a five-minute furlough.

Love Always,
Leland

[Plymouth, England]
May 27, 1944

My Dearest Letty:

It is evening and I have finished my work for today, I hope. Now I wish I could think of some way to add variety to my letter, but that is not easy.

If you read the paper—and I know you do—you know more about what we are doing than I would be permitted to tell. But the paper would never tell you that I am in love with you. Hence, I must write and tell you that.

Love Always,
Leland

[Plymouth, England]
June 3, 1944

My Dearest Letty:

Here I am doing my good deed for the day, or maybe it is my naughty deed. Maybe I shouldn't go around telling little girls I am crazy about them, but I simply can't resist the temptation, especially if it is a wonderful little girl whom I have been in love with for such a long time.

But some time, if you are still around, I can tell you all about how it is to see the spring parade majestically across England and know that you are still waiting for me. It is a helpless feeling.

Love Always,
Leland

[Plymouth, England]
June 4, 1944

My Dearest Letty:
Wish I could find time to write a long, long letter in which I could tell you all the nice things in the world, such as:

How this country is like a painted picture of the quaint landscapes, how the old houses peep out from behind majestic hedges, or about the nice black cocker spaniel that has adopted A Troop and is pestering me now, and, of course, how much I love you. But I don't have time just now. So,

Love Always,
Leland

[Plymouth, England]
June 10, 1944

My Dearest Letty:
Hope you have not missed my letters, but I have written little. I am still crazy about you.

Things have been nice today. It was quiet, but this afternoon three genuine American girls showed up in a Red Cross clubmobile and served us coffee and doughnuts. It was the first American girl I had seen since I was in [censored]. Gosh, it was great to see a girl with a Texas accent, and those people appear in the oddest places.

Then later the cooks turned up with some ice cream. We had tasted it only twice since we left the states. When mail came in, I had a letter from you with a picture. Yes, it was great.

Love Always,
Leland

[Minehead, England]
June 20, 1944

My Dearest Letty:

No, I have not forgotten to write you. Other matters, though no more important, have at least been more urgent.

My mail is regular, but I still don't know how you finally came out of your bout with measles or if you decided to go to Kansas City. I am waiting to learn. I only hope you don't take a job that you can't quit when you wish, such as joining the Women's Army Corps. You see, we want to make our own plans when I get home.

Love Always,
Leland

[Tilshead, England]
July 5, 1944

My Dearest Letty:

Yes, you are still my pin-up girl. Your picture came today, and after looking at it closely I have decided that you are as beautiful as ever. (How do you carry your age so well?)

Seriously, it was a good picture, and you will never know just how much I liked it. Hope to find time to write you an airmail letter tomorrow. Meanwhile, suppose you take time off and write me a nice, long letter about what happened.

Love Always,
Leland

[Tilshead, England]
July 13, 1944

My Dearest Letty:

Just had a nice bunch of letters, including two from you. That alone makes it a nice day.

Say, what's this I hear about you asking questions of a swami? And did he say I was still in love with you? If not, he is a fake, and you must not pay any attention to him. But if, on the other hand, he said that I love you more than you ever guessed then he is right.

I'll bet the city was beautiful on the night of the third. Gosh! I'm beginning to wonder what a really lighted city looks like. It is one of the things I want to see most.

Love Always,
Leland

[Tilshead, England]
July 16, 1944

My Dearest Letty:

It is Sunday afternoon, but if I were in Kansas City at this time of day we would call it evening. You see, it is nine o'clock but the sun is still shining.

That is the odd thing about this country. We have so little darkness. The sun goes down around ten o'clock, but we don't have to worry about darkness until almost midnight. Then it begins getting light around 4:30, so we have five hours of night. Sleep is something of a problem.

So you, too, have become conspicuous with your Southern accent. I have had the same experience many times and there is a definite advantage to it if you will make the most of it. It has been my passport into many interesting acquaintances that I could not have made if I had spoken New Jersey or California.

This was especially true in New York and Pennsylvania. I would seldom speak more than a dozen words until someone would say, "You all are from the South, ain't you?" And I would proceed to play the part of Bob Burns' cousin Wofford. In this way, I have been able to meet some interesting people.

But Aaron, when I saw him last, had developed quite a Brooklyn tinge in his talk. Youngsters do that, I suppose, without noticing it.

I only hope you don't change too much. The way you talk is one of the many things I love about you. In fact, I love you more than a little and that would be true no matter how you talked.

I had intended to write a long letter but certain things make that impossible now.

Love Always,
Leland

THREE

Normandy

An armada of landing crafts left the port of Southampton during the night of July 25 and arrived the next morning on the Normandy beaches. Most of the armor and troops went ashore at Utah Beach, which had been made ready for the heavy equipment. The soldiers of Leland Duvall's cavalry troop pushed ashore farther east at Omaha Beach, scene of the fiercest fighting on D-day. The division spent three days assembling its equipment and on August 1 began its first assault on the Germans. It was to breach the German line, cross the Sée and Sélune Rivers, and capture the town of Fougères. Duvall's and three other platoons of the Eighty-Fifth Cavalry left at two thirty in the morning to probe ahead of the armor and infantry. Duvall saw the first combat that he had seemed eager to experience. Fougères fell two days later.

Major General Lunsford E. Oliver, the commander of the Fifth Armored, had organized it into three combat commands. Each would comprise a tank company, an infantry company, and a reconnaissance platoon, which would always go into battle together. The innovation proved so effective that it would become the standard in armored-force training. The division broke through the German line and, in its first twenty days of combat, drove 405 miles through German-occupied France to the Seine River and then fought its way through Luxembourg to the German border. Troops of the Eighty-Fifth Cavalry, who traveled much farther, would be the first Allied soldiers to enter Germany. During that period, according to the commander's confidential report at month's end, the Fifth Armored troops killed 2,811 Germans, captured 2,960 soldiers, destroyed 203 tanks, eight armored cars, and 384 motor vehicles, and captured 36 tanks, three ambulances, eight airplanes, and 184 weapons.

Duvall would discover that actual combat for a reconnaissance scout was far different from his preparation. The men were trained to sneak behind enemy lines, reconnoiter the terrain, and radio back to the armor, artillery, and infantry units the location and strength of the enemy. The reconnaissance platoons did that, but the division traveled so fast across France that the cavalry could barely stay ahead. When the brutal combat began against the entrenched German defenses, the cavalrymen found themselves assigned infantry roles and fighting alongside the infantrymen and tanks.

Nothing about the division's exploits in its first forty days got into the newspapers. General George S. Patton, the commander of the Third Army, ordered that the armored division be kept a secret. The soldiers became known as Patton's ghost troops. Duvall, of course, wrote nothing about the action until October, when he told Letty Jones that Patton had decided to let people know that his outfit was in the war and that its exploits had gotten a nice write-up in the papers. Until the brutal winter of 1944–45, Duvall continued to offer reassurances that he endured no great hardship and faced no grave peril and that she should not expect to hear of any heroism on his part. He would never talk of any combat recognition except a presidential citation for his troop during the Battle of the Bulge, but his discharge papers recorded that he was awarded five Bronze Stars for bravery or meritorious service, a distinguished unit badge, and a Purple Heart.

[Normandy, near St. Sauveur-Le-Vicomte]
July 28, 1944

My Dearest Letty:

Now that I have found an opportunity to write again, I also find that I can think of nothing to write except the same sentence I always use. Just for variety's sake I am not going to say that. We will see if you have imagination enough to guess what I mean. Anyway, it is still true.

Maybe some day the situation will permit the censor to permit me to say where I am, where I have been and what I have been doing. Even that may fail to improve the interest of my letters, but (if I also have time) it will increase their length.

Love Always,
Leland

[Pacy-sur-Eure, France]
August 19, 1944

My Dearest Letty:

Just have about five minutes to write this so please don't expect me to say more than "I love you" and "Please keep on writing." Will try to answer all your letters and questions when I find time.

Believe me, I am in a hurry now.

Love Always,
Leland

[Near Paris, France]
August 28, 1944

My Dearest Letty:

Just had about five or six letters from you this morning so I am giving you a short note in return. Not a fair trade you will say, and you will be right. But that is the best I can do just now. Some time when we have nothing else to do I'll sit around the fire and write you dozens of long letters and just hand them over to you. No mailman, no stamp and no censor. (*No offense toward the censor.*)

Sorry you can't decide whether to accept your transfer, but I don't think you have anything to worry about. There is really no danger and I am sure you can handle the situation. It's obvious that you cannot be content at home. You are now a cosmopolitan.

Love Always,
Leland

[Nanteuil-le-Haudouin, France]
August 30, 1944

My Dearest Letty,

Well, I am back on the one-a-day schedule, for I wrote you yesterday and am writing again today. But I don't think I will be able to keep it up for long.

Wish I knew just where you are and what you finally decided to do. But I guess I will learn in a few days when your letters catch up with me.

The circumstances make it hard to write. I can't tell you what they are, but it is hard to concentrate. Add to that the fact that I am in a hurry and you will see why your letters are short.

About the only thing that I can make clear is that I am still in love with you. So long as I am sure you remember that, nothing else matters. It can all wait until I am able to talk to you. That will save paper, etc., and will be much more delightful.

Love Always,
Leland

FOUR

The Siegfried Line

With September came unrelenting rain, which turned roads and fields into gelatin and made progress by heavy armor nearly impossible. Throughout the autumn, gains by the Fifth Armored Division had to be measured in yards instead of hundreds of miles. Units of the division lined up along the Luxembourg and Belgian borders across the Our River from the Siegfried Line, the long German fortification of tank traps, bunkers, and tunnels. Leland Duvall's troop would probe the German defenses along the border in Luxembourg and Belgium and then move north into the Netherlands before engaging the Germans in October and November in the Hürtgen Forest, in the longest battle of the war and by far the bloodiest for the Fifth Armored Division and the cavalry. The commander of the Eighty-Fifth Cavalry, Maj. John P. Gerald, was killed during a patrol in Belgium in October. His predecessor, Lt. Col. Kent Fay, had been killed forty-five days earlier.

It was along the border in Belgium that Duvall's troop was trapped for the first time in a farmhouse surrounded by Germans, apparently a common peril of scouts. It is the subject of a letter to his girlfriend, apparently unscanned by the censor, in which, for the first time since the Normandy landing, he describes what is happening, although in Duvall's typical amused way.

[Meischdref, Luxembourg]
Sept. 14, 1944

My Dearest Letty:

At last I get a chance to mail you another letter and remind you that I still love you. And I am doing this while the other guys in the car crew are cooking their chow. May even have to miss supper if I write all the letters I should.

Say, I have several souvenirs of various countries and cities, which I intend to send you if I ever get a chance. Hope I can send them before long. Of course, you may not be interested in them, but you can keep them and I'll tell you the story that goes with them when I see you.

Love Always,
Leland

[Beidweiler, Luxembourg]
Sept. 16, 1944

My Dearest Letty:

Just had three letters from you yesterday, so I feel that I should try a little note now. I may not get this into the mail for a few days, but I can always change the date on it if it gets too old.

After all, I would probably say the same things in any letter no matter when it was written. So the date means little: I would always say that things are going smoothly and it is raining (as usual) and that I am still in love with you.

Oh yes, I shaved off my beard. Didn't know I had grown one, did you? Well, I had a nice one. Weeks old. But it looked so much like an Airedale terrier and was so uncomfortable that I shaved it off.

I am sending some money to give you an idea what the stuff over here looks like. Have several coins from various countries but cannot send them now. Must sign off now as I am in a grand rush.

Love Always,
Leland

Dearest Letty

[Beidweiler, Luxembourg]
Sept. 18, 1944

My Dearest Letty:

Since I have not made a report on the condition of my ears, etc., for a few days, it might be a good idea to give you the condensed version. At the moment, they are dirty. I slept in the mud last night and have not been able to get rid of the debris.

But that is unimportant. The main thing is that I am still in love with you.

Bet you never would have guessed that, but it is true. Maybe you will not be interested when you learn that I have got into the habit of being dirty and not washing my ears. I promise to change all that later.

Love Always,
Leland

[Luxembourg, on the Our River]
Sept. 28, 1944

My Dearest Letty:

I am writing this under very trying circumstances. The mud is three inches deep and my writing case has just fallen into it. The boys are frying eggs and potatoes, and since I have not eaten in several hours I am plenty hungry. The aroma is tantalizing.

So why am I writing? It must be because I am still in love with you.

Haven't had any mail in quite a while, so it is not easy to write. Don't suppose you have been so loaded with mail from me either, as I have been rushed for writing time. May get around to writing more often in the near future.

Love Always,
Leland

[Luxembourg, at the German border]
Sept. 30, 1944

My Dearest Letty:

All morning I have been waiting for the rain to cease so that I could write this in comfort, but I give up. It will not quit so I am in a pup tent doing the best I can. Hope you can read it.

Have just finished eating three delicious American doughnuts. You see, three American girls with a Red Cross clubmobile were around dishing out doughnuts and coffee. Unfortunately, they did not come up here where I am. (It is too near the Germans, and I don't blame them for not coming up.) They stopped at squadron headquarters and sent the doughnuts up, but I had to make my own coffee.

Say, I may have not told you but I have a new girlfriend. She is a pretty little trick (not as large as you) with big blue eyes and the softest blonde hair you ever saw. Her name is Anna something or other—her last name is unpronounceable for me. Of course, I cannot talk to her, but she is trying to teach me her language. Already I can count to ten and say a few words.

She brings me eggs as fast as the hens will lay them, as well as butter and such things. But she is a mercenary little cuss and will not give me anything. I have to trade. An egg, for example, costs me a stick of gum and some candy. But the trading is not as profitable as it sounds. When she has no more eggs and wants another piece of candy, she merely goes across the hedge and picks up two or three green apples and I have to trade for them, too. You see, she is only five or six years old, so she would not understand if I tried to tell her that I did not want the apples. So I have to give her the gum and pretend I enjoy the apples.

You keep insisting that you are growing too large. Personally, I think you should weigh 121½ or 122, so you see it is not necessary to eat the extra slice of bread. It so happens that I am losing a little weight. Am down about 15 pounds. If I keep on losing weight and you keep gaining, well, I might not fare so well when I come home.

Must sign off for now.

Love Always,
Leland

My Dearest Letty:

Well, I hope I have time to finish this, but a guy never knows. Anyway, I just had a flock of letters from you and a few other people and it is high time I tried to answer some of them. Everyone except you and the family has about quit writing to me. They can't remember to write if I don't answer their letters, and that is not always possible.

Say, you should have been with us a couple of days ago. It was Jim Modlin's wedding anniversary, and we had to do a bit of celebrating. So we did it with a dinner.

We are staying in an abandoned farmhouse just now, so we had a stove. One of the boys acquired three fryer chickens for the occasion, and we did them in grand Southern style. I must break down and modestly confess that I am not a bad cook when it comes to preparing fried chicken. (But I cannot compare with your mother, of course. You may tell her that truthfully.)

Anyway, we fixed up quite a tasty meal. We had genuine milk gravy (we also have a cow, which we milk twice a day), salad, cheese, onion, French-fried potatoes, milk and coffee, toast and jam. It was very good. The best part of it was that some of the boys discovered a white tablecloth, so we ate from China plates on a nice clean table.

And to add a bit of the feminine touch, some guy produced two big beautiful dolls (one blonde and one brunette) and set them up on either side of Jim's plate. A party is a dull affair without girls, you know, and the dolls were the best we could do.

There was only one hitch to the whole party. While we were lingering over our coffee and cigarettes, the jerries opened up with their artillery. One shell landed on a side room of the house and blew the roof away. It knocked soot into all our coffee and we had to pour out a gallon of good milk. They have very bad manners about such things. (Naughty boys!)

We had a good house when we moved in, but the usable part of it is getting smaller by the day. The roof is gone from one room, and the artillery knocks out the windows from a new room almost every day. Very soon now, we shall have only the cellar. Luckily, that has no windows, and there seems to be no way for the shells to damage it.

I was pleased to learn that you would probably go to work at Russellville before long. It is a pleasant little town, and you should enjoy working there more than at Kansas City or Fort Smith. Then, too, you will be easier to find when the war is over.

Hope you don't mind my starting this note with ink and finishing with pencil. My ink supply is exhausted and there is no drugstore on the corner.

Love Always,
Leland

[Belgian border, near Aachen, Germany]
Oct. 10, 1944

My Dearest Letty:

Since I have time to write a little today, I hope you won't mind my using wrapping paper for stationery. It is all I have and they say the American Army is supposed to be good at improvising. That is, we do the best we can with what we have.

Things are going pretty good here, but it is still as muddy as the Delta country. It rains regularly, but that is to be expected. Otherwise, conditions are good.

Chow is plentiful, and we even get plenty of cigarettes. Writing paper is not so plentiful, but we get plenty of envelopes. My only complaint is that I cannot get a new pipe. I only have one now and, being a bit on the absent-minded side, I keep it lost half the time.

Oh yes, they finally took the Fifth Armored Division off the "secret" list and admitted that we were in the war. Gave us quite a write-up in the paper, too. They told how we gained 400 miles in our first 20 days in action, and listed many of the towns we had captured. They also gave this division credit for being the first Allied troops to enter Germany. I intended to send you the story but lost the paper.

I suppose you are working again, but I can only guess at that. Your letters have been scrambled as to the dates, and many of them have not arrived. It is like missing several installments in a serial story or movie. I simply have to guess at what transpired in the preceding chapters.

Guess mine are the same, but the saving feature is that nothing happens in my letters. The only point I don't want you to forget is that I am still in love with you. Remember that and even if all my letters fail to arrive you have missed nothing.

Love Always,
Leland

[Heerlen, The Netherlands]
Oct. 14, 1944

My Dearest Letty:

Well, here it is almost the middle of October and Saturday, too, but I have not seen a single football game this year. Tragic, isn't it? But if I were home we would see one today.

That is not so bad. Football can wait. But for several days I don't even get a letter. Can you imagine that? And all the time you complain that you cannot get mail. We both seem to be in the same boat.

I just learned that Ardis shipped out for overseas some place. Don't know where he is going, but his postoffice is New York so he might be on his way to Europe.

I am investigating to see if it is possible to send you a box of souvenirs, etc., which I have collected. They are all utterly worthless, I suppose. I could get nothing of any special value, but you might want to take a look at some of them.

I have a few coins from various countries, including England, Hong Kong, Belgium, Germany, Holland and Luxembourg. Also have a couple of decorations of honor for Nazi soldiers and even an identification button for a Nazi underground worker from Miami. But I don't think he will ever get back to Miami, so I am sure he won't need the button again.

Guess I might as well call this off. I have quite a cold (had a chill last night) so the thinking wheels in my head simply won't go. Will try to be better when I write again.

Love Always,
Leland

My Dearest Letty:

Things are looking much better at the moment. Had about 15 letters in last night's mail, including four from you. The old morale went up about 30 points in spite of the rain.

It seems that your vacation had ended and you were working again. Too bad little girls like you have to work, but it seems to be a rule now. At least I should have no trouble calling you on the telephone when I come home. That will be some consolation.

Started this last night but did not get to finish it. That is not unusual. There is always some odd job turning up to be done, so such things as letters have to wait.

Guess Ardis must be on his way over here now. Had a letter from him and his address was through the New York postoffice. He had not shipped out, for he had just been on pass in New York City. Guess he was at Camp Kilmer, but he won't stay there too long.

Aaron is in Camp Atterbury, Ind., now. It seems that he is chief carpenter in an infantry regiment, and I don't suppose he will be there too long.

But I keep kicking around from one country to another, and seeing some new things in each place. Guess I will forget most of it when I see the U.S. again. Anyway, nothing I have seen has made me change my mind about being in love with you. That seems to be rather a permanent state of mind.

Love Always,
Leland

[Heerlen, The Netherlands]
Oct. 21, 1944

My Dearest Letty:

It's getting to be a habit this writing to you. I do it almost every day now. It's a lot of fun.

I can tell you all sorts of stories, and there is no way for you to check up on me. But I suppose you are laughing in your sleeve and saying, "Why, the dumb ox. I've been doing him the same way for years and he never thought to try to check up on me."

Like the way you go on telling me you are still in love with me. Nice story! And I don't even try to prove it one way or the other. Suppose I should investigate and learn that you were only kidding? It would only spoil a beautiful dream, and I like to go on dreaming.

A kid came by with an accordion today and gave us quite a concert. He was a little white-headed chap no more than 10 years old but he was pretty good. Played quite a variety of music, but "Barrel Polka" more than anything else. So he played it about a dozen times. Collected a pocket full of chocolate on the strength of it, too.

Well, I seem to have exhausted all the printable news and besides it is almost time for chow.

Love Always,
Leland

[Heerlen, The Netherlands]
Oct. 21, 1944

My Dearest Letty:

I may have time to finish this before dark if I hurry. I always find myself racing against time when I start writing, and there is really no need for it if I would only budget my time and allot a certain portion of it as writing time. But I never do that.

Was never any good at budgets or planned programs. Always went along in a haphazard style and hoped the ends would meet. Don't guess it was such a good system, for I never managed to accomplish much with it.

You may try to change all that. You might even succeed to a certain degree, but I warn you now that I am not easy to reform. But I must admit that this weather has changed me some. I noticed when I took a shower today that I had started growing webs between my toes like a duck. They are really necessary if a guy is going to get around here.

We did have a bit of drought today. It quit raining last night and only started again a few minutes ago, and for thirty consecutive minutes the sun actually shone. Of course, it was a sick bit of light (the sun seemed to be mildewed) but it was sunshine nevertheless. The local people were amazed. Many of them had never seen anything like it. Thought it might be a good omen or something.

Say, I can't remember just what kinds of money samples I have sent you, and I don't know if you are interested in any of it, but I am enclosing a sample anyway. I also have some coins that I will send some time. Some of them are pretty odd in appearance such as the square 5-cent piece from Holland and the curiously shaped threepence of England.

Well, the darkness is closing down so I must say I'm still in love with you and call this a letter.

Love Always,
Leland

[Belgium]
Oct. 29, 1944

My Dearest Letty:

Lady, if you could only see me now! You would never suspect that I am not a gentleman. You see, I have a clean shave, a new haircut and I am sitting in a chair to write this. Yes, a real honest-to-goodness chair. Odd things come into the path of a soldier, and he uses them and leaves them.

But sitting in a chair and doing the other civilized things we do occasionally has its good points. It helps us to stay in the habit of the conventional life. We have lived in the open and slept on the ground so long that there is a real danger of forgetting what a bed or a table is like. And we sometimes bathe and shave so infrequently that we lose the knack and grow careless of all personal appearance.

But it doesn't seem to impair the fighting qualities of the boys. I have seen some of the guys—Infantry, Artillery and Engineers as well as the Armored Force—with beards like Santa Claus and mud to their helmets doing plenty of the kind of work it takes to get this mess ended. I sometimes wonder if they will be capable of going back to their normal way of living. Most of them will, I suppose, but a few, especially the younger ones, will be changed a lot. But I guess men of the age of Drittler and me will be about the same. Our habits are fairly well established.

For example, I go on being in love just as I always have. No amount of mud or Army field rations can change that.

So you have settled into your new apartment and your mother doesn't like it. Well, I can see why. I could see that she has lived so long in her old place that any new one would have to have a lot of merit to make a favorable impression on her.

You seem to be curious about where I am, and it is too bad that I cannot tell you. It is just one of those things. I can tell you to not imagine anything too unpleasant. It is really not so tough as all the papers would make it seem. Those stories come from guys who are in a habit of sleeping on a Beautyrest mattress in a steam-heated room. They have to make a living so their stories must have a certain amount of color.

I can tell you this. I have been in France, Holland, Belgium, Luxembourg and Germany. Saw Paris but briefly and wished I could spend some more time there. I learn from the local papers that soldiers are going there on pass now, but we are too far away for that to mean anything to us.

The city of Luxembourg, too, is nice. Always one of the most beautiful cities in Europe, it has not been changed too much by the war. There was little strategic bombing of the place and most of the buildings are intact. I attended church in the cathedral there, and it was one thing to be remembered, even though I couldn't understand a word that was spoken.

Love Always,
Leland

Monschau, Germany
Nov. 1, 1944

My Dearest Letty:

If I can keep my thoughts together I will try to get off a note tonight. It is not so easy as it sounds for there is a lot of noise around.

Just had two V-mails from you this afternoon. One was dated 17th October, and you forgot to date the other (absent-minded girl). But that did not take any of the enjoyment out of the letter.

So they have you working nights now. Too bad. But maybe you will enjoy it as well as any. Personally, I never liked a night shift, but I never liked the day shift either.

You see, I never liked the idea of working. It takes up too much time that could be employed in other things that are more interesting. That is the reason I am planning to have a small garden when I come home. You see, I figure you can tend a small one without taking up too much of your time.

By the way, since you are working for Mr. Bell (it is the Southwestern Bell system, isn't it?), I should be able to call you up easily enough when I hit the states. Keep a line open when this is over and I will call you up the moment I hit New York. That will be doing you a great favor. It will give you plenty of time to get the other soldiers and 4Fs out of your life before I get home. Hope none of them are the persistent type that insists on staying around until the last minute, for I don't want to have to dispose of them personally.

Well, the noise is too great, and I can think only when there is quiet.

Love Always,
Leland

Monschau, Germany
Nov. 4, 1944

My Dearest Letty:

Have been debating whether I should cut this paper in half and make it at least near the conventional letter size, but I decided to make this a big letter instead of a good one. It is a case of sacrificing quality for quantity, but that is not unusual.

It is that way with my cooking (yes, I do a bit of cooking). You see there is a group of us together here, and we have Army field rations plus a few odds from the kitchen truck. I usually cook breakfast for the bunch. That is where the quantity comes in. The big job is to cook plenty. They all break down and confirm that my meals are delicious, but I sometimes suspect they are only feeding my vanity to induce me to go on cooking. But I do make delicious coffee.

And you should taste the jam I made yesterday. The ration we get contains a fruit bar that no one will eat. I saved up about a dozen bars, cut them into a pan, added lemon juice, powdered sugar and a bit of candy and boiled it into a nice dark jam. The whole gallon disappeared in nothing flat. They might even give me a medal for making Army rations edible. They have given medals for that, you know.

Say, I traded for a pair of shoes for you a few days ago and have not been able to send them to you yet. With shoe stamps as they are in the states you may need them this winter to keep your feet off the concrete. Will try to get them into the mail within the next few days. Wait until you see them! They are not built for either style or combat, but they are durable enough. Apple wood is pretty tough, you know. They cost me two packs of rationed cigarettes and a bar of candy. But when you consider that the Dutch value cigarettes at $3 per pack they were not so cheap as they look.

I also sent you a bag of odds and ends a few days ago. Don't know when they will arrive, but they will be there sometime. You may not find them interesting, but there are a couple of war stories that go with some of them. The stories will keep until I see you.

Must say I am still in love with you and run along for it is getting too dark to write.

Love Always,
Leland

Monschau, Germany
Nov. 6, 1944

My Dearest Letty:

Well, the big daily newspaper is going to press again, and the poor editor doesn't have a single scoop. In fact, he doesn't have a decent front-page story. Boy, is he tearing his hair (what he has left).

You see, all the stories that are available come under the heading of military information or could possibly "give aid or comfort to the enemy" so we don't write those stories. Such stories would include our location, assignment, experience, etc. A guy could write a long letter with that.

He could also write a pretty good gripe letter by complaining about the rain, mud and all the little things soldiers gripe about. But that would not make interesting reading. No one likes to read complaints. But, believe it or not, it is the little things that get under my skin. A guy can fight back against the big problems, but the little ones must be endured, and they are a constant annoying factor, like gnats and mosquitoes. And they get into my hair in a way that keeps me from being the kind of guy who stays in the Army after the war is over.

On the sports page there is also a dearth of news. Nothing except the checker tournament (which I won) is happening. The boys have a five-frame blackjack game going on the next blanket, but the results are still in doubt.

In the Walter Winchell column, you will still read that I am crazy about you, but that is not news. It has been there for so long that even the neighbor's children know about that.

Mail has just come in but the clerk has not sorted it yet. Haven't had a report in a few days so I hope there are a couple of letters for me.

Guess you have settled into the routine of your job by now. It is about time you grew into the habit so that you can get up at exactly the right minute, eat breakfast on the dot and make the office just thirty seconds before time to go to work. When you get it down that fine, you are really on the ball.

Love Always,
Leland

Monschau, Germany
Nov. 7, 1944

My Dearest Letty:

After the huge letter I put out recently there should be no reason for me to write now and, to tell the truth, there is none except to remind you that I am still as much in love with you as ever. But I seldom sit down to write when I don't include a letter to you. Matter of habit.

No, I have not seen Anna in quite a long time now. She lives in a little village in Luxembourg and I am in Germany. So I am eating no eggs except the kind that comes in cans. They are marked "chopped ham and eggs," but you would never guess it by the taste.

Love Always,
Leland

Roetgen, Germany
Nov. 14, 1944

My Dearest Letty:

The smoke from my fire makes it impossible to see the paper at times, and so I am not entirely responsible for what may come out of the pen. But it is out of the question to move away from the fire, so I will have to take a chance.

Of course, I will have to make sure that I get over the fact that I am still in love with you, but beyond that the letter will be unimportant anyway.

Snow came to the Western front a few days ago. It started with flurries such as you would expect to see there around Christmas, but in a couple of hours it settled down to the serious business of changing all the landscape. It placed a quaint little white nightcap on all the fence posts and draped a heavy robe over the complaining fir trees. It carpeted the whole earth with a soft white rug so that not even a mouse or rabbit could move without tracking up the floor like a small boy who had forgotten to wipe his feet.

It was all beautiful, but it did not make me happy. My pup tent is not designed for snow.

It brings up the nostalgic picture of a warm quiet room. I dream of the glow of an open fire, a deep easy chair, a thick robe and—oh, well. You know the picture.

Let the snow fall outside. The room is pleasant. The music on the radio is clear and soft. The light is turned down.

"Shall we go to the show?" you ask after you have checked on the fire to see that it has plenty of fuel.

I glance out. It is still snowing hard.

"Suppose we skip it and spend a quiet evening at home," I decide. "It is pretty cold outside and I can see the show tomorrow."

Of course you are hoping I will say that, and you have already learned to agree me with anyway. We spend the evening at home. Too, you know you will have to be up early tomorrow to go to work. It takes long hours to support a husband.

Maybe I'd better stop before you start throwing things in my direction.

Love Always,
Leland

Roetgen, Germany
Nov. 16, 1944

My Dearest Letty:

Just had two letters from you today, and one yesterday, so I owe you some kind of a note. Of course, it cannot be much for there is nothing happening that would make interesting reading. I suppose it will be all smudged with oil, for I have just finished cleaning my guns and my hands are greasy. Now don't tell me I should wash them. It is cold.

You should see one of my guns. It is a beautiful double-barrel shot-gun I acquired in Luxembourg. The stock is a checkered hand-made job and is really a beauty. I wish the postal regulations would permit me to send it home or (if you want to practice up your quail shooting) to you. It is a light 16-gauge job so you could handle it without trouble. If I can get it home after the war I will make a quail hunter out of you.

Do you remember the bird dog that Houston and Ruby gave me several years ago? Lady was her name, I believe. At least that was what I called her, and she was really a pretty little trick. But she died that fall from some unknown malady. Now I have only one dog so you see I am about out of the canine business. Guess I'll have to acquire a new stock when I come home, for the one I have is no longer a pup and will be too old to do anything but scratch fleas when I see him again. I have always wanted a cocker or springer spaniel and a really good Irish setter but have never owned either. So I have quite a bit of dog buying to do.

I have to run along.

Love Always,
Leland

Postcard from Germany
Nov. 17, 1944

My Dearest Letty:

This is a fair picture of the "Fatherland" in winter. At least the view reminds me of my present surrounding, which is why I don't think so much of Germany. My idea of punishment for jerries after the war is to send them home and make them stay there. Nothing could be worse.

Love Always,
Leland

[Postcard from Germany]
Nov. 17, 1944

This is how Berlin is supposed to look at night, but our Air Force claims to have changed the picture somewhat. Haven't seen it—yet. Will tell you more about it when I come home.

[Walhorn, Belgium]
Nov. 19, 1944

My Dearest Letty:

While you are pining away in a sad state of dejection waiting for me to come home the least I can do is write you a cheerful letter occasionally.

I apologize. Just wanted to make you mad with the first paragraph. Now I can be serious and tell you I still spend all my leisure time thinking of you and waiting impatiently for this mess to end so that I will see you again. Now I hope you have forgiven me.

Most of our snow has melted. I think today's sunshine will finish it off, and I am not sorry to see it go even if it was beautiful in an uncomfortable sort of way. After this winter I don't think I shall ever be able to appreciate the beauty of snow and the sharp hardness of cold weather again. I once thought I would like to spend a winter season at Lake Placid, but I have changed my mind. Placid is inviting enough in the summer, and I think I shall go there again. But I much prefer the Rio Grande in winter.

Had a letter from Ardis, and he has already had a couple of passes in France. I have not been so fortunate, for I have not even had a six-hour pass since we left England. However, a few of our boys have had passes recently and my time will come eventually.

A few of the boys went all the way back to Paris. Of course, it is quite a distance, but that is where I would like to go. We only saw the glamorous city briefly and from combat vehicles, but I saw enough of it to make me want to go back. By comparison, London is a stack of unsymmetrical bricks and stones and I could have no special regret if I never saw it again. But I sincerely hope for a few days in Paris while I am on the continent.

Love Always,
Leland

[Walhorn, Belgium]
Nov. 23, 1944

My Dearest Letty:

You will probably not get this letter for many days. My supply of V-mail forms is exhausted and I have no airmail stamps, so I will be forced to send it free. However, I have a supply of both on order and should get them any day now. I guess the writing habit is pretty strong when a guy writes letters he knows will not arrive for several days, but I know of no way to remedy the situation.

Someone just reminded me that today is Thanksgiving. I had not thought of it before, and if they had not mentioned it the day would have passed without my noticing it. Now that it has been brought out I remember other Thanksgiving days that were more festive.

There was one, in 1926 I guess, when Dr. G. W. Jones and I jumped the gun on the season and went quail hunting. We watched for the game warden with one eye and tried to keep the other on the doctor's untrained pup. I think we got about a dozen birds, including one that the doc shot into sausage with a load of buckshot. He had the one shell of heavy shot left over from a deer hunt and loaded it into his pump gun by mistake.

But on many Thanksgivings I watched Tech and Ouachita battle to a scoreless tie on the football field. Those two always played a dull game against each other. Each team was afraid to cut loose, and I have sat in the driving rain and gnashed my teeth and vowed I would never go out to see them again. But I always did.

Last year, with many of the boys on furlough, an order came out that Thanksgiving would not be a holiday and the normal training schedule would be followed. And did the boys cuss about that! But they were in a better humor after the dinner Tony served us.

Who knows? Next year, you and I may be sitting in the rain watching Tech and Ouachita play another scoreless tie.

Love Always,
Leland

[Walhorn, Belgium]
Nov. 24, 1944

My Dearest Letty:

By this time I hope you have gotten over your Thanksgiving indigestion. You really should not eat so much, you know. I think I have told you before that you should weigh 122½. With my losing weight I would be taking a big chance if you were to get bigger than that. I might even have trouble with you if you were large enough to think you could be the big boss around the place. But with the kind of food your mother prepares I could forgive you for eating too much. Occasionally, say on Christmas and Thanksgiving.

Had about four letters from you today. You might say I hit the jack-pot, for few of the other guys got any mail at all. It was a nice dessert after a swell Thanksgiving dinner.

Yes, we had a good dinner, in spite of the mud, rain and the war. The menu included roast turkey with dressing and brown gravy, real cranberry sauce, creamed potatoes, green beans, peaches and cream and coffee with an issue of hard candy.

Not bad.

Of course it was not served up in the style of the dinner last year, but it was the best possible to fix in a field kitchen.

I just happened to remember one Thanksgiving when I was in Memphis with two guys known locally as Shorty and Horse. We were in work clothes and were dirty after a sixty-mile ride on a cottonseed truck. When it came time for dinner, we crashed the main dining room of the William Len Hotel. Don't know yet why they didn't throw us out for a trio of bums, for it is quite a fashionable joint.

Pshaw. Out of paper in the middle of the story.

Love Always,
Leland

[Walhorn, Belgium]
[Postcard of Paris]
Nov. 26, 1944

My Dearest Letty:

How is this for a Christmas card? You might call it a bird's-eye view of Paris, created by an ultra-modernist. But I was only able to get two of them, which gives you an idea of how limited is the supply. I got seven of another type. But there is no point in trying to write a letter here when I intend to write tomorrow anyway—if I have time.

Love Always,
Leland

Dearest Letty

FIVE

Christmas in a Snowy Woods

The snowfall that inspired rhapsodies in Leland Duvall's letters from the American West and New York turned into a curse on Germany's western frontier in the winter of 1944–45. Snow would fall almost ceaselessly from early November through February in the coldest winter on record. Frostbite and trench foot—so named because men typically got the necrosis from freezing snow and mud in trenches and foxholes—were about as lethal as German shells.

After nearly a month of probing and rebuilding, Fifth Armored units during the last week of November joined a massive Allied assault on the German defenses in the Hürtgen Forest, a dense evergreen woods between Aachen and the Roer River. The Americans would see the fiercest fighting of the European war. They were at a terrible disadvantage in the canopied woods because armored vehicles could not maneuver, the Germans were solidly entrenched, and the Americans were unaccustomed to hand-to-hand fighting in the woods. Progress through the forbidding forest was impeded by minefields, barbed wire, blockhouses, and booby traps hidden by the snow. Artillery shells exploded in the treetops, mortar shells fell randomly, and the Germans, embittered by their retreats across France and Belgium, fought savagely in what they believed was their last stand. While the Americans fought heroically, Hürtgen would prove a disaster, the greatest blunder in the European theater. The Allies eventually retreated. In the long slugfest, all the Allied units would suffer heavy casualties.

"We lost a few good men here," Duvall scribbled in the margin of a book on the Fifth Armored many years later. His close friend, Lt. Ed Sherman, with whom he always shared passes, was gravely wounded in the woods. Duvall took shrapnel in his buttocks, which were unprotected by a tree that he thought shielded him from mortar shells. He had taken grenade fragments earlier in the day. He told Letty Jones months later that they were only scratches, but the mortar shrapnel gave him considerable discomfort as an old man. Altogether, American casualties totaled twenty-three thousand from battle and another nine thousand from trench foot, pneumonia, and other causes.

No sooner had the Americans given up on chasing the Germans from the forest than Adolf Hitler ordered the final desperate campaign to stave off defeat. The Russians were advancing from the east, the Italian peninsula had been lost to the Allies, and his soldiers and equipment were badly depleted by the massive assault from Normandy and air attacks. Hitler figured the Allies expected a sort of Christmas respite in the deep snow, and he ordered a blitzkrieg through the middle of American and British lines in the vicinity of the densely forested Ardennes Mountains. He intended to split the Allied defenses at the unlikeliest place and plunge all the way to the vital supply port of Antwerp on the North Sea. Then, he thought, the British and Americans would sue for an armistice and he could turn his attention to the Russians. It would be highly successful for the first weeks of December, but the offensive collapsed, speeding the war's end. It would be known as the Battle of the Bulge but officially as the Ardennes Offensive.

Duvall's cavalry was on the extreme northern edge of the German offensive, but for him those would be the most harrowing days of the war. For Duvall, the Battle of the Bulge began on November 30 with orders for his combat team to take the heavily fortified "Hill 401" near Kleinhau, Germany, and to clear an area from Kleinhau to the Roer River of Germans. The Americans would take heavy casualties for the next week. Fifty percent of the Eighty-Fifth Cavalry would be killed, wounded, taken prisoner, or sidelined by trench foot or other illnesses by the third week of December.

Down to 40 men from its full strength of 120, Duvall's Troop A held a hill overlooking the Roer River gorge for four days against heavy German artillery and then was dispatched during the night of December 19 along the west bank of the river to a bridge on the northern outskirts of Untermaubach, a pivotal town held by the Germans. The men were to plant themselves inside the pocket of German forces outside the town and block attempts to reinforce the garrison at Untermaubach from the north or from across the river until ten o'clock the next morning, when an infantry force would arrive to capture the bridge and relieve the troop. They sneaked into two country houses on the road into town within sight of the bridge. The relief troops did not arrive the next morning. They were pulled away to stop the German march to the south, the Battle of the Bulge, and the overnight siege turned into a week. Troop A repulsed artillery shelling and one tank and infantry attack after another. The men had K rations for a day and then found what sustenance they could in the cellar, mainly moldy potato bread.

"They couldn't move us," was all that Duvall remarked about the siege in the margins of the Fifth Armored history, but he described it in detail in an interview for the University of Arkansas oral-history project in May 2000 and in an article in the Gazette on June 15, 1980, after he and Letty had made a driving tour of Belgium, Germany, and France to retrace his travels with the Eighty-Fifth Cavalry thirty-five years earlier. Two of his buddies from Arkansas, Ray Hallam of Huntsville and Othella Harris of Prairie County, were killed trying to escape into the woods back of the houses. A German 88-millimeter gun across the river occasionally shelled the houses. Duvall was smoking in a second-floor library with a wayfaring French soldier who had hooked up with the troop when an 88 shell came through the roof and killed the Frenchman. On December 22, the Germans came across the meadow to put an end to the siege, but A Troop's captain called in an artillery barrage that saved them at the last minute.

It must have been at the Roer River house that Duvall experienced combat at its closest. Though he never told Letty, in his *letters or afterward, about killing men, he once told his son-in-law, Fred Tisdale, that killing was not so hard when it was done at great distance and one could not be sure that his bullets caused men in the valley below to fall but that it was unforgettable when you could see their eyes and know unmistakably that the fatal bullets were yours. He recalled being holed up in the living room of the house at the first glint of dawn on the first morning when a halftrack rumbled out of the heavy fog and rain and up the driveway, accompanied by a couple of squads of German soldiers. The vehicle stopped a few feet from the house and the soldiers headed for the front door. Sgt. Duvall was manning a machinegun on a tripod inside the doorway and began firing. Most of the Germans fell within a few feet of the door or around the burning halftrack. The lone survivor, an officer, crawled to the door and handed Duvall his pistol draped with a white handkerchief.*

Leland and Letty searched for the house at the end of their 1980 vacation and drove upon it at dusk. The hole in the roof caused by the artillery shell that killed his French friend had been replaced by a skylight. He got out of the car, photographed the house, and sobbed. It was the only time Letty ever saw him cry.

His article in the Gazette *on June 15, 1980, some of which follows here, described the search for the house and recounted Troop A's ordeal. Duvall's third-person account did not identify himself as one of the soldiers, but he is the sergeant firing the machinegun and examining the old newspapers found upstairs.*

Snow muffled the sounds as the soldiers strung out single file and followed a little draw down the hill they had been holding. They moved carefully. With the countryside frozen in predawn silence, small noises would have carried well.

The wall of the gorge was steeper than the roof of an A-frame and the soldiers clung to bushes as they eased themselves down the wall of the canyon. All knowledge of the terrain had been gathered from maps and each move was a step into the half-known.

The house was no more than a grotesque shape against the background of the trees along the river, and the solders found the

Dearest Letty

back door by feeling along the wall. A room-by-room search revealed no living creature, but the sheltered beams of flashlights picked out massive pieces of antique furniture in the ground-floor living room, neat beds with clean linen in the second-floor rooms, and supporting evidence that the occupants lived well. It was as if the family had gone away for the night.

The deep basement was a bonus. Its masonry walls, rising a couple of feet above the ground, were protected with window openings. A rick of black bread, already stale with age, was stacked neatly on a shelf, and a pump in the corner tapped underground water. At the moment, these things did not seem important. Each soldier carried a breakfast K-ration and a canteen of water, which would be adequate until the infantry arrived.

Weapons available for the assignment consisted of a .30-caliber machinegun, each soldier's rifle, and an assortment of sidearms and grenades. Some of the rifles were equipped with grenade launchers. The communications sergeant had lugged in a small two-way radio.

A sergeant set the machinegun on a tripod in the doorway facing the road and soldiers took positions at the windows on the different floors.

Heavy winter fog along the river delayed daylight so that the sergeant heard, rather than saw, the column of soldiers approaching from the right and the clank of vehicle tracks to the left. The ammunitions truck and the soldiers were impersonal shapes when, as moving objects, they came together in front of the door.

By sheer chance, a tracer from the machinegun ripped through the fuel tank of the truck and a yellow, smoking explosion dissolved the fog in a suddenly formed dome. The fire illuminated the road and cast alternate light and shadows on the trees that fringed the river. While the machinegun arced along the column, some of the soldiers must have plunged into the river, which was only a few feet away. Others dived behind the little parapet, but it offered no protection from the riflemen at the windows on the upper floors. Still others sprawled on the pavement in grotesque and contorted shapes. One surrendered.

A Troop still had its 40 men and things were going well. The enemy, stunned by the surprise, would be a bit uncertain. In a couple of hours, the infantry (bless 'em) would trudge down the river and capture the bridge in a cakewalk. There was a good chance the columns that had marched into the sights of the machinegun represented most of the unit that had been assigned to guard the bridge.

As 10 o'clock approached, the soldiers in the house glanced at their watches and peered through the windows in the direction whence the infantry would come. Nothing happened.

By noon, the company commander decided to have the radio operator inquire about the delay. The information was not reassuring. No one came right out and said so, but there had been a change in the plan.

Perhaps it was the next day or the one after that before the details were provided. Somewhere to the south, the Germans had begun their offensive—it would come to be known as the Belgian Breakthrough, which set off the Battle of the Bulge—and there was a bit of confusion. The attack across the Roer no longer was operative and that part of the front was in a holding stage. The little group was to hold its position since the infantry division had been ordered to turn south.

The order to sit tight made no difference. A Troop was completely surrounded and there was little chance it could go anywhere.

There was, at the top command level, a matter of priorities. Two of the three regiments of the recently arrived 106th Division had been wiped out and the 101st Airborne was surrounded at a place called Bastogne. The commander of the 101st had replied "Nuts" (or some stronger expletive) to an offer to let it surrender. No one made a comparable offer to A Troop, and there is little chance the German high command knew the outpost existed.

About noon, the Germans made a tentative effort to unsettle the nerves of the soldiers in the houses. From somewhere across the river an 88mm gun ripped a few holes through the upper floor—perhaps it could not aim lower because of the terrain—and the first projectile killed a Frenchman who had abandoned his connection with the FFIU [French Forces of the Interior] and attached himself to A Troop when it passed through his village. The massive armor-piercing slug knocked the hole in the roof that has now been patched with a skylight. The soldiers who had positions at the upstairs windows retreated to the basement. After a few rounds, the firing ceased and the little valley was quiet again.

Later in the day, another kind of firing developed. American artillery, from guns far back in the forest or only a couple of miles

Dearest Letty

away, lobbed an occasional shell into the valley and, with the A Troop operator acting as forward observer, adjusted their range and windage. On the afternoon of the second day, the value of the aiming became apparent.

Soldiers, in some strength that was never determined, appeared at the shoulder of the hill downstream and fanned out along the far rim of the meadow. No one fired. It was the sinister approach of an overwhelming number. The tactic was readily apparent. They were working their way into position for an attack from two sides.

Then the matter became further complicated. Five tracked gun carriers, lightly armored for protection against rifles, pushed their snouts around the point of the hill. Four halted at the edge of the meadow but one rushed forward well ahead of the infantry.

The radio operator was calling for artillery, but nothing happened. The venturesome gun crew arrived at the edge of the yard and began cranking the cannon barrel around toward the basement window when a sergeant tested his grenade launcher on the track of the vehicle. He beat the gun crew to the draw and the explosion set off panic in the disabled junior tank. Perhaps it would have made no difference if they had remained behind the shield of armor. At about that time, the American artillery arrived.

By some feat of timing never understood by nonartillerymen, shells from a wide assortment of guns—the 75s a couple of miles away, the 105s farther back, and the 155s and the 240s that must have been in the next county—seemed to arrive simultaneously. The frozen turf of the meadow erupted in overlapping geysers and the sounds merged in a sort of ground-level thunder. The coverage was complete. After two successive barrages, the radio operator appealed to the artillerymen to cease firing. The threat had been eliminated, but the shells were peppering the house with shrapnel. It could have become downright dangerous if the wind had changed.

A quietness settled over the little valley and the soldiers in the basement crowded at the windows to survey the mutilation of the meadow. Those who ventured upstairs in search of a better view discovered another minor threat. The house was on fire.

Wisps of smoke floated down the stairs from the top floor and a quick investigation revealed that the deep pile rug on the library floor had been ignited, perhaps by hot shrapnel. The circle of six-inch flames, like a fire set in the middle of a meadow, was working its way toward the walls. The floor-to-ceiling shelves were jammed with books and probably would have burned slowly. The potential flash point was a neat stack of newspapers, glaucous with age, that obviously had been preserved for a purpose.

When the house succumbed to solitude, the sergeant who had helped extinguish the fire, and who remained in the room to make certain the fire did not reignite, developed a gnawing curiosity. He wondered why the owner of the library had preserved a pile of newspapers, some of which obviously dated back to World War I.

The sergeant was hampered by an inability to read German, but the thread of the story was apparent. The papers dealt with the Treaty of Versailles, reparations demanded of the Germans, and the maneuvering of the French army as part of the effort to collect. The wrecked German economy during the postwar period seemed to be offered as the result of reparations that demanded intolerable sacrifices of the losers.

(So far as could be determined, there was a concentration on the demands imposed on the Germans. No mention could be found of the fact that the Germans borrowed more than twice the amount of the reparations from one source: the United States. Most of the loans went into default, but that was not a part of the continuing story.)

The examination of the newspapers, concentrating on one continuing story, seemed to suggest that war is a sort of fungus. Occasionally, when conditions are favorable, the parasitic plant develops into a giant puffball that, when it explodes, scatters billions of spores to the four winds. The spores from World War I had settled in the centers of political power, the halls of industry, and in the attic library of the house beside the Roer. When conditions became favorable, the spores flowered again. Hitler rose to power and war came.

Christmas must have passed while the 36 soldiers (four had been killed) remained in the house, but no one noticed. The concept of "Peace on earth, good will to men" was incompatible with the environment. [Duvall's memory of the dates may have been faulty. His troop left the house in time to rejoin the unit by Christmas Eve.]

The rick of black bread became the major source of nourishment and the guard stints at the windows were part of the normal routine. Occasional reports over the radio with the weakening bat-

Dearest Letty

tery revealed that the Allies were regaining the initiative in the Bulge. In time, the circle of soldiers around the house seemed to melt and the remnant of A Troop climbed out of the gorge. They departed at night, as they had come, and no shots were fired.

A Troop's stand was memorialized by a presidential citation for heroism the next spring. Duvall copied it and sent it along to Letty in a letter. From the library of the house he kept the two books that were in English, an anthology of German short stories and The Poetical Works of Lord Byron.

[Hürtgen Forest, Germany]
Dec. 3, 1944

My Dearest Letty:

In order that your mailbox may not always be empty I have to keep up a constant string of letters. At least that is what you say, but no doubt if I were to miss days on end there would be only an infinitesimal difference in your letter total. The postman would probably not even notice the difference.

Well, the picture came. You know the Daisy Mae pose of a beautiful girl, Dogpatch Style. Gosh, it was wonderful. You really let your hair down on that one.

I didn't show it to the general, as you suggested. I don't see the general often. But I showed it to the captain and asked his advice. He said: "Son, stay in the Army, where it is safe. If you get out, you are a dead duck. That girl will be impatient if you offer resistance. So stay in the Army if you want to go on living the safe, free life of a bachelor."

But he is an old recruiting officer and a married man. So I understand his point of view.

Then I showed it to the chaplain, but he only looked wise and smiled. Then he gave me his home address, and I think he was only drumming up a marriage fee, or something. He will have to make a living when the war is over, and maybe his church doesn't pay so well.

So I stored the picture in an *Esquire* magazine among the cartoons and Varga Girls. Perhaps you don't read *Esquire*. It is supposed to be a men's magazine, but you must have seen Esky. Esky is the innocent-

looking little chap with the long yellow moustache and the eyes of an English nobleman. But he is not as innocent as he looks, for the camera always catches him while he is making a play for some girl.

Well, in this particular *Esquire* (it was the October issue), the wolf is in GI clothing, and he has enticed a pretty French maid into her wine cellar to get him a glass of wine.

But that was before I put your picture in the magazine. When I picked it up this morning, Esky was not on the cover. The French maid, looking a bit disappointed, was still holding the candle, but she was alone.

Now, here was a mystery of the greatest magnitude. Never in the history of the magazine had there been a cover without Esky. Pictures of movie stars in scant bathing suits had not caused him to budge. There have been Varga Girls in the most beautiful poses, but Esky never turned so much as the corner of his moustache. Pictures of American beauties, Eastern and Western style, could not cause him to desert his traditional place on the cover. But an American beauty, Mountain Style, was too much for him. As I turned the pages slowly and pondered the mystery, suddenly there was no mystery. For there on page 20, opposite your picture, was Esky. He had worked himself into an advertising picture of Hart Schaffner Marx clothes, a Stetson hat, Arrow tie and a pair of Nunn-Bush shoes. He looked very much the man about town and as innocent as ever. But there was no doubt about the fact that he was trying to impress you with his cosmopolitan bearing and his worldly knowledge.

But if he had only known you as I do—

Seriously, I liked the picture. Now, you will say, why the heck didn't you say so, and let it go at that?

My only answer is a guy has to write about something. He cannot simply say "I love you, the mud is terrible, we are winning the war as fast as possible, but it is not over yet" and call that a letter. Nor can he tell you where he is, except to say "somewhere in Germany." Nor what he has seen. He can say this letter was rudely interrupted three times but he cannot say what caused the delay.

This should explain why I write as I do. This and the fact that I still love you.

Love Always,
Leland

[Kleinhau, Germany]
Dec. 6, 1944

My Dearest Letty:

Writing this letter is going to be no fun. My supply of pipe tobacco is exhausted and I am forced to rely on the effeminate stimulation of cigarettes to supply the mental support and inspiration. Being entirely masculine in taste and habit, I find the cigarette insufficient. One should never attempt to write anything, not even a letter, without the proper environment and atmosphere. To do so impairs the quality of the finished product and reflects the writer as inferior or incapable, for we tend to judge people not by their best work or even their mean or average production but by their worst.

By this rule, news stories should be written at the scene of the happening. Mysteries require that the writer install his typewriter in a large deserted house with plenty of rusty hinges and swinging shutters and a candle for light. If a puff of wind extinguishes the candle occasionally, it only adds to the effectiveness of the setting. The philosopher should be installed in a room whose walls were lined with tiers of books. There must be an open fireplace, but the fire does not dance and flame with too much enthusiasm, and from the throne of an Oriental idol a lazy column of blue incense smoke crawls toward the ceiling. The key adjective to describe the atmosphere is tranquil.

But, fortunately, if one is to only compose 500 words or so of Ozark Mountain prose (such as this), no special props are needed. All that is required is that he be in love with the one who is to read it.

That and a pipe full of Kentucky Burley. Unfortunately, I do not have the tobacco. Therefore, I find that I am repeating myself. The letter is a failure. But this is where you came in.

Love Always,
Leland

[Kleinhau, Germany]
Dec. 7, 1944

My Dearest Letty:

This is some sort of an anniversary. At least you might call it that, for the war began three years ago today. Remember?

Now, don't come back with the story that in your youthful innocence you paid no attention to it in those days. You may be young, but not that young.

I think I remember it too well. All the details are still vivid, but we will save that for one of the subjects to discuss when there is plenty of time.

Dearest Letty

Things are about as usual here. It is still muddy, but we are beginning to learn how to beat it. They issued us all Mae Wests (that is the Navy term for life preservers) so now when we step into a mud hole that is too deep we merely float around until someone pulls us out. I hear they are planning to install a sea-air rescue squad and attach it to each unit. That way, almost none of us will drown.

Say, I had three letters from you yesterday, and two of them were written the same day. Now you are really getting on the ball. That is the way you should conduct yourself, young lady.

When you behave like that, I can know you have less time to get into mischief. The way I figure it, if you work eight hours a day and write me two letters, you have to be good at least part of the time.

Then, too, it is a pretty good hint that you still think of me occasionally. And I am still crazy about you.

Love Always,
Leland

[Eupen, Belgium]
Dec. 24, 1944

My Dearest Letty:

Now don't tell me. I know you have not had a letter from me in a few days, but that is one of those situations that could not be avoided. I thought of you all the time (when I had time to think) but could not write. I do not have too much time now, hence this note. Will try to get off a longer letter tomorrow.

Incidentally, tomorrow is Christmas and I have just been down to the kitchen truck. The cooks are roasting the turkey tonight, which we will have for dinner tomorrow. Already they are beginning to look delicious. I insist that we have the best kitchen crew in the Army.

Love Always,
Leland

[Verviers, Belgium]
Dec. 27, 1944

My Dearest Letty:

I guess you are expecting a long airmail letter by this time, but I am afraid you will have to wait a couple of days and be content with this. But I am also sending you a telegram today, so that is not so bad.

Christmas passed quietly, and I worked all day. If we had not had such a swell turkey dinner and a small platoon party in the evening, I would not have even guessed it was Christmas. Hope you had a nice time.

Your letters have been arriving regularly and giving the old morale a boost in the right places. Must sign off, but I still love you.

Love Always,
Leland

[Verviers, Belgium]
Dec. 29, 1944

My Dearest Letty:

I am still in the V-mail business, but so long as I am in any kind of business I go on writing when I find time, and I shall go on loving you as usual.

The guys in the tent are busy telling of their girls back home. Boy, are they giving one another a line! To hear them talk, they were all Casanovas in the good old days. But I only sit and listen. They would not believe me anyway if I told them how nice and wonderful you are.

I am sending you another package today. Don't know when you will get it. I may be on the road quite a while.

Love Always,
Leland

[Verviers, Belgium]
Dec. 30, 1944

My Dearest Letty:

Since I am still out of airmail stamps you will have to be content with another V-mail tonight. However, the mailman has promised me some stamps tomorrow, and I shall try to get off a decent letter when I get them. About the only purpose these letters serve is to let you know I am still in love with you.

By the way, when the package I just mailed finally gets to you, don't let the Purple Heart medal stimulate your imagination. You see, I was only scratched but all medals count for points toward a discharge in the demobilization plan, and I am taking all the points I can get. I could have gotten the medal long ago but it had no value then, so I passed it up. So save the medal for me. It may mean that I come home sooner after the war is over. Hope you enjoy the volume of Byron that I am sending.

Love Always,
Leland

[Verviers, Belgium]
Jan. 1, 1945

My Dearest Letty:

I am writing a New Year date into my letter, but please don't anticipate a philosophical dissertation on the passing of time—what the New Year will bring and all that sort of thing. I do not have time or space for that.

About all I can say here is that I am still in love with you and that your letters are still coming in regularly.

That and the fact that I am happy at the moment. I have just been down to the kitchen truck and they are cooking turkey for dinner. The smell of the food stimulated my appetite, but it is still two hours until chow time. Maybe I can sweat it out.

Love Always,
Leland

[Verviers, Belgium]
Jan. 2, 1945

My Dearest Letty:

Since I have been giving you only V-mail letters and a telegram for the last few days I guess it is time I gave you a little longer letter. Of course, you never complain about short letters, which is considerate. You seem to know that there are times when any kind of a letter is out of the question and other times when a note has to serve the purpose. Some people can't seem to realize that, because they are always wondering why I don't write. When the war is over and I am loafing around waiting for a discharge, I will snow them under with letters and work them over if they don't answer, but now they will have to wait.

The Christmas package you sent has not arrived yet nor has the package from Mother. Guess the mail clerks were snowed under, but they will get it to me sometime.

I sent a leather case full of trinkets and souvenirs several weeks ago, but I guess they are still on the road. Also sent a pair of shoes and quite recently another package with my Purple Heart medal in it.

These you are to keep for me, but don't let your imagination go to work on the reason for my being awarded the medal. I only got a scratch out of the deal and the only reason I accepted the medal is because it will count points toward a discharge when the war is over. You see, the guy with the most points will get out first, so I am accepting all the points I can get. I was dumb enough to pass up the medal last summer, but at that time it had no point value. Now I wish I had taken it, but it is too late.

Well, the boys are fixing up a snack. They always do, every night. Last night, we had cold turkey on toast, and tonight we are having bacon sandwiches. You would be surprised how well some of the boys fix up their chow.

This is my last sheet of paper, so I had better say "I'm crazy about you" and run along. Besides, if I don't call an end to this all the bacon will be gone. A guy has to get there early or be left out.

Love Always,
Leland

TELEGRAM
Jan. 6, 1945

Miss Letty Jones:
All well and safe. Best wishes for new year. All my love.

Leland B. Duvall.

[Verviers, Belgium]
Jan. 7, 1945

My Dearest Letty:
When I get three letters in our mail call from you, as I did today, it is time for me to do something about it. Two of them were V-mails of Dec. 22 and 23. The other was an airmail written about Thanksgiving. So you see there is no way to predict the behavior of the mail.

But it is nice stuff to get, even if it is tardy, so please don't be discouraged about writing. A few of the letters will get through on time and the others will find their way eventually.

Wish I could tell you what I did today, but I will only stir up your curiosity by saying it is one of the things I shall save until I see you. Remind me then and you will get the whole story. There are such a lot of things for us to talk about that we may not find time for this one for many years.

Say, I saw an excellent movie yesterday. It was "Old Acquaintance" with Bette Davis. Maybe it is an old picture. I am a bit rusty in the entertainment field and cannot say what is old and what is new. But I had not seen it before, and it was definitely good.

Miss Davis is a wholesome character for a change: the kind of person I would like to be. Maybe that is why I enjoyed the show so much. That is, she has the necessary strength of character to absorb a lot of undeserved punishment, and she does not allow it to alter her natural sweetness. All the time you know she has the ability to be an excellent cynic with a natural knack for acid retorts, but she seems to be a person who has developed a habit of deriving a nostalgic pleasure in wanting things she knows she can never have.

But I started out to write a letter and not a movie review. Hope you don't mind the interruption, but see the picture if you have a chance.

Have just taken time out to eat a sandwich. We had steaks for supper, and some were left over. The boys brought up a few of the steaks, and we heated them and toasted some bread. It was pretty delicious. There is always chow around and the kitchen serves us two meals a day. Guess you will find that I have funny eating habits when you see me again. But I will still like the chicken your mother cooks.

Must sign off now, as I have other things to do. But I am still in love with you.

Love Always,
Leland

[Verviers, Belgium]
Jan. 10, 1945

My Dearest Letty:

I may have time to write this before I have to go to work, but our hours are pretty uncertain. Never know what time we will have to start or when we will quit. The heck of it is there is no extra pay for overtime.

Have not heard from you in a few days. In fact, all the mail I have had came from guys over here. So I guess the mail boat did not come in. It will be around in a few days.

The mail situation over here is rather funny. It comes in bunches. Recently, there was a story in *Stars and Stripes* to the effect that one per cent of the packages had been lost due to enemy action. Every guy I have met since then is sure he had a least one package in the bunch.

Well, the sun came out this morning for a change. It is the first clear day we have had in quite some time. It has snowed every day for about a week. The wind blew while it was falling and the stuff drifted like a West Texas blizzard. I should know. I have been stuck in the drifts a couple of times.

As I presumed, I did not get to finish, so I am doing it this afternoon.

Just had a letter from Ardis. It was the first time I had heard from him in quite some time. He is somewhere down on the Seventh Army front, but I don't know just where he is. Have not heard from Aaron in quite some time, but he is around somewhere.

Letty, I keep trying to remember how far up the street the 900 block is. I never paid any attention to the house numbers in Russellville. So I can't picture just where you live. But you should be fairly close to Tech. Hope you don't get involved with the faculty and alter the course of higher education.

By the way, did I tell you that I have just ordered a course from the University of Texas? I will have to find time to do the work. Must sign off.

Love Always,
Leland

[Verviers, Belgium]
Jan. 11, 1945

My Dearest Letty:

I am writing this before breakfast, so please don't expect too much from this effort. You know how the inspiration comes only after a good cup of coffee.

You should see our part of the country this morning. Do we have the snow! It is six inches or so deep, and it is still falling. The wind has been blowing and the stuff is drifted in great piles.

Another boy and I had to go to headquarters last night, and it was dark when we came back. The first time we ran into the ditch we managed to get out without help, but the second time it was not so easy. We had to have enough men to lift the jeep and set it on the road. But it was a cold job. Must say I love you and run along to chow.

Love Always,
Leland

[Verviers, Belgium]
Jan. 12, 1945

My Dearest Letty:

It is only about twenty minutes until I have to go on guard, but I can spend that time writing. There is no need to go to bed until after guard and, besides, I owe you at least half a dozen letters. But you must settle for just one until I find time for the others.

Guess you are wondering what the enclosed scrap of paper is all about. Well, it is a sort of souvenir, of the kind an autograph hunter collects. It was given to me by the major, and there's a story goes with it, as Damon Runyon would say.

Recently we had a little scrap, which drew some favorable comment from the high-ranking officers. When it was over and we came back to rest a bit the captain suggested that I write the story, to be submitted to the Public Relations Office. This scrap of paper is a bit of interoffice communication from the commanding general via the chief of staff to our squadron commander and indicates that the story has been submitted to the *Stars and Stripes* to be published there. If they use it, I shall try to see that you get a copy. But I am not sure it will get by the censor, therefore I cannot send it in yet.

Well, I have finished my guard and even though it is almost midnight I will finish this, too. Now, lady, there is a sure sign that I am still in love. Otherwise I would go to bed immediately. It is even more convincing if you remember that I worked at squadron headquarters until after two o'clock last night and did not sleep any today. Now, I guess you will believe me.

My Christmas packages are still coming in. I had one from home yesterday. The other guy and I were hungry as bears when we came in last night. The package was here so we opened it immediately. When we had finished, most of the edible stuff was gone, but the package had served the purpose well. There have been few times when I would have appreciated it more.

Your package has not arrived, but it will in due time. Must get some sleep.

Love Always,
Leland

[Scrap of paper] CG—
This written by Sgt. Duval who "was there"—has been given to PRO for S&S publication.
Jim [indecipherable]

[Verviers, Belgium]
Jan. 14, 1945

My Dearest Letty:

I am writing you again tonight, but I have a reason besides the fact that I am still thinking of you. Your package arrived today and I liked it. In fact, my old shaving kit was getting pretty battered and I was beginning to need one. All the other stuff fit in nicely, too. All in all, you have a pretty fair idea of what a soldier needs.

Saw a U.S.O. show today. It was a pretty fair show, and the first I have seen in some time. One girl was a fair singer and could imitate anyone from Mae West to the Ink Spots. All the guys enjoyed her act. Must sign off.

Love Always,
Leland

[Verviers, Belgium]
Jan. 16, 1945

My Dearest Letty:

I have been writing V-mails for a few days now, so I may get a complaint about the shortness of my letters. But you have given me no argument so far that I could not win, and I think I can go on telling you what you should do.

Just had a letter from you today in which you said the box of souvenirs finally arrived. I don't remember all the things that were in the box, but I do recall the blue and white necklace. It came from Holland. A little girl named Ellie something (her last name is unpronounceable) gave it to me. I have her picture at home, which I shall show you sometime. She and her brother came around quite often while we were up there. They are the children of the town's most prominent doctor and were quite interesting. The boy was about 14 or 15 years old and Ellie was about 10.

The other stuff was from Luxembourg, France, Belgium, Germany and England. Of course, there was a coin from Hong Kong, but I did not pick it up there. An old salt—maybe I should say an old soak—gave it to me in a British pub. Said it would bring me good luck. Maybe you will need it more than I do, so I sent it to you.

Have sent a couple of packages since then, but I guess they will not get there for several weeks.

It is still plenty cold here, and it snows a little every few days. The stuff keeps getting deeper instead of melting. The way it looks now we will have to put up with it until spring. If you think it cold there you are mistaken. When I woke up this morning my top blanket was frozen stiff and that in a tent where a fire had been going most of the night. There was about half an inch of frost all over the inside of the tent.

No, a guy doesn't get cold. We have excellent sleeping bags, plus blankets, so we are all set. I have a sleeping bag at home that I bought, but there was no way to bring it over. I often wished I had it until they issued this one. Guess I will have to use it for fishing trips when the war is over. Maybe you can get along with a couple of blankets if you like to fish. Must sign off for now, will write again when I can.

Love Always,
Leland

[Verviers, Belgium]
Jan. 18, 1945

My Dearest Letty:

Am not in the mood for a long letter nor do I have time for it, so I am depending on this. Hope you don't mind.

No, we are not too busy. It is just that the boys are having quite a session just now and it is something of a job to think of something decent to write. If an obscene word happens to get into this, please don't be surprised. Such a thing has been known to happen.

Have not had a letter from you in a few days, but our mail is not too regular. They had a couple of bags of mail tonight, but it was mostly old Christmas packages. I only got an old C.D. out of the deal but there were only a small bunch of letters.

Dearest Letty

One of these days I shall write you a letter that will take two stamps to carry, but not tonight.

Love Always,
Leland

My Dearest Letty:

Guess I will have to write this before I have to move back out of my comfortable shack. I am on duty now, but it is not too tough and I can find time to write some.

Had a nice airmail letter from you a couple of days ago, and it was quite new, too. Dated the last of December. It seemed that the souvenirs did create quite a sensation at that. Guess the gals were curious about where the stuff came from.

Anyway, I enjoyed the letter, and I am glad you liked the trinkets.

We had quite a blizzard last night. The wind brought in the snow at about 60 miles per hour and draws it through even the smallest cracks.

Must say I love you and sign off.

Love Always,
Leland

[Verviers, Belgium]
Jan. 23, 1945

My Dearest Letty:

Having three letters from you this afternoon put me on the spot. I simply had to write you a note even if I have to make it a short one.

Was especially glad to get the picture, which was in one of the letters. You insisted that it did not look like you. Must say it looks more sophisticated than you were when I last saw you. At that measure it did not look like you. From it one would judge that you are the quietest, most serious and conventional person alive.

I remember that you are not like that. You are mischievous, provocative and tantalizing, so the picture can't deceive me. The picture I like most is the one from Kansas City, when you insisted you were trying to amuse a baby. My second choice is the one that got "Esky." Those pictures are really you.

Love Always,
Leland

[Verviers, Belgium]
Jan. 26, 1945

Dearest Letty:

My periodic report is past due, and I am planning a longer one than you have been receiving. In this way I hope to appease you a little, even if the longer letter says nothing that could not be stated on a V-mail form.

On that I could say, as I always do, that "I love you," "It is very cold," "We have plenty of snow" and "I am still in good shape."

In order to properly use the additional paper, I must elaborate on the above statements. There are no additional subjects.

I

On the first subhead there seems little to add. I have told you long ago that I am in love with you and nothing could change that. In fact, I was sure of it long before I could convince you that I was not joking. Remember when I first mentioned it to you and you insisted that on that subject you refused to *tête-à-tête*.

That day, we were on the bluff at the edge of the mountain. It was cold and a wind was blowing your hair wildly around your face. You were beautiful, but that was not the only thing that made me want to talk of being in love with you. For the most part, it was because of YOU. It was because you were so disturbingly mischievous, so lively and so full of fun that a guy was never safe when you were around. So what was a guy to do? It was so tantalizing to be around you, yet there was nothing to do but go back. Well, I solved it neatly by falling in love, but it did not turn out so well. Here I am in Europe, and you are a career woman. But it will not always be this way, I hope.

II

As for the cold weather, there is little change in that except that it is even colder than it has been. Last night was perhaps the champion, and it must have been zero or below.

III

The snow keeps coming. No sooner does the weather clear than everyone says, "Well, we won't have any snow for a few days." But that night it always snows again. But I reserve my opinion and hope that we will have an early spring.

III

As for myself, I am in good condition, as usual. Guess I must have gained back some of my lost weight, and I must be back to around 170 or so. However, I am not large enough to fill out the last pair of pants Uncle Sam gave me. The quartermaster only had a size 36, so I took them. Size means nothing for we aren't going anywhere where it will be noticed.

Love Always,
Leland

[Verviers, Belgium]
Jan. 31, 1945

My Dearest Letty:

In spite of the fact that one of the boys just came in with a load of newspapers (the first we have had in about four days) I am still writing this letter instead of reading them. You see, we can always take the papers along and read them later, but writing takes a bit of time.

Then, of course, it is much more important that I keep checking up on you than it is for me to check up on the war situation. You see, you fit snugly into my postwar plans, and the present situation is well under control.

Say, I wonder if you have ever received the telegrams I have been sending? I thought they would be faster than letters when I found it impossible to write for several days.

Love Always,
Leland

[Verviers, Belgium]
Feb. 5, 1945

My Dearest Letty:

It is pretty difficult for me to write tonight for a personal reason, which you will understand. I had a letter from Mom recently that leaves me in no condition to think of anything pleasant.

You, of course, know the contents of the letter, but you cannot know how utterly helpless it makes me feel. He was my youngest brother, you know, and we always understood each other to a degree that most brothers never reach. I was always able to help him get out of the little jams in which all boys become involved, and if he had any problems he came to me, even when he knew Dad would help him as readily as I.

Now I have to wait for someone to tell me when I can go in and see if he still needs me.

Please forgive me for writing like this but I need to tell someone.

Love Always,
Leland

[Verviers, Belgium]
Feb. 6, 1945

My Dearest Letty:

As usual, I am a bit rushed when it comes to writing to you. But I hope you don't mind my short letters, and I am sure you remember when I had plenty of time and wrote you long and boring letters almost every day.

I thought I was pretty busy when I only had a full day of schedule, but there was always time in the dayroom after supper to write a few letters or read a book if a guy did not have a pass and went into town. Now there is no town to visit, but there is also no dayroom and a guy has to write anywhere he has a chance.

Still have heard nothing more about Aaron, but I have reason to think he may be a prisoner.

Love Always,
Leland

[Verviers, Belgium]
Feb. 10, 1945

My Dearest Letty:

Well, I had three letters from you today, which was pretty good in any language. One said the wooden shoes had finally arrived, but I think you were only kidding when you said they were too large for you. I thought they would be about your size.

Seriously, people really wear shoes like the ones you have. They claim they are not as uncomfortable as they look. The people who wear them shuffle around in a way that looks uncomfortable to me, but they do serve an excellent purpose. The countries that use them have muddy seasons, and when they go out into the mud they use the wooden shoes. But they are also clean people, and they leave the wooden shoes outside when they come into the house. It saves a lot of mopping and also keeps their feet dry.

Will write a longer letter and tell you how much I love you when I have time.

Love Always,
Leland

[Verviers, Belgium]
Feb. 11, 1945

My Dearest Letty:

We are about even on the letters now, and I am writing as often as you do. That is, I am writing almost every day now.

I did not expect to scare you with my cablegram. It was just that I had not had a chance to write in a few days and thought you might be curious about what had happened to me. That is one of the things we worry about here. When we know that the situation here is under control and yet have no way of letting people know it, we know they worry needlessly. It is quite a pity that we do not have direct telephone communication with the states.

I am glad to learn that you have the commendable habit of enjoying a Dagwood lunch about bedtime. That will mean that you can be persuaded to fix me sandwiches, too. That will be nice after I have grown into the habit of fixing my own.

Remember the chow we had at the Hut one night? All the other places were closed, I believe. Until then I did not know you were not in the habit of sleeping. Boy, did you consume the coffee. I'll bet Chase and Sanborn are glad when you go on a party. Their sales are sure to go up.

I'll bet you girls sent up the sales of Johnnie Walker Scotch on your last party, too. At least I would hate to supply the Scotch for a party of career girls, if the prices are as high there as they are here. Of course, there is no whiskey to be had at any price. Some of the boys occasionally find a bottle of watered cognac. This costs ten to twelve dollars a bottle and is mostly water. No one manages to get even a buzz out of it, but they drink it anyway.

The trouble is there is more money in this country than there are goods to buy. This is true not only of drinks but of everything. Anytime a man buys anything here he is a sucker. The Army issues everything that is really necessary, so the logical thing to do is to save the salary. Most of the boys do this, and I suppose most of the boys in this troop are saving a greater percentage of their money than they ever did before.

Must remind you that I still love you and run along, as it is time to go on guard.

Love Always,
Leland

[He attached this article from Stars and Stripes. It perhaps is the one that he wrote and mentioned in an earlier letter.]

5th Armd. Takes 400 PWs, Battles Snow, Terrain

WITH FIFTH ARMD DIV.—When tanks and infantry of Combat Command A of the Fifth Armd. Div. fought through extreme cold, shoulder-high snowdrifts and prepared defenses to take a German town, it was an old story to tankers and men of the Victory Div.

Fighting weather and terrain as much as they fought the enemy, 46th Armd Inf. Bn. Troops slogged more than four kilometers through almost impassable terrain to attack the town successfully.

Tanks of the 34th Tank Bn. spearheaded the thrust and assaulted the town with tank guns while the infantry quickly passed through and mopped up. More than 400 German prisoners were taken in the attacks.

Mines Laid Thickly

German minefields were laid in thick belts on the approaches to the town, and sappers of the 22nd Armd Engr. Bn. had to gap several minefields before the command could pass through. The combat commander, Brig. Gen. Eugene A. Regnier of San Antonio, Texas, personally complimented the Corps commander for the quick success of the mission.

The Fifth Armd. Div., commanded by Major Gen. Lunsford E. Olivier of Vicksburg, Miss., was the first Allied unit to cross the German border in September. To reach Germany, the division had battled its way 800 miles through France, Belgium and Luxembourg. In the two weeks after it jumped off in Normandy August 2, the Fifth Armd. Div. drove 300 miles behind enemy lines to reach Argentan and close the southern jaw of the Falaise trap, then thrust on to the Seine River.

March Through Paris

The division marched through the newly liberated Paris, and on the outskirts began its fighting drive that carried it to the Belgian border in two days. Turning to the east, the division crossed the Meuse River, captured Sedan and passed through a corner of Belgium to liberate the Grand Duchy of Luxembourg.

The first patrol of Fifth Armd. Div. troops crossed the German border near Wallendorf on September 11 to engage enemy troops holding the Siegfried Line defenses. Patrolling continued until September 14, when the division's Combat Command "R," commanded by Col. Glen H. Anderson of Bedford, Iowa, crossed the Our River and completely cut through the Siegfried Line in 28 hours. Combat command "B" under the command of Col. John T. Cole of Halesite, N. Y., next pushed into the enemy's defense line, and the two armored forces held their positions in the Siegfried Line under increasingly heavy artillery fire and German attacks as the enemy built up overwhelming forces in the sector.

Mission Accomplished

The division units, their diversionary mission accomplished, were ordered withdrawn, Combat Command B being the last to leave on

September 21. During the week that the division's troops occupied the Siegfried Line positions they drew to their sector and contained strong German forces that greatly outnumbered them—forces powerful and mobile enough that they might otherwise have resisted the main assault by other First Army divisions at Aachen, or the Allied Airborne Army landing in Holland. During the drive, Combat Command A was responsible for the protection and defense of the entire Grand Duchy of Luxembourg.

Herleen, Netherlands
Feb. 14, 1945

My Dearest Letty:

I shall have to hurry if I finish this, for we have something to do tonight, and it is almost time to start. But I have not written in a few days and it is certainly time for me to remind you that I am still in love with you. From one of your recent letters I gathered that you were not sure of it. There was that gleam in your eyes when you wrote it. You know, the way you look just before you start out to ensnare a new victim.

You had the same gleam when you trapped me, but the funny part of it is I enjoy being trapped, and the next guy might, too. So I can't afford to take a chance.

Gosh, is it raining tonight, and will our job be a dark one!

Love Always,
Leland

[Herleen, Netherlands]
Feb. 16, 1945

My Dearest Letty:

The boys are retelling stories of their Army and civilian experience, and the talk is loud, if dull. If I can break through all the noise I may be able to construct a letter. If not, you will have to wait until tomorrow to learn that I am still in love with you and that I am still around.

I am in Holland at the moment. It is a pretty nice country, but from what I have gathered it has felt the effect of the war pretty stiffly. But that is true of every country through which the war has passed or is passing, and it leaves many pitiable individual cases as well as the tragedy of all the country.

There is no way of knowing which of the people in this country are Nazi, but they all act friendly. Of course, they have to act that way, and you cannot trust any of them farther than you could throw a Sherman tank by its gun muzzle. But there is no damage done in feeling pity for those who act friendly.

What I am trying to do is introduce an old chap who is an example of the tragedy of war. Judging from appearances, he was never an example of the prosperous Dutch farmer, but I am sure the war has played a part in bringing him to his present position.

At present we are billeted in a barn, which is a part of a house-barn combination such as they build here. A middle-aged man operates or manages the farm, but Pop does the greater part of the work.

Pop, as the boys call him, is 67 years old and is a dried-up little man with a bristling moustache. His gray hair was curling over the greasy collar of a ragged coat when we moved in, but one of the boys gave him a haircut. Two days later, he managed to get 20 cents, Dutch money, and was puzzled because the barber would not accept it as payment for the trim. One of his feet has been frozen, and a nasty gash runs across the arch of his foot. Because of this he wears a wooden shoe over the wrapped foot, and a leather shoe on the other. With this odd combination he hobbles about, cleaning stables, chopping wood or doing any of the odd jobs that come up.

The farm manager seems to eat regularly, even if his menu is limited for variety, but during our first two days here the boys noticed that Pop only ate twice a day. On these occasions his meals consisted only of a few scraps tossed to him in the same manner that I would feed my foxhound.

The third morning Joey, the mess sergeant, served hotcakes. When the troop had finished eating, one of the boys brought up seven big cakes in his mess kit. Pop had finished his regular breakfast, but he ate all seven of them and practically licked the butter and syrup from the plate. He mumbled the Dutch equivalent of "thanks" but the grateful and satisfied look on his face was more eloquent than Woolcott. He is not an expressive talker, even if one could understand him.

Since then the boys have fed him regularly, but his appetite has not diminished. He seems to have built up a hunger over a period of years that a few meals cannot satisfy.

Letty, I have used a whole letter in trying to tell you of an old man whose name I do not even know. If I wrote thirty or so pages about him, then a similar number about the children who hang around the kitchen truck at mealtime and watch us eat, I might be able to convey some of the meaning of war. If I could describe the eager way they look at a pan of pork chops and tell how they crowd around when the troop has finished eating to carry off the scraps and leftover food, I could convey the point I am trying to make.

The tragedy of war does not confine itself to the shooting and the waiting. It is not content to embrace those who shoot and those who wait to see if someone comes back. It touches everyone: the old, who cannot live long enough to appreciate peace, and those who are too young to have a personal knowledge of war.

But this is growing a bit involved and perhaps boring.

You hinted recently that you might cut down the number of letters you wrote, and just when I was wishing you would increase them. Letters (especially yours) are about the only wholesome contact I have with the kind of living I hope to do when this is all over. Hating is not my habit, but it is a way I have learned. If I cannot also love, there is nothing worth the effort of living in this place. Your letters and the others serve as a counterweight, and help to balance my behavior. Without them I would completely lose contact with normal living.

I hope this tells you how essential your letters really are without giving the impression that I am a victim of battle fatigue.

Love Always,
Leland

[Herleen, Netherlands]
Feb. 18, 1945

My Dearest Letty:
I had half a page of a letter already written and was well on the way to a long epistle when the dog that belongs to our host came in. But he

is too darned friendly, and the first thing I knew he had planted a muddy foot in the middle of the page. So I had to throw the whole thing away.

Now I like a dog as well as anyone and have owned several, but I insist that they follow certain rules of behavior. The first rule says they are not to make any attempt to send their footprint to the girl I happen to be in love with. To do so intrudes on purely personal affairs of mine and will not be tolerated.

There are other rules, of course, but they are not important now. I will show you a well-behaved dog when I come home and acquire a pooch. He will not annoy you by barking at night nor will he raise any objection when a visitor comes into the yard. My dogs must be friendly with everyone.

Letty, of course you are curious to know where I am and what I am doing. It would make my writing job easier if I could discuss those things, and the letters might be more interesting. But such subjects are dangerous in more ways than you could imagine—not to me, especially, but to thousands of guys. Lack of security was probably responsible, in part, for the fact that Aaron and a lot of other guys are listed as missing.

Perhaps I am too security conscious, but I don't think so.

I put out quite a laundry today. Don't guess it is clean, but at least I got some of the dirt out. It is not easy to wash clothes when there is no washing machine and not even a rub-board. If you know any tricks of the trade, please tip me off. Also, tell me how to get the clothes dry when it rains every day and all the guys want to use the space around the stove at the same time. I managed to work in four pairs of socks, but the rest of the stuff is hanging out in the rain.

Am trying to manage a quail hunt. Modlin and I have found the quail, but there is one little item that is holding up the sport. I have no shells for my shotgun or, to be exact, I have one shell. If we can find no more shells, we are going anyway. We can dry run for half a day, then shoot the shell just before we come in. But I have the location of a guy who has shells for sale and we may be able to get a few.

Letty, you have not said anything about whether the package containing the medal and book ever got to you. Or maybe you did and the letter has just failed to get to me. It is not important, but there is a story that goes with the book, and I hope it reaches you. If it is on hand, the story will be more effective when I tell it to you sometime.

Love Always,
Leland

My Dearest Letty:

Things are so dull around here that I am becoming bored with the whole war. Wish they would decide to call the whole thing off.

Have even resorted to quail hunting, but have yet to get a bird. We were out all afternoon and chased partridges all over the country, but they were too smart for Jim Modlin and me. However, we have managed to build our supply of shells from one to five.

Letty, you may think I'm crazy because I seldom answer your questions. The letters I write are not answers but simply disjointed ramblings about any subject that happens to come to my mind. But, you see, I destroy all the letters as soon as I read them. This is for security reasons. It is the smart thing to do, even if it sounds cold and unsentimental. So I often forget what questions are asked.

For example, you asked if I knew Floyd McGee. Yes, Floyd (or Bill) was a good friend of mine and I was certainly sorry to learn of his death. His father was one of my teachers when I was in grade school, and I have known Bill since then. The last time I saw him he was a wholesale candy dealer for Curtiss Candy Co. and seemed to have a well-established business.

This would be an interesting country if a guy had an opportunity to study it and could speak the language. One of the things that attract my attention most is the ancient buildings. Within sight of our present billet are two castles that must have been built around the fifteenth or even the fourteenth century. There is no date on them, but their age is indicated by the fact that they have moats around them.

It is an odd contrast. When such places were built the moat or ditch was dug for defensive purposes. With the drawbridge pulled, the moat provided an effective barrier. A guy in a suit of armor found that it was no cinch to swim a thirty-foot ditch while a lot of guys were tossing rocks or shooting arrows at him.

Then came gunpowder.

Now an army unit can set up headquarters in one of the places and find itself crowded for room. Half a dozen shells from a light field gun could take the place apart, and we are reminded that the place once housed the whole army and was capable of resisting a siege of weeks. The art of war has made great progress.

But we do not have time or the opportunity to inquire about individual places. I am afraid I shall leave here in total ignorance of an interesting bit of history. That will make little difference. You will probably cause me to forget all this anyway, so I would profit little by it. After all, I expect to spend most of my time when the war is over behaving like a normal American. That and loving you. This country will play a small part in either occupation.

Love Always,
Leland

SIX

To the Elbe River

With the first stirrings of spring in Western Europe in 1945, the worst of the war was over, except for the German soldier. The catastrophic ending of the Battle of the Bulge sapped the last remaining ability and will of German soldiers to wage offensive war. For them, the only remaining questions were how much they could slow the Allied advance to Berlin and the collapse of the Third Reich, and at what cost.

The Fifth Armored Division moved out from its moorings in the Netherlands the last week of February and returned to the Roer River, the scene of so much savage fighting since October. This time it had to dislodge the Germans from their fortifications and drive to the Rhine River and ultimately to the Elbe River, forty-five miles west of the capital. Better weather, drier ground, and the enfeebled German air force restored the armored division's great strengths: speed and firepower. The Germans fought ferociously in defense of the homeland at first, and the Allied advance the last week of February and the first week of March had to be measured in yards, but when the Rhineland defenses collapsed, it was a race to the Rhine and then to the Elbe. It was reminiscent of the sprint across Normandy and Brittany in August, except this time surrender flags met them everywhere. Duvall would recall that Germans seemed to look for opportunities to surrender. While his unit was patrolling a section of the Elbe in April, one of his men found himself in a stable, with a houseful of Germans in a distillery stable next door. Duvall jumped in a scout car with a 37-millimeter gun and raced *down the road to the stable. He pointed the gun at the door and all the Germans came out with their hands up. One of them had a sporting Mauser, which the relieved GI took and gave to Duvall for saving him.*

The troops of the Eighty-Fifth Cavalry returned to their recon-naissance roles, roaming far ahead of the armor, infantry, and artillery and securing bridgeheads. Duvall's platoon was the first to move out from Holland on February 24. It was ordered, along with a tank battalion and an infantry battalion, to cross the Roer, traverse the cabbage fields of the Rhineland, and capture five towns, which they did in less than seven hours on February 26. His A Troop reached the Rhine on March 31, secured the bridge, and then streaked northeast toward the Elbe. It captured two bridges on the Weser-Elbe Canal, interrupted the German dem-olition of a bridge over the Oker River by cutting the wires for the last charges, and then sped to the Elbe. On April 11, Duvall's com-bat command made a fighting run of sixty-three miles in thirteen and a half hours. They reached the Elbe the third week of April and cleared out the remaining pockets of Germans. Duvall's com-pany raided a large oil dump at the river and captured 170 soldiers and their officers.

The Elbe was as far as the Americans were to go. The mop-ping up east of the river and the first occupation of Berlin were to be left to the Russians.

Duvall's letters to Letty Jones recount none of the action in which he was involved but betray the exuberance that he and the other GIs felt about the approaching end of the war. In repose behind the final fighting, he found typewriters—he always typed with his forefingers—and the letters flowed in torrents.

[Munchen-Gladbach, Germany]
March 8, 1945

My Dearest Letty:

For days I have not had a chance to write, and this is not exactly a golden opportunity. The guys have picked up an accordion, guitar and a lot of other noisemakers and are having a jam session. Also, the artillery is rattling the windows so that they seem ready to fall out. So, you see,

if you want a letter you will have to wait a couple of days until things quiet down some.

But some of our mail caught up with us today, and among the letters was your picture. Now, that picture was the kind I wanted. Exactly. It is you, as I think of you, and as I dream of you. That is the vision that dances out to me in the darkness through the mud and snow and across the thousands of miles of water. It is the same gay, laughing creature that is forever tantalizing me when the game gets rough and it becomes difficult to remember that all the world is not hatred. It is the image that shows me a smile when I forget how to smile myself. It is the woman I love.

Always,
Leland

[Munchen-Gladbach, Germany]
March 9, 1945

My Dearest Letty:

I am sitting at a real honest-to-goodness desk to write this. Can you imagine that? It is a good one, too. Complete with telephone desk lamp, pen rack and ashtray. I am smoking a good cigar and feeling like a big captain of industry.

Of course, there are a few things lacking. The lamp won't work (there is no electricity), and I am writing by candle. The phone wires are cut, and they did not lead to any place I am interested in anyway. There is no secretary and no typewriter. I have a typewriter, but it is broken and one of the boys is trying to repair it.

Now this could easily be back home. I could dictate my letter more easily than I could write it. Then I could pick up the phone and dial your number, but only to say: "Darling, I'll be home early tonight. Could you have a steak for dinner?" Naturally.

Hope you understand that I am only dreaming, which is pardonable at the present. But, I still love you.

Love Always,
Leland

[Munchen-Gladbach, Germany]
March 10, 1945

My Dearest Letty:

If I can break in on the conversation that is going full blast, I will let you know that I am still in love with you as much as ever. In fact, I am quite sure that I love you more now than I ever did. It must be the result of the last picture you sent.

I always see you just as you were in the picture, but I sometimes asked myself if you were really so wonderful as I remembered you. The picture confirms my dream. I knew all the time you were, but I wanted to be showed again, just as it is nice to be told that you are still in love with me, even when I am sure you are. The picture was wonderful.

Have not heard from Aaron yet, but Ruth writes that she has had letters from the wives of several men who were in his company. These boys are now prisoners and I have hopes that he is a prisoner. In that case we may get him out before too long.

Love Always,
Leland

[Rhineland, Germany]
March 12, 1945

My Dearest Letty:

It might be a better idea if I only attempted a V-mail for I may not have time to finish this today. But I have written so many of them that I tire of seeing the little red-bordered sheet. It cramps a guy's style when he knows the letter is definitely limited to a certain number of lines and words.

He knows it would do no good if one of those rare inspirations came along that could conceivably be woven into a fairly interesting letter. The loom is too small, no matter how good the material might be. So when writing that small, efficient letter there is no necessity to grope for ideas that could not be used.

Letty, I liked your picture of Main Street on Saturday night. It was just as I remembered it, but I needed to be refreshed. Perhaps it is hard for me to make you understand what I mean, but it is an acute and very real situation with me and with all of us. The kind of existence we go through makes it a little difficult to retain an acute memory of the thing we love and the things we hope to go back to when this is all over. We try (at least, I try) to reform the picture of those things, but at times it is not easy. The picture dances and blurs at the edges like a movie when the projector is out of focus. It is not easy to shut out the war, distance, absence, and time by merely shutting the eyes and trying to imagine what the things at home are like.

But through it all there is one beacon that is still sharp and clear. That is the fact that I am still in love with you. The guns and the miles cannot alter that fact, nor can it change the edges of the picture.

Maybe this is a little involved, and I may have failed completely in my attempt to tell you how a soldier reacts to war. If I have, I apologize for attempting it in the first place.

Just at the moment we are living in luxury. We are in a house that is neat as a pin, and there is plenty of room. It was formerly an apartment house and there are several beds. However, I have a nice comfortable spot on the floor. It has been so long since I slept on a bed that I am not sure I would like it. I know I would have to relearn the tricks of using one.

When this is over I hope the Army provides a two-week school on how to be a civilian. It would have to include such subjects as "eating," "sleeping," etc.

One lesson would, for example, go something like this:

"If you should be invited out to dinner and should desire, say, a second helping of butter you will find that it can be obtained merely by expressing a desire for it in a moderate tone. The phrase 'May I have some butter, please?' is the accepted form, and usually gets results. It is not necessary to yell 'Throw me the —— grease,' for such practice is frowned upon in polite society."

Or:

"After a visit with friends, if you do not find your hat where you think you left it, your hostess will usually produce it with a minimum of excitement. It is quite likely that she has put it in a closet, which was built for the purpose. As a civilian, you will find that it is not necessary to stand in the middle of the room and yell, 'Don't nobody leave the house. Some lousy —— stole my hat, and I'm gonna find it before anybody gets away.'"

The course would cover every phase of civilian activity, and would save many a poor ex-soldier a lot of embarrassment.

But I will take my chance on it when this is over, and I don't care to spend two weeks learning to be a civilian. Can you trust my behavior?

Love Always,
Leland

[Rhineland, Germany]
March 14, 1945

My Dearest Letty:

There are a couple of hours in front of me during which I could become acquainted with some new books, which are on my desk, or I could go downstairs and bat the breeze with the boys. But I'd rather write you than do either.

The books will bear further discussion. They are textbooks from the University of Texas and are part of a course I am taking from that school. I wrote you that I had ordered it and yesterday the textbooks came, but as yet I have no assignments. The course is promising and should be helpful.

I have three volumes. One is *College Handbook of English Composition* (Wooley & Scott). The second is *College Readings in English Prose* (Scott & Zietlin), and the third is *Composition for College Students* (Thomas, Manchester & Scott). If I have to do all the work outlined in them I should fill all my spare time for six months or so, but it should eliminate any chance of my finding myself unemployed and bored.

Such a situation could arise, you know. If the war should end and if we were part of the Army of occupation while waiting for ships to Japan we might find ourselves with spare time. This is my insurance against such a possibility.

Didn't know you were going to marry such an industrious man, did you? Well, you are, and there are a lot of things you will learn about me that you have never suspected.

Spring seems to be here at last, and it is quite a relief after a cold winter. We were fortunate in that we were not too busy during the coldest part of the season, but many men were. While they were literally freezing, we were in tents with stoves and such. It was a great help.

Spring here is much like the season at home so far as temperature is concerned. However, there seem to be no violent changes, nor are there any heavy rains. There are only drizzles and showers without thunder. Such days are not followed by bright sunshine, but the clouds hang around indecisive as to whether they should go away or continue to make us miserable.

I prefer decision in such matters. Rain should come in torrents and should be followed by an equally positive period of sunshine.

By the same measure should a man's behavior be governed. When at peace, he should make the environment a positive force and be actively friendly, not merely in a state of passive half-belligerent existence. When circumstances force him into a fight, he should be a positive force and should finish the job as quickly as possible.

But I am drifting into a subject that rightfully belongs to the philosophers, and I have no business kicking it around. My intention in this letter was merely to remind you that I am still in love with you, and this fact has no possible connection with the above subject.

Love Always,
Leland

[Rhineland, Germany]
March 17, 1945

My Dearest Letty:

This is only a prelude to a letter that I hope to be able to write a little later when I will not be limited by time. I am writing this in a race with the chow truck and mailman. If I finish it before the truck arrives it will go out with the evening mail. If this sounds like a confused schedule, it is no more so than your habit of working a couple of hours in the afternoon and finishing the day after you have slept.

Well, you asked for some kind of picture and I am sending you the only available sample. I had even forgotten I was on a picture when I had your request. It takes so long to get film developed from here. But today the forgotten prints arrived. The group picture was made about Christmas. The country is Belgium, in the vicinity of Eupen and Verviers, and the names are on the back. The picture of my girlfriends was near Simpleville (Holland). These are the gals who got all my candy and gum ration while we were in that vicinity. (Notice Anna's wooden shoes.) Maria, at the extreme right, was my favorite, but Anna got her part of the gum.

The snow scene is near Monschau, Germany, and shows a guy named Broccani with his machinegun. Will have time for no more now except to say I still love you.

Love Always,
Leland

[Rhineland, Germany]
March 19, 1945

My Dearest Letty:

All day I have intended to write you a letter but circumstances have prevented it. Nothing of any consequence, you understand, but trivial matters that kept me annoyingly employed in jobs and left me feeling that I have accomplished nothing toward ending the war and seeing you again. It is maddening.

Your two letters helped, of course, as they always do. But I did not like the tone of one of them. In it, you threatened to quit work when I come home and grow lazy. Now, I ask you, how can you support a husband if you quit working? And I would be terribly disappointed if I found that I had a lazy wife. So you may as well quit toying with dreams of a time when you will have nothing to do except sit around and look beautiful, mow the lawn, tend the garden and do odd jobs like that. They are to be done in your spare time, you understand, when I have plenty of time to give you advice from the lawn chair in the shade.

Love Always,
Leland

[Rhineland, Germany]
March 22, 1945

My Dearest Letty:

When I sat down here I fully intended to write to another person who deserved a letter, but my pen is in such a habit of writing your name that it slipped up on me and had a letter started to you before I knew it. Now, it would be a shame to waste a sheet of scarce paper, so you get the letter. The other one can wait.

We are eating like kings in the days of Robin Hood now: deer and pheasant and things like that. My shotguns are paying off for all the time I have carried them. You remember the one I got in Luxembourg last summer. It is a nice little bird gun and I also have a twelve-gauge model now. They are a big help in giving a relief from the monotony of war. For a few hours a guy can forget he is in Germany and imagine he is shooting upland game birds in America. Maybe it will help me be not so different when I see you again.

One part of me will not be different. I will still love you just as I always have.

Say, Letty, some weeks ago I paid a membership in the Book-of-the-Month Club for you. By this time you should be getting books from them, but I know you have not received them, for you have said nothing about them in your letters.

Of course, I am utterly selfish in sending you the books. I shall expect to spend my evenings (the quiet evenings we spend at home, you know) reading the best books that were written during the Great War. Right now I have little chance to read, for I cannot carry a library around with me. So you will find me far behind in the field of literature and it will be up to you to re-educate me.

I am having plenty of trouble with my lights. The Air Force must have knocked out every generator in Germany. At least I have not seen one in operation. Our house is a honey but we use candles for lights, and our supply is about exhausted. We experiment with every sort of wax and grease, but none of them works well.

I am writing this by the light of a wax heat tablet, issued for field cooking, and a can of shoe impregnite, used to protect the feet from gas. So far, they work well, but I am not betting they will last.

Letty, if this war should end, as I dreamed it did last night, I don't want to come home and have you tell me you have only been writing to keep my morale up. That's what you did last night, so I had to give up the idea of marrying you and join the Army again. Now you know you shouldn't string a guy along like that.

Love Always,
Leland

[Rhineland, Germany]
March 24, 1945

My Dearest Letty:

This is really not a letter. There is no time for that just now, but maybe the clippings I'm enclosing will substitute for one, for they will give you some idea of what part of the world we are in. Now get your war maps and geography and start looking. Maybe you can figure it out.

Anyway, it is a nice, pleasant spring day here. All the Heinies (Germans to you) are out working in their gardens as if there was no war going on. I don't guess the German soldier can be as nonchalant. He is taking quite a plastering just now. Will write more later.

Love Always,
Leland

[Rhineland, Germany]
March 25, 1945

My Dearest Letty:

This is supposed to be a demonstration in how to write your only girl a letter in twelve minutes. That is exactly how much time I had when I sat down.

The first step, of course, is to write the address. That takes up too much time, for they insist that addresses are written in duplicate on V-mail forms. Then the heading "Germany" must be inserted under the date. Somehow there is a pride in being able to write it. It means that the war is nearer over than if I had to write "England" or "France" or "Holland." The greeting is a matter of habit and I could write that with my eyes shut, but habit does not mean that it has lost any significance. It has a real meaning and improves every time I write it. Then, of course, there must be a declaration that "I love you."

There, I made it with three minutes to spare.

Love Always,
Leland

[Rhineland, Germany]
March 26, 1945

My Dearest Letty:

You may find it difficult to understand why I should write you so often and yet show so little originality in the body of my letters. It would seem that the experience of a dogface would provide plenty of subject matter for long letters.

In truth, we may see little that could be of value in a letter. Rather, I should say, we retain little, but we pass many places that should be interesting. In Aachen, for example, is the cathedral where Friedrich Barbarossa was crowned and buried*, but when I saw the place I thought nothing of the ancient ruler or what part he played in bringing about this war. At the moment, we are in a quaint Rhenish village, but it looks dull enough to me. Sometimes we stop in a castle built by a robber baron of the 16th century, but we are more interested in the bullet resistance of the walls than in the beauty of the woodwork or the history of the guy who built the place.

With this explanation of why my letters are dull, I can now write as freely and as uninterestingly as I please. Surely you cannot condemn me since I put up my defense in advance.

Letty, you and Polly were a little mixed up about the "wigwam" she told you about. I had nothing to do with it. You see, Ardis was the sponsor of the shack. I was too mature to have a part in the Shack Club, but it was a colorful organization. In those days, Ardis was a natural leader of younger boys. He did not care for the usual games of sport but preferred to collect a bunch of youngsters and stage such acts as an amateur rodeo or a boxing tournament.

It was such a group that built the shack and comprised the club. Long winter afternoons were spent in the clubhouse on such boyish projects as construction of coaster wagons or planning a 'possum hunt. There was tobacco, yes, and it was not always rabbit tobacco as Polly supposed. The club treasury usually contained enough money to provide a package of makings and a book of paper. They handled this in much the same way that a drinker handled his bootleg whiskey. They concealed it in various ingenious corners and assumed bland, innocent expressions when a non-member entered the place.

The stove smoked and the roof leaked, but I envied them even in

---

*Leland was in error about Friedrich Barbarossa's crowning and burial in the Cathedral at Aachen. The Holy Roman emperor was crowned in St. Peter's Basilica and interred elsewhere. The emperor Charlemagne was buried in the Cathedral at Aachen. —Ed.

Dearest Letty

my maturity. I was always a welcomed visitor but could never invade the intimate circle of membership.

Aaron, the youngest brother, was first to outgrow the club, but Ardis continued to acquire younger members. These were initiated into the club, but they only became full members when they had learned to smoke the strong tobacco without being nauseated. Many a fond mother suddenly discovered that little Rollo had acquired the nasty habit of smoking. Many suspected that Ardis in some vague way was responsible for it, but they could never prove it.

On one occasion, Ardis took a group of prospective bronco busters into a neighbor's pasture to practice riding. The owner came by and Ardis retreated with his group to the security of a thicket. He proceeded to tell the boys how they were liable to arrest and would no doubt be in jail before the end of the week. The boys took it seriously, and Ardis suggested that they infiltrate back into the village so as to not attract attention. The boys crept and crawled back to town, and Ardis came home with a brilliant idea.

I had an envelope mailed at Russellville, so he erased the address and changed it so that it came back to him. He then took the typewriter and constructed a legal-looking letter, as if the sheriff had written him a letter about the incident, threatening immediate arrest of the whole gang on a charge of trespassing and malicious mischief. He circulated the letter among the boys and advised them to stay out of town until the whole thing blew over. The forgery not only fooled the boys but their parents also took it seriously. For two weeks, a strange car pulling off the highway was sufficient to send a dozen boys scurrying out of the village to the comparative safety of the shack hideout, where Ardis was always ready with legal advice and instructions. Anxious mothers spoke in hushed whispers of the possibility of Junior being sent to the Reformatory. Mothers whose sons were involved banded together and pooled their ideas on how to meet the grave situation. It was only when they decided that the suspense was too great that the case was broken.

They concluded that the smart thing was to employ Bob Bailey to represent them in court and to take advice from him. Ardis decided the case had gone far enough, so he confessed the fraud. Then it was his turn to hide.

A dozen women went on the warpath simultaneously, and they were all after his scalp. It took a good deal of explaining and some smooth diplomacy on my part to establish friendly relations again.

Most of the boys are in the Army or Navy now, and their mothers are worrying over more serious problems. But it was there that they learned the basics of depending on themselves and their buddies.

It has been more than three years since I saw Ardis, for he is with the Seventh Army now and I wonder what the Army has done to him. Mother said when he was at home last he had traded his drawl for snappy accents with the nasal twang of New Jersey. I am afraid he has lost his slow smile, too, for that was his greatest asset. People trusted that more than anything else. But I must not make this into a biography.

You may consider this an introduction to a part of my family that you have not met. To make it complete you can take a look at the enclosed picture. It may help you to see what he is like. You can send it back to me when you have looked at it, for you will not want it and it is the only one I have of him.

Do not be surprised if I cover any kind of subject in my letters. But always imagine that I am merely talking to you and not writing. We will no doubt talk of any number of subjects sometime.

But I always get up on the wrong side of the world and cannot talk to you now. That is why I have to write "I love you" instead of whispering it to you, which is what I am waiting to do.

Love Always,
Leland

[Rhineland, Germany]
March 28, 1945

My Darling:

Must finish this in a hurry for I have another job to do, but I could not do it efficiently until I said I love you.

Letty, I am afraid I neglect telling you how much I need you. Perhaps I could not tell you even if I tried harder, but I can see how it is easy for the girl back home to imagine that a soldier grows independent and doesn't need her. This may seem reasonable, but in my case it is not true. Every day I am reminded in a thousand ways that it is always you I need and that it is you who keeps me dreaming of a future that is worth waiting for.

Love Always,
Leland

[Porta Westfalica, Germany]
April 7, 1945

My Dearest Letty:

For several days I have had no chance to write or to think. You have noticed a break in my chain of letters. From the papers you have guessed the reason. It has been quite a busy time. Days have lost their individuality. They fall and merge like raindrops on a windowpane, but all the while we move toward Berlin and toward the end of the war. That fact keeps us going, and even makes the whole adventure interesting and enjoyable. This may sound crazy, but a guy learns to live and enjoy himself under almost any conditions.

Several letters from you came today, and this was a big help. If you think you enjoy letters there you should watch an Army mail call. The only letters I had today were from you, but I did not mind that. Your letters were so good they made up for all the ones that did not come.

I am glad your membership in the book club finally came through. I had begun to wonder about it. Hope you enjoy it until I get there. Then I shall eliminate the necessity of your books for entertainment. But we will always need books to build up our library.

Love Always,
Leland

[Pattensen, Germany]
April 8, 1945

My Dearest Letty:

I never thought I would have time to write today, but the unexpected happened as it often does here, and I have a few minutes free time. The package came today and I am enjoying my first really good cigar in several weeks. It is seldom that we get anything better than the rope and cabbage-leaf brand of cigars, so we naturally appreciate a good one even more for that reason. The pipe is the first genuine Dr. Graham I have had in a couple of years, and my tobacco supply was about exhausted. So it seems that you could hardly have picked a more opportune time to send just that kind of package.

Letty, I may not find time to write again for several days. You can see how it is when a guy is moving and the APO has trouble keeping up with the drive. There is simply no time to write and no way to send mail out, even if he could write. But please don't worry about me for I can take care of myself.

Love Always,
Leland

[Elbe River, northwest of Berlin]
April 28, 1945

My Dearest Letty:

I am sure you have not been puzzled over your lack of mail from me in the last two weeks or so. By this time you have learned many of the reasons for the long gaps between letters, and you know it is not a situation I can control. We simply moved so far and so fast that there was no mail service of any kind.

So you see, I have had no mail from anyone during the whole time. It is simply annoying to know there are dozens of letters only a couple of hundred miles back, and none of them can be brought up. But they will get here in a few days now, and I will have plenty of reading for several hours. A longer letter will follow. Meanwhile, this will remind you that I still love you.

Always,
Leland

[Elbe River, northwest of Berlin]
April 29, 1945

My Dearest Letty:
There was a time when I thought nothing of writing you a dozen pages at one sitting. But that was long ago. Now I am fortunate if I can fill a single sheet.

But it will not always be so. If I am lucky, in a couple of days I may be able to write something like an acceptable letter. Now I must confine myself to this.

Letty, I have a confession to make. Remember the toilet case you sent me? The one I liked so much? Well, I lost it, and with it my razor, toothbrush, soap, towel—everything. It was the Germans who caused it so I cannot hold myself at fault, but now I must depend on the other guys for soap, razor and comb, and I have no toothbrush. Aren't you sorry for me? I shall manage a new supply when I get back to my troop again.

Just came from a movie. They showed us "A Song to Remember." Superb acting, but the story paid little attention to faces. Just room to say I love you and be always waiting for me.

Love Always,
Leland

[Vicinity of Elbe River, Germany]
April 30, 1945

My Dearest Letty:
The machine on which I am trying to write this is so huge and ponderous and fitted with so many gadgets that I really feel that I am sitting at the instrument panel of a B-29. It is not really a typewriter at all, but a combination typewriter, adding machine, calculator, Linotype and Teletype all built into one. It has everything, including three keyboards, and is wired for electricity. I am not sure what would happen if the socket were plugged in, but I shall try it when I have finished writing. Who knows, it might even make sound movies. On the other hand, it might be a booby trap and blow the whole room through the ceiling. If you don't hear from me again you can guess the awful truth. My curiosity got the better of me.

The truth of the matter is, I have used every known means at my disposal to impress you with the fact that I am still crazy about you, but this is the first time I have had the opportunity to employ so much machinery in the process. Maybe I can make it more impressive this way. Please inform me of the results.

We have been in this building for a couple of days now, but we only discovered this machine today. It was cleverly concealed in a huge desk, and we had missed it all this time. Can you imagine anything so huge escaping the prowling eye of a G.I. for two whole days. Question mark. There, I have beaten the screwy punctuation system. If I merely write it you will be able to get the idea.

The boys are cooking noodle soup, and you should hear the argument that is going on. One of them is trying to cook it the way they do it in Philadelphia, and the other insists that it be done the Kansas City way. I don't know how it will turn out, but I am afraid there is truth in the adage, "Too many cooks spoil the broth." On the other hand, they say, "Many hands make light work," but I do not like that one so well. I am afraid you will insist on using that one on me when there is work to be done around the house. Now that I think of it, I shall stick to the one about too many cooks.

Letty, you would be amused at my car crew. Parenthesis. I hope none of them is looking over my shoulder as I write this. Parenthesis again. They must have offered a wide contrast in character before the Army molded them to its pattern. My driver is from Kansas City and was just old enough to get in on the boom money of the war spending before he came to the Army. He is, as a result, a happy-go-lucky kid with seldom a serious thought. But he is as cool under fire as any man I ever knew, and if I were choosing up for a fight he would definitely be on my first team. One day we had two cars stuck in the mud and the jerries were throwing everything from 20mm to artillery at us. All the guys were taking cover while Charlie and I were trying to get chains on the car. I guess I was scared, but there was no time to stop and take stock. Charlie was calm as if it were a problem on maneuvers. His movements were unhurried, and he seemed surprised that the other guys should be hitting the ditches. "Where are you going Question mark," he would ask them. "I am going to sign up for thirty years when I get back to the troop." I don't know how he does it, but he does it.

My radio operator is an Irish lad from Philadelphia. He is Catholic and was probably devout in his youth, but the Army has changed that and he seldom goes to mass now. His voice is pitched high, almost to the feminine key, and when he is excited he sounds like a kid whose voice is just changing. He and Charlie carry on a perpetual argument on any subject that happens to come up. It moves from one topic to another without a break, for they have a standing agreement to never agree. But it is always in fun and always entertaining.

The gunner is from Leslie, Arkansas, and he is known as the "best man in the troop." His jokes are quiet and carefully inoffensive. I have never known anyone to doubt one of his statements. If any situation ever scared him he is actor enough to keep it from showing. I have never seen him change color or allow a single face muscle to quiver, no matter what kind of a spot he was in. It will take a lot of luck or a lot of Germans to stop these boys.

All of this may not interest you in the least, but you might like to know the kind of guys who go along with me.

I have not had a letter from anyone in so long that I shall probably have to learn to read all over again when my mail finally does catch up with me. But that should not be too hard, and I am willing to undertake the task any time now. Charlie is clamoring for the machine. Wants to try the electricity.

Love Always,
Leland

Germany
May 8, 1945

My Dearest Letty:

No matter how monotonous the subject matter of my letters may be, there is at least one factor in them that has variety. No two consecutive letters are written on the same kind of stationery. No doubt you have noticed this characteristic and wondered why it is so.

The reason is simple. There is a shortage of paper up here, due to the fact that truck space is used for a more essential purpose. So we have to improvise and use whatever is at hand when we start a letter. Usually, it is German. Just now we are in the office of a sugar refinery, and there happens to be an abundance of paper in various sizes and shapes. It is all inferior quality, but as O. Henry said of the stew without an onion, "'twill serve."

Letty, I have not had a letter in so long that I find it difficult to write. When I sit down I find myself wondering what is happening in the old town. This consumes my mind to the exclusion of everything else. If I only had one letter, something to furnish a tiny bit of inspiration, something to give me a hint of what you are thinking or what you are doing, it would be so much easier to construct some kind of letter.

You see, I have not been with the troop in quite a while now, and before I left them we were moving so fast that there could be no thought of mail. I worked (that is, my section did) with various combat teams and finally with the British Army. Then my car broke down and Ordnance picked me up. I am with them now, waiting for the repair job while the letters stack up.

But this is like being on a pass. Nothing to do but loaf and sleep. They feed us well at the kitchen, which is something of a novelty to us. (Usually we have to cook our own chow.) My crew and I have the whole factory and offices at our disposal. There is a nice hot shower, so we have it made. I could spend the duration doing this if there was only some way to get our mail.

Letty, did I tell you that our troop was given a Presidential Citation? It happened weeks ago, but I don't recall writing it to you.

The citation was given for "heroic action against the enemy in the highest military tradition," which is another way of saying we pulled off a non-habit-forming job. The action was not one a guy would do often enough to form a habit of it. We slipped behind the German lines and set up a roadblock with nothing to defend it but small arms and grenades. Once we were in, there was no way to get out, so they said we were heroic because forty men held off a tank-infantry attack, knocked out a tank with grenades and two full-tracks and a staff car with rifles. But I contend that the guys merely did what they had to do to keep from getting wiped out. But so are most of the heroes of war made.

Must say I love you and go to dinner.

Love Always,
Leland

Dearest Letty

Germany
May 8, 1945

My Dearest Letty:

Well, today the war in Europe is officially over. It is hard to grasp the fact. At times, I find myself imagining that it is all a dream and in a few hours I shall be awake and the burp guns will be stuttering at me like an ambitious woodpecker. Again I get the feeling that there has really been no war at all and I am awake for the first time in months. In short, you might say that I am a little confused.

All the other guys seem to be in the same condition. They listen to the radio blaring the news, and no one seems to realize that it has anything to do with him. There is no celebration and the only thing that shows the nerve tensions is the talk is a little louder than usual, but that could be because the radio is turned up loud.

The stories are going around about what we will be doing next, but they are all in the rumor stage and I have learned to pay no attention to any of them. Will let you know as soon as I learn anything definite and the censor will let it go through the mail.

Incidentally, my mail caught up with me a couple of days ago, and you should have seen the package. I had exactly 50 letters plus assorted papers, packages, etc. Of course, there is no chance to answer them all. That would be impossible, but I shall write at least one letter to each of those who wrote and let that serve.

I was thrilled to hear of the oil painting and I wish I could have it here. But now I don't think it would be safe to mail it due to our uncertain status. Then, too, I have no decent way to carry anything. If we should stop some place I might write for it but, if not, you will have to keep it for me.

Letty, how do you like my new typewriter? It serves very well to say such words as "I love you" but it is no good at spelling the difficult words. In fact, it spells almost as badly as my pens. But you can tell the letter I was trying to make unless I hit the wrong key and have to double. A couple of letters are out of place on the keyboard and I can't blame all the wrong letters on that. But with this machine I can make all sorts of clever little doodles, like this: 1/ § ü ß Ç π _\ + = Q. Bet you can't do that on your machine.

To the Elbe River

239

May have written you that our troop was given a Presidential Citation. Well, the restriction has been taken off the story now and I can give you a copy of the official document that should make this letter long enough to satisfy even you. Barring typographical errors the story is exactly like the copy approved by the president.

Love Always,
Leland

Presidential Citation

Headquarters 5th Armored Division
A.P.O. 255
U.S. Army
General Orders
Number No. 12

1. CITATION OF UNIT: Under provisions of Section IV circular 333 War Department. 22 December 1944. Troop A 85th Cavalry Reconnaissance Squad Mechanized is cited for outstanding performance of duty in action from 15 December to 22 December 1944. During a series of attacks eastward from Klinehau, Germany, onto the high ground north of Untermaubach, Troop A, though previously trained and experienced in mounted reconnaissance, exhibited remarkable adaptability in dismounted infantry tactics and was successful in the seizure of its assigned section of Hill 253. In spite of terrific barrages of enemy artillery and two savage counterattacks, Troop A held its sector firmly against overwhelming enemy numbers and firepower for a period of four days. On 19 December, having suffered 50 percent losses, the troop was assigned the mission of penetrating to the rear of enemy positions and severing the main enemy supply route. This small force, half of whom were suffering from battle wounds, deftly cut the supply route and established a roadblock, which they held for three days even though the operation planned for relief the first day. Although completely surrounded by strong enemy forces, it decisively defeated a concerted tank-infantry attack with no more powerful weapons than rifle grenades. One Mark V tank was destroyed after it had advanced to within ten yards of the troop's position while two other tanks shelled the houses, which the troop occupied, from a distance of 200 yards. Simultaneously,

75 enemy infantry charged the position but were repulsed with losses of 60 killed and 6 taken prisoner. This force of 4 officers and 40 enlisted men was responsible for an effective block that cut off large enemy forces from their base of supply, greatly facilitating the capture of these forces and the sector which they held. The heroism, fighting determination and versatility displayed by the members of Troop A are worthy of emulation and reflect honor upon the Armed Forces of the United States.

By Command of Major General OLIVER
EDWARD G. FARRAND
COLONEL G.S.C.
Chief of Staff

Germany
May 10, 1945

My Dearest Letty:

I have spent most of the day writing letters, and it would be a shameless waste of time if I did not include a letter to you. Not only would it be a waste of time, it would also be dangerous. Suppose someone mentioned that they got a letter from me on this date and you did not get one. I would have to see you in person to cool your ire, and I am still a long way from home.

I wonder how the old town celebrated the end of the war in Europe. They must have staged quite a party. I can remember the end of the last war. (Don't tell me. I know you can't remember that long ago.) Even that was something for the books. Everyone acted as if they were drunk or doped. One particularly sober chap, Mr. Elbert Hanks, breezed up the road in his T Model Ford like a high school boy. His normal speed was 20 miles per hour, but that day he was doing at least 30. One of the neighbors had a bird dog that had a habit of chasing cars. Everyone knew Joe and avoided him. It was also considered hazardous driving to hit a dog. But Mr. Hanks gave no thought to that, and when Joe charged out the Ford made no attempt to avoid him. In fact, it deliberately swerved in his direction and it was a surprised setter that found himself being wallowed around in the frosty road. This is one of the pictures I retain of Armistice Day 1918.

How different is this one. All of the boys seemed too tired and exhausted to care if the war was over. A few of them tossed out some smoke grenades or shot a few flares, but it could not be called a serious celebration. Two or three years had exhausted their capacity for excitement.

Just now we are doing nothing. We are in that restful period when the Army has not decided what we are to do next, so we sit around and do nothing. But this will not last. Before long, someone will wake up to the fact that armies are not supposed to sit around, and they will put us to work. The job may be only picking up paper and cigarette stubs, but we will be busy.

There are all sorts of wild stories of what we will do next but none of them is official. In fact, none of them has the least basis of authority, so we have no idea if we will go directly to the Pacific, occupy Germany, go to the states for furlough, or be discharged.

Maybe the war has made me a little crazy. Maybe it is you, or maybe it is the sensible thing to do, the thing I should have done long ago, but if I should get a furlough to the states, even a short one, I am sure I would ask you to marry me as soon as I got home. If you don't think it is the sensible thing to do you could always refuse, you know, and I could easily understand your reason. In fact, it was I who convinced you in the first place (if I am not flattering myself by assuming that you needed to be convinced).

But I have some cooking to do and must sign off for now.

Love Always,
Leland

Germany
May 12, 1945

My Dearest Letty:

It is such a beautiful day that I can barely muster the energy to do anything but stretch out on the new grass and watch the shadows slide silently across a peaceful countryside. It seems funny to know that the war is over and to realize that the planes that pass over will not take a shot at you and that there is no necessity to shoot at them. Even those

Dearest Letty

with black crosses are probably being flown by American GIs who are getting a chance to try out the machines they have been hunting, just as our boys like to try the German motorcycles and armored cars. A soldier likes to experiment.

Today, the air is heavy with the scent of lilacs and apple blossoms. Strange how soon the smell of powder and burning flesh can be filtered out by growing shrubs. Yesterday, we drove about 150 miles through the heart of Germany. Of course, the war had passed lightly over much of it, for the Germans were on the run when this part was taken, but there were plenty of signs of the fighting. Factories were scattered all over the landscape and there were hulls of burned-out tanks and skeletons of guns at the side of the road. But already the hulls of the tanks had begun to look as if they had been knocked out a long time ago. They were beginning to rust and new blades of grass were creeping up through the tracks.

What I am trying to get at is the war is not permanent and the world will soon forget it. Not literally, of course, nor completely. It will live on as a terrible dream and will be something that youngsters will find on page 435 of their history books. But the edge of the picture will be blurred and there will be no sharp outlines of black and white.

We will forget the sharp crack in the wind that a bullet makes when it passes overhead, and how it sounds like the gun is behind you and you begin to imagine the enemy has filtered through the lines. The sharp sting of the tiny pieces of shrapnel will be forgotten and we will find ourselves trying to remember exactly how German powder smelled.

The disrupted fragments of lives will form new and more tranquil patterns—yours and mine together.

Look, I only started out to say that it is a beautiful day. How the heck did I get tangled up in this sort of subject? A lot of guys claim they have trouble finding anything to say in letters, but if my time is not limited I find that my problem is stopping with a letter that will go through the mail for one stamp. I guess I talk too much for the comfort of my listeners, which is supposed to be one of the gravest offenses of social behavior.

Well, it happened. I had to go to work in the middle of the letter, and now it is afternoon. Since I wrote the above I have washed and painted a car and cleaned some of my equipment. Still have plenty of that sort of work to do, but I do it in small doses. It is a pleasant way to do things. A good motto is, never do today that which can be postponed until tomorrow.

Love Always,
Leland

Germany
May 14, 1945

My Dearest Letty:

If this is to be a long letter I will have to write in a hurry for I have to go out on a patrol in a few minutes. So if I should happen to hit all the wrong keys you will have to try to figure out what I mean.

But part of the jog will be pleasant. It will not be like the combat patrols we were making a few weeks ago, when you never knew when someone would start shooting and make themselves unpleasant. Now, all we have to do is show the Germans that we are still around and that there is no reason for them to get ideas. And it gives us a chance to leisurely look at the country.

Yesterday, I covered a lot of this part of the country. We are in the Province of Saxony, and if a guy knew enough about the history of Germany it might have been an interesting drive. We could have gone to Leipzig, but that city is said to be almost completely destroyed. All ruined cities look alike and I have seen too many of them already. So we went through parts of the province that were less mutilated. The German army was pretty well beaten here so there is surprisingly little damage to many of the towns. Some showed no signs of scraps while others had only a few pockmarks where machineguns had spattered the walls and broke out a few windows. A good gang war in Chicago could have done as much.

Some of these villages are supposed to be old. One town has some buildings that were reported to have been built in the 13th century and the old part of the town is surrounded by a well-preserved stone wall that dates to the Middle Ages. The wall was for defense purposes and must have served well against spears and the early muskets, but I doubt if it would have any lasting value against a 37mm, and I hate to think what would happen if it were hit by a 90 and then attacked by a bulldozer.

I am writing too fast. See what happened to the sheet.

But there is a reason. My time has expired and I have to run along now. Meanwhile, I will be thinking of how much I love you.

Love Always,
Leland

Germany
May 16, 1945

My Dearest Letty:

All of your recent letters indicate that they were written when you were getting no letters from me, and you seemed to be worried over the fact. By this time I suppose you are getting plenty of the long ones I have been writing to keep you reading most of the time. So there is really no point in my explaining that I did not have time to write for quite a long time. Had hoped to be able to send you a telegram as soon as the war was over and let you know that I had made the grade, but that was not possible so I had to let you wait until my letters finally arrived.

By this time you have probably figured out that I do not have enough points to get a discharge from the Army with the guys that get out on the point system. There are so many men who have been in longer than I have and have seen more action, so they naturally get the preference. I do not know where we will go next or when we will move. That has not been handed down yet. As soon as I learn I will tell you, if the censor will permit. It is possible that we will get a furlough before we go to the China Theater, but no one knows.

As I said, I am short by a few points of the discharge figure. Could have done more, I guess, if I had tried for them. You see, they give five points for a Purple Heart. I have been hit three times and have taken one Purple Heart. I was nicked by a rocket in France, but it was not serious and we were in a hurry so I did my own first aid and did not report it. On another occasion shrapnel from a mortar cut across my back but it did more damage to my overcoat than to the skin. It was more of a burn than a cut, but I have known men to take five points for less. But when the grenade fragment hit and stuck I went in to let them see if they could pick it out. They could not, but they gave me a Purple Heart. However, I did not miss any time on the line, so you see it was not serious. I wanted to tell you then just how insignificant it was, but the censor would not permit discussion of those things.

This letter probably sounds like an afternoon sewing club with the women discussing their operations. Since I have only attended a few of these and on no occasion were the conversations as frank and intimate as I have been led to expect, I am no authority on how women gossip about their operations. But if the letter is in that tone and if you do not find it to your taste, please believe that I am only trying to say that you worried needlessly over the extent of my injuries and that censorship prevented my telling you how infinitesimal they really were.

What is more important to me is an idea that I expressed in another letter. It will bear repeating on the chance that the other letter was lost in the mess of V-E Day mail.

In my letter I gave you a warning that I would probably ask you to marry me, even if I only had a furlough. Well, I still feel the same way, so you can begin now to think of all the reasons you might have for refusing, if you should have reasons.

This is not a proposal, you understand. I want to make that in person. This is merely a warning of what you can expect. After all, I have spent the best years of my life trying to convince you that I am in love with you. You doubted me for a long time, but I think you are convinced at last. I will not have time to argue with you so long if I only get a furlough.

Must sign off for now as I have several letters to write.

Love Always,
Leland

Germany
May 19, 1943

My Dearest Letty:

It is almost sunset and I am sitting on a sun porch that is exactly the kind of porch I would like to sit on every day for a long time. It is small, perhaps 8 by 10 feet, but this serves to give it an intimate air that is so pleasant, in contrast to the promiscuous habits of Army life. Sleazy lace curtains hang over the long glass-fitted shutters. The door is stained glass: blue and green and amber and old rose so that you can look at the world through any kind of glass you choose. Small murals on a cream wall show a tiny cabin set on the bank of a stream that is picking its way through a gap between snow-covered mountains. A tiny canoe is moored to a silver birch with the paddles tossed carelessly on the grass. Gray smoke curls up from the stack chimney and two people, a man and a woman, sprawl lazily on the short grass. It may not be a good mural—I am no judge of art—but it seems to fit neatly on the wall of that particular porch.

In a place like this, one should be able to write the things he feels. If he is crazy about someone he should be able to tell her about it in a way that would leave her no room to doubt it. But my trouble is I keep getting up on the wrong side of the world and it spoils my mood and consequently my command of the language. Something should be done about it.

Have been painting today, and there are streaks of GI green all over my hands. It is persistent stuff, too, and refuses to come off for anything but gasoline. Have not used that yet.

Have to change to German paper in the middle of this letter.

Have had several letters from you recently and in all of them you were wondering what had happened to me. I tried to tell you before we jumped off on the last drive that it would be some time before I was able to write, for we were going to be busy. But I knew you would expect at least a V-mail. The truth is that I wanted a letter, too, but we had no mail service of any kind. It was more important that we get gasoline and ammunition than that we get mail, so that had to wait.

You were wondering about the First Army. Well, all the time I was in the Ninth Army. If I could have told you then you might have been able to keep up with me better. We changed last winter, but it was supposed to be a military secret then. We went through Kerfeld, Munchengladbach, Munster and Stendal. All of these were much in the news of the papers we got later.

Well, I have some work to do for the benefit of the university. This is one time it is interfering with one of your letters, but it must be done.

Love Always,
Leland

Thamsbrück, Germany
May 21, 1945

My Dearest Letty:

It is a bit dreary today for the sun quit shining after a long session and now it is raining. No, you could hardly call it rain in the sense that you have grown to think of rain. This is really just a slow drizzle, but it is enough to get one wet if he stayed out in it for a while. I will have to do just that for we are on a roadblock.

The G-2 finally decided that it would cause no great military disaster if we gave our exact location in our letters. Now, I can tell you the name of our town, but I dare you to find it on one map. I know you do not have Sheet R5 "Central Europe, 1:100,000" and you would not find it on a smaller scale map. The name of the town is Thamsbrück. Now, I don't think I made a mistake when I put the ü in there instead of the u. It is spelled with a ü. The place is 75 miles or so west of Kassel, which may give you a better idea of where it is.

I may have told you that it is an ancient village, somewhat larger than Pottsville, but it is unlike Pottsville or any other American town in every respect. It is so different from them that to use an American town for comparison purposes in a description of this place would mislead you. The streets, the houses and especially the church are interesting, but the customs and habits of the people are even more interesting.

There is, for example, the town crier. It must be an honored position in any German town, for the position is always filled by one of the oldest citizens. He is everybody's newspaper, and he seems to give advice in matters of law. When something noteworthy happens or when a new decree goes into effect, it is the job of the town crier to see that all the people get the news at once. This is accomplished in the most direct manner. He seizes a copy of the document and heads for the main street. On the busiest corner he starts ringing a bell that is exactly like the one teachers used to end recess periods in the old days when you went to school. When a crowd gathers he reads his paper in a loud voice. He then moves to another part of town and repeats the routine until everyone has heard the message. No job is so important that the bell of the town crier will not interrupt it. Women allow dinners to burn, children drop their toys, and young people pause in their lovemaking when they hear the bell of the town crier. (Let him try to interrupt me when I see you.)

Then there is the public well. It is on the main corner of the town, and most of the citizens get their water there. Part of the necessary household equipment is the kind of yoke the people use to aid in the task of carrying water. It is a heavy stick about three feet long. The middle is whittled out so that it fits roughly the outline of the neck and shoulders. To this they suspend two heavy pails so that they hang down to the level of the hands. Most of the weight is carried on the shoulders. It is at the town well that the women meet and exchange the latest gossip. Here the boys loaf and wait for the girls to come for their evening supply of water, and the girls, no doubt, volunteer for the job when they see who is waiting at the well.

But none of this, picturesque as it is, can make me like the place. It is as good as any in Germany, perhaps better than most places, for the war has passed lightly through this section.

But I must say I love you and call this a letter, for the boys are making an awful lot of racket.

Love Always,
Leland

Germany,
May 23, 1945

My Dearest Letty:

It is not often that I get as excited as I have been since yesterday. I just learned that Aaron had been returned to military control from a prison camp somewhere. There were no details, of course, for the War Department telegrams never give any, but that is enough.

All this time I had thought he might easily be a prisoner, for there were many that were unreported. At every prison camp I tried to look at every face to see if he might be there, but he never was. I knew it was foolish to even look, for there were so many odds against it. Every time we met a bunch of prisoners I asked about the outfit they had been with. At one time we freed a boy from Aaron's division, but he was from an antitank outfit and knew nothing of what had happened to any of the rest of the division.

Of course, I have no idea how he has been treated and what physical condition he is in. Some camps were not so bad while others were terrible. But he was pretty strong and would be able to stand up under a lot. I am hopeful that he is not in too bad shape.

You never knew him, but I think you would like him. I am not saying this because he is my brother, but because he is the kind you would like. He is some nine years younger than I am, but he and I often did things together, even more than we did with the other boys. He wore my clothes, after he grew up (I did the same with him, incidentally) and I always helped him get out of the little jams that boys get into. Above all, we always understood each other. We liked the same things in general and probably had more in common than most brothers have.

He is probably on his way to the states by this time for prisoners are given high priority on travel facilities and usually move pretty fast. We often get them on their way in two or three days when we liberate a camp, and it was never more than a day or two. One time we had to capture a fleet of German trucks and repaint them so that they looked like American trucks, but it worked.

Don't know when we will move or where we will go. But if the war in the East does not get too hot we have a chance for a break. That is only my opinion, of course. We have had quite a bit of combat and all that is bound to help. We have five major campaigns to our credit and that is above the average in this theater. You see, we took part in the Battles of Normandy, the Rhineland, the Ardennes, Northern France, and Central Europe.

Incidentally, that gives me twenty-five points toward a discharge, but even with that I only have eighty-three. The necessary score is eighty-five, so I am like the candidate for office who came in second. I also ran.

The authorities have decided on the five campaigns in Northern Europe after announcing at first that they were only giving three. It gave us a ten-point boost and made several of the boys eligible for discharge, but it failed to put me over. Now, if I only had another medal of some kind or a cluster on my purple heart I would be over the top, but I refused two chances because the wounds were so slight.

I have an appointment at squadron headquarters in a few minutes, and the funny thing is I have no idea what it is all about. Can't think of any law I have violated or any crime I have committed so it could hardly

Dearest Letty

be a threat of a court martial, but they seemed to think it was necessary that I be there promptly.

Must say I love you and get started. One cannot keep the colonel waiting. There is no need to say that this letter is poor, for you will understand why. I am thinking of Aaron, so I again am in no mood to write.

Love Always,
Leland

Germany
May 27, 1945

My Dearest Letty:

Now that I have a new ribbon in my typewriter and nothing else to do for a little while I can think of nothing better to do than write my girl a love letter. Not the sentimental kind of letter that some guys write. I have never learned to put that kind together. I guess my lack of practice comes from the fact that I have never been in love before. It may sound strange that I should live all these years and still say that, but it is true anyway. Yes, I know I have suffered from a form of infatuation on different occasions, but it was always temporary. On none of these occasions did it show any signs of being permanent. Nor did I ever seriously consider marrying the girl. I offer this as proof that it was not love.

Nor was it anything like the way I have felt about you for ever so long, longer than I will ever be able to convince you it was. If I tell you I was strangely disturbed when I saw you and when I thought of you (and this was quite often) long before you thought of me as anything but a big boob who kidded you unmercifully, you will not believe me.

I can tell you that once upon a time I was in a crowd, at Hector, I believe, when one of the younger girls of the Mars Hill crowd told me that you were engaged. It is true that I had never thought of myself as being exactly in love with you at that time, but I had known a vague feeling that sometime I would wake up and find that you and I were together. There was no reason for me to feel that way. Love does not need a reason, but I always felt like I was waiting around for you to grow up, but you had grown up faster than I had anticipated.

And here I was learning that you were engaged. I felt no sharp pain at that knowledge. In fact, I could not bring myself to realize that it was true. I remember kidding you about the ring and telling you that you had at last begun to show signs of getting beautiful. For weeks I searched the paper for an announcement of your marriage, but it was never there. I was always afraid it would be.

One day I met you in town; you were with Mr. Teeter, I believe, and you were still not married. There was no use kidding myself after that. I was lost. But with the war coming up there was nothing for me to do. At least, that is what I told myself, but my good resolutions were for nothing. I held out a long time, but finally lost. You do not have to guess at the rest.

The boys, no doubt, want to go to sleep and this is not a pleasant sound. Typewriters are not built to write love letters on, but there is little choice with me. When I write with a pen no one can read it. So I must forego the lavender stationery and the faint perfume, and since I lack experience—you have taught me all I know about the gentle art—this will have to serve as a love letter. Perhaps I can do better with practice. Should I try to improve my technique by writing to a lot of other girls?

Love Always,
Leland

Germany
June 4, 1945

My Dearest Letty:

Just came in from a pass to Paris and will have to go out on a patrol in a few minutes, but I can get a short letter written before I start. Tomorrow will be another day and another letter, but I had to write tonight and tell you that I still love you more than ever.

Letty, it is obvious that you do not understand me. All this time I have been trying to convince you that I am a reasonable man who takes no unfair advantage in an argument, but I seldom lose one. That is why I warned you that I was going to ask you to marry me as soon as I get home. That way, you could figure out all the arguments in advance, but I was still sure that I would win. I had no intention of taking No for an

Dearest Letty

answer, but I did not want you to be able to say that I took you by surprise. If I knew in advance just what I was going to say and you had to grope for words I would definitely have the advantage, but this way it is even. But I still expect to win the argument.

It would be silly to try to tell you what Paris is like with so short a time to write. That will have to wait. But I can say that it is beautiful and gay and all that you have ever heard it was. There is no food in the cafes, and we had to eat at the Red Cross clubs, but that was not bad. I found little for sale and the inflation is out of control, but I did manage to pick you a gift that I think you will like. It is not elaborate, but it is one of the few things that I could find and it seemed to fit your personality better than anything else that was for sale. It will be on the way as soon as I can get it into the mail. Patrol time.

Love Always,
Leland

Germany
June 5, 1945

My Darling:

Ever so often (every five minutes) something happens to remind me of you. You would be surprised at how my imagination stretches to include you in everything I happen to encounter. Just now some guy from New York sang a ballad called "Goodnight, Sweetheart" and all the time he was singing it I saw visions of myself saying the same things to you. It is a sentimental ditty and maybe you don't care for it, but I liked the way he sang it, for it seemed that you were near while I listened to it.

And when the lilacs bloom or the birds sing I think of how nice it would be to live them with you. It is always you.

Even when I see some contented housewife patiently pulling weeds in the garden I think how nice it would be to sit in the shade while you grew radishes and lettuce. (I'm sorry. I really meant the first part of the letter, but we will compromise on the garden. I'll discuss terms of that later.)

Yes, I remember Athleen, and the times I fished by her house, but I probably would not know her now. It has been quite a while and she has grown up. I also know Mary Nell. In fact, there are quite a few people in the county that I know and would like to see again. But there are many I knew once that I would not recognize. It will be fun to meet them all again and see how many faces I remember. Maybe you will go with me on a tour of the streets to see how many faces have changed. We did once, remember?

Letty, I wish I could tell you all about Paris, but there is too much to tell. It is the world's most beautiful city, and it is never dull. It has all the glamour, the poverty, the pathos and the beauty that you could imagine, but it would be easier to describe the places than the intangibles.

The place that interested me most was Notre Dame. It is quite a church and I am sending you a booklet that will describe it in detail. You might be interested to know that in the main auditorium it is 135 meters (150 yards) from the altar to the back of the room. This will give you some idea of the size, if you will remember that this is only a small part of the building. You would also be interested to see the strange figures of legendary animals that are carved in the stone along the eaves. These include huge bats, giant lizards, owls and dragons. The idea was, so it was explained to me, to scare people into acting like Christians.

Letty, I have a torturous job in front of me. They have us scheduled for a big parade tomorrow, and you know how I like parades. The heck of it is I have to sew on all the stripes, patches, Hershey bars that I never wear. They say I will also pin on my Good Conduct Ribbon and look like a soldier. So I have to get busy. I may wear my ribbons once more for you when I come home, but it is not my habit. Must get out my needle and thread.

Love Always,
Leland

Thamsbrück, Germany
June 10, 1945

My Dearest Letty:

There is nothing quite so satisfying as a good after-dinner cigar and the opportunity to write you a letter. But today is a lazy day. The sun is hot and the flies are terrible. Even the sparrows seem reluctant to stir. They

Dearest Letty

are as saucy as ever, and they sit at the eaves and scold but refuse to move.

Strawberries are ripening in my garden, but I am not allowed to pick them. They are the property of the German family whom we dispossessed, so I can merely look out the window and wish they were mine. The roses, too, are blooming now. The old lady who lived here spends a lot of time with them. She has them all staked and pruned, but I don't like the way she has them fixed.

Now, years ago when I enjoyed a local reputation as an expert in the field of roses I could give good solid advice on the culture of the plants. I could talk learnedly on budding, grafting, spraying and fertilizing. I could also discuss the advantages of the Radiance, the Sunburst, Paul Scarlet or Mrs. Charles Bell. I even made speeches on the subject before garden clubs. Didn't know that, did you?

It was a far cry from the speech I made yesterday. My subject on this occasion was the Japanese war machine. Tomorrow I shall discuss "What's Next in the Far East?"

Now don't get all excited. All this does not mean that I am off to China. It is merely that I am the lecturer on the Army's I & E Program. Naturally, I do not like the job. It requires some extra work and that is out of my line.

Which brings me to the question you asked me recently, viz. "What am I going to do after the war?" Frankly, I have no plans, except one. Even it is not necessarily a postwar plan. If I should happen to get a furlough before I am discharged it could only be a furlough plan. I plan to marry as soon as possible, and beyond that who knows? It is more fun to live without plans and take life as it comes. Of course, my wife might not like that. She may be the conservative type who likes to live by the budget and the clock. If she is, I shall have to convince her of the joys of living dangerously. If we should find that we could not live by our combined wits and we spent all the money I have in the bank and in soldier's deposit, then I might even be forced to take some kind of job. Or maybe she could be induced to support a husband. But I have no fear of the future. The way we love one another it will make no difference if I make fifteen dollars a week or ten thousand per year.

Incidentally, I got back a report on my first lesson from the university. I might even mail it to you and let you look it over. You would get nothing out of it for I cannot mail the books, but I could send the questions to give you an idea of what they are like.

Love Always,
Leland

Thamsbrück, Germany
June 12, 1945

My Dearest Letty:

Today I am getting a break, so I am using the time to write you a letter. The lecture I was supposed to give has been postponed, due to the fact that a Red Cross doughnut truck is scheduled to arrive at the same time the speech was to come off. What a break! Now I can get some decent coffee, omit the lecture and write you a letter.

You see, I am scheduled to speak about four times a week on the I & E program. That is the Instruction and Education program, in case you are wondering. They give me such subjects as "What is Germany's Place in the World of Tomorrow?" "How Strong Is the Japanese War Machine?" "Phases of the Pacific War." On each subject I am supposed to entertain the men for an hour and it is not easy. For the most part they are not even interested, so I have to resort to the tactics of Billy Sunday to get their attention.

Letty, you asked me how many points I have. I have a grand total of 83. The number necessary for discharge is 85, so you see I am just two short. But this does not mean that I am off to the Pacific. In fact, I doubt that I will ever get a tumble for the place. It seems that they are taking the low-point men there and I am in the upper bracket.

Surely you guessed that when I warned you that I was going to ask you to marry me as soon as I saw you. You knew I would never do that if I thought I would be off to fight again. As soon as it became apparent that my fighting days were over I began to think of marriage. The fact that I might not get a discharge for a few months did not matter. I only wanted to make sure that you did not find yourself married to a Joe who had lost a couple of legs in France.

I shall always love you.
Leland

Dearest Letty

Thamsbrück, Germany
June 13, 1945

My Dearest Letty:

There were no letters today or yesterday, which gives me a chance to catch up on some of my back mail. But I always have to take time out and write to you, no matter how high the pile of other letters happens to be.

But I have a better opportunity to write here than any place we have been. In the first place, I have a room to myself, at least it is supposed to be my room, but I have as much privacy as a goldfish. All the guys breeze in and out like it was a poolroom, for it is on the ground floor and is handy to reach. I don't mind that, but most of them have problems and that takes up time that I could use.

It is a comfortable room even if the old lady did take out all the good furniture. She left me enough. There are three tables, and most of them are piled high with magazines, mess kits, papers, shaving equipment and that sort of thing. The couch, under the south window, is one of those old velvet jobs, but it is deceivingly comfortable. The high straight back doesn't look like much, but it is a nice place to loaf. It also serves as a bed. One end is equipped with hinges so that it can be folded down to make it long enough for a man.

All the pictures have been removed from the walls and in their place is Army equipment. My coat hangs at the right of the door, a dozen bandoliers of rifle ammunition is above the couch and over my desk are a pair of German binoculars and a German pistol in shoulder holster. These two items I plan to bring home with me, if some man doesn't offer me a lot more than they are worth. Leaning against the right side of the desk are my other two guns. One is an Army Springfield with a telescope sight. These are rare. Then there is my pet gun. It is a German Walther patent automatic shotgun. I have sent several guns home but am afraid to risk this one in the mail, so I plan to carry it with me.

The only other pieces of furniture in the room are the wicker chair I am sitting in and the desk. The desk is a simple job and is about as neat as you might expect it to be, which means it is piled high with all the odds and ends that happen to come my way. Heading left to right, you find:

One reading lamp with parchment shade and shining brass base, a pile of unanswered letters, one letter I have just finished (to Aaron), a

To the Elbe River

257

stack of books that includes three college texts, a dictionary, the Lord Charnwood biography of Abraham Lincoln, White's historical novel, *Look Away, Look Away,* a guidebook to Paris, a leather notebook, and a package of pipe cleaners. In the center of the desk, directly behind the typewriter, are a pack of envelopes, three pencils, and a mahogany alarm clock, time 1000. The right side is the most cluttered. Here are the assignments for the correspondence course, an unfinished lesson, four magazines, three unfinished lectures (which reminds me, I must get to work on them), a fountain pen, a penknife, a pack of cigarettes, two pipes, a box of matches and an ashtray.

The ashtray would give you a laugh. It is the bald head of a typical German, mounted on a porcelain base. The pate is bald as an egg, and the ears stick out like sails on a yacht. The face is a study in horror. The eyes protrude and the mouth is wide open. This forms the receptacle for cigarette stubs. Beneath the chin are the words "O, diese Stuern!" I have no idea what they mean, but diese means "these."

Not much of a room, you will say, but, believe me, if I had had one like it last winter it would have looked like a dream cottage. Now it is merely a room of dreams, if you know what I mean. I keep telling you my dreams so much and so often that you should be familiar with them by now. But I must tell you again that I am still in love with you. My dreams begin there, but that is only the beginning. There is no end.

Love Always,
Leland

Thamsbrück, Germany
June 17, 1945

My Dearest Letty:

Even though I should be preparing the lecture I'm supposed to give to B troop tomorrow, I am busily writing you a letter. But you are always giving me an excuse to get out of something that I do not want to do anyway. Nice girl. Thank you.

But if I keep this up what am I going to tell the boys in B troop tomorrow? Drittler is over there, you see, and he will be expecting me

Dearest Letty

to tell them something. Now, what will happen is that I shall fool around with this letter and all the other things I really want to do until I barely have time to throw something together. Then I shall go to work like a beaver until the last minute to find a thing to say. But I always make it at the last minute.

Letty, did I tell you that this division has been placed in Category IV, which means that it is to be demobilized? That will have little effect on the men who are in it, but those who have enough points will be discharged and those who do not will be sent to other units. In other words, there will be no more Victory Division when they get around to splitting it up. The men will go in every direction and it will be like starting all over again. Of course, I have no idea where I shall end up, but we have long since passed the stage where we sweat out such things. I have decided that, no matter what they give me to do, I have already seen something worse so there is nothing to worry about. However, there is an excellent chance I shall be in the states before too many months.

I was glad to learn that you decided to take the Mauldin cartoon book. There are many cartoons in it that you will not appreciate fully, for you have not seen the things that inspired them. But I think you will find an appealing humor in all of them. I have a collection here by Sgt. Baker of the Sad Sack, which I shall send you to go along with Joe and Willie. Between those three characters you would be able to form a pretty sharp picture of what life in the Army is like.

Letty, this may border on gossip, but it is a situation that I am sure has affected enough people to demand a place among the postwar problems. Only a slight knowledge of biology is sufficient to understand why it is so common, but biology does not offer a solution.

The wife of one of my good friends has written him that she wants a divorce and has wanted one for many months. She did not tell him sooner because she felt that it would not be good for his morale while the war was going on. Now that it is all over and she does not think he is going to the Pacific it is time to inform him of the state of her affections. The inference being that she waited this long on the odd chance that a sniper's bullet might save her the trouble of telling him that she did not love him any more.

It hurts him more than anyone could guess. In fact, there are only a couple of guys in the troop who are close enough to him to even know that it has happened. He is an excellent actor and no one else suspects that there is anything wrong. He is the last man I would have guessed would be a victim of a thing like that. I did not know his wife, of course, but I knew him to be a settled man and I was also sure that he did not marry on a sudden impulse. I also knew that he was much in love with his wife, for he was always sending her little things and talking about her in a way the devoted husband talks. In his behavior he never did a single thing that would have caused her to be the least bit jealous, even if she could have made herself invisible and followed him everywhere he went. It just did not seem possible that a thing like that would happen to him.

We can see why it happens, but we cannot find a way to make it easier on the victims. Not all of the wounds of the war will have been caused by shrapnel or bullets. No doubt you have seen examples of the same thing, and I have seen men who forgot that they had wives. This will result in a drastic change in moral values, just as all wars do, but it will be painful, for there are many who are victims of the change who were perfectly satisfied to behave along the old patterns.

Letty, you remember my writing about Jim and Hattie Ling. Well, Jim was missing in action just before the war ended and Hattie is almost wrecked from worry for him. I have written her a couple of letters and tried to sound as hopeful as I truthfully could. I told her how Aaron and a lot of other boys were missing for so long and still came through in good shape. I knew Jim was captured, but I did not tell Hattie that he was captured by a bunch of SS men. I am almost certain that they killed him, for they had a habit of doing that sort of thing. Jim and Hattie were a couple of the nicest people I knew. When we were at Indiantown Gap and Pine Camp, I often went to their place for supper and enjoyed the evening thoroughly. There is some hope that Jim is still alive but it is slim.

Well, I have given you a long letter without even telling you what you wanted to know. One of your letters just came and you repeated the question of what they wanted with me at squadron headquarters. Lady, they were assigning me the dubious honor of making the series of speeches I have been complaining about. And it is no fun. But it does take a lot of my time. If I did not love you so much I would be at the job of preparing something to say right now instead of giving you all the latest gossip. But

I do have to get on the job or the boys in B troop will have nothing to listen to tomorrow.

Love Always,
Leland

Heldra, Germany
June 23, 1945

My Dearest Letty:

Well, they finally gave me some time off from the lecture tour (it really amounted to that) and I am now able to do some of the things I want to do: a bit of reading, writing and playing. Nothing could be nicer.

That is, nothing could be nicer as long as I have to stay in this place. Frankly, I don't like the Fatherland or any of the people in it. The feeling does not seem to be shared by as many American soldiers as I thought. Everyone seems to be coming around to the idea that they are pretty nice people after all.

We read stories and see pictures of the treatment given to the prisoners and it makes me wonder who won the war. A couple of months ago when we were still fighting, all the men seemed to resent the fact that the Germans whom we were sending back to the prison cages were getting better treatment than the average soldier could have. They made violent speeches on the subject while they huddled in the rain and waited for the order to move up. Of course, I shared the resentment.

Now I find that these same soldiers are thinking the same thoughts that led to the easy treatment of prisoners. They are saying that the Germans were poor, misinformed saps and are not really what they thought. It is not too hard to see why they get this impression. On the surface, these people seem to be simple country folk with not a touch of ambition and no thought of cruelty. They are obedient and seem anxious to do anything the soldier wants done. They even act as if they are glad enough that we are here. The boys fall for the line.

But when I look at these same simple country folk I do not see the harmless people who are glad we are here. I see the same little men who yelled "Heil Hitler" the loudest at all the party rallies. I remember the thin, scared look on the faces of the slave laborers who once worked these farms. I cannot forget that the plan was clear to me then, that they wanted the laborers so that they would not have to do all the work, for their job would be simply supervision and carrying the whip. Most of all, I remember the stories of the American men who had spent months in German prison camps. Civilians claim to know nothing of what happened there, but the men tell me that on many occasions it was the soldier who saved them from being beaten by these same harmless civilians. The only reason the soldiers wanted to save them was to make them rebuild the railroads.

I remember all this and they seem to forget. Perhaps I hold a grudge too long. I may be all wrong and they may be right. If they can think of the whole war as if it were a baseball game they took it much more lightly than I did. If I did not know better I should say that they had never been as badly scared as I have been. But I know better than that. Therefore I cannot understand them.

But this is supposed to be a letter to let you know that I am still crazy about you and to remind you that we are going to have plenty of time to discuss all this later. Then we can talk of the Germany of the postwar months or of Paris or Kansas City or any other place we choose. Or we might only discuss the art of growing cabbage or any such prosaic subject.

Since I started this, we have moved to a new town. It is only about forty or so miles from where we were. The name of the town is Heldra. It is west of the old town so you see we are moving in the right direction. But we still have some work to do, and I do not know when there will be ships to take us to the states.

Hope you don't mind this political letter, but I just happened to have that on my mind when I sat down to write.

Love Always,
Leland

Heldra, Germany
June 25, 1945

My Dearest Letty:

All afternoon I have been working on my lessons like a devoted schoolboy and now I am taking time out to do what has been on my mind all this time. I could hardly quit in the middle of one of the questions, and I kept thinking that I would finally match the end of an answer with the end of a page, but it would never come out that way. I ended up by simply finishing the whole lesson, except for the English grammar, and now I am free of the whole thing. The only trouble is it is 2300 hours (eleven o'clock to you) and I shall have to sleep some. So you will have to be satisfied with a couple of pages and the assurance that I am still in love with you.

I said it is eleven o'clock, but I am not sure of it. I have three timepieces and they seem to be like women at a Home Demonstration Club meeting; they never agree. There is my old pocket Elgin. It has been dependable for years, but of late it has shown signs of going temperamental. Perhaps this is because it has not been cleaned since long before I left the states, and there is bound to be a lot of battle dust in the case. Or it might be that it has grown jealous because I acquired the other mechanical contrivances for measuring time. The clock on my desk is a marvel of symmetrical design and beauty. It is a miniature of the huge grandfather clocks so popular in this country. But it, too, has picked up a lot of dust while riding in the pocket of an armed car. But while dust makes the Elgin run faster it makes the clock go slower. Then there is the new wristwatch. A few watches were sent in with the P.X. rations and they drew my name as being one of the lucky men who were allowed to buy one. It is a nice-looking watch with a modern design done in stainless steel and soft leather. It is supposed to be shockproof, and the odd numbers on the dial are represented by luminous dots. The sweep second hand completes the modern touch, but the catch is that the hand will not keep sweeping. It stops at four-hour intervals just like it belonged to a union. A touch of the stem is enough to start it again, but I have to refer to one of the other timepieces to see how it should be set. Which one? That is always the question. The only solution seems to be to send the two watches to Uncle Richard Roberts at Moreland and have them repaired, toss the clock into the gutter and take my GI watch back from my radio operator (Rafter), who has been carrying it since my life became burdened with so many tickers. There is a sand glass in the kitchen, which the lady used for the purpose of timing the boiling of eggs, and I could get that. But the sand runs down every three minutes, so it is no better than the new watch.

To the Elbe River

Letty, we are now in the country of the famous wild boar, and I have been out hunting him this morning. All I saw were tracks and wallows. The hills are steep and rugged and there are plenty of places for the hogs to hide. These are supposed to be the genuine Russian tuskers, and if this is true they should be pretty fierce. They tell me it is non-habit-forming to wound one of them if you do not manage to climb a tree in a hurry. A 300-pounder with a four-inch tusk could make a man climb a tree in a hurry.

This is also a sample of Germany's vacationland. People come here for the scenery and for the mountain climbing. Yesterday, we climbed to one of the clubhouses used by the hikers. There are no hikers now, of course, and we had the place to ourselves.

It is on the point of one of the highest mountains. The front overlooks a cliff and from there the mountain drops steeply to the valley floor and the river. The place is lonely and quiet. There is no sign of human life. Far below, in the checkered fields, the naked eye picks up tiny moving dots like bugs crawling across a checkerboard. Binoculars reveal that these are men plodding slowly behind yokes of patient oxen. The towns become splotches of red in the green carpet because all the roofs are red tile and the grass covers the rest of the valley.

There is one break in the green. That is the river. The river is a ribbon thrown carelessly across the floor as if a child had cast it aside, or as if a seamstress had been in the act of sewing it on some tiny garment and the telephone had told her that her husband was home from the war. She dumps it on the floor but trails one end of it with her as she hurries out to meet him. This is the river and it marks a crooked trail until it disappears through a door between two hills.

But I am nearing the end of a third sheet when I had thought to write only two. As you always say, there is no news, but to me there is no place to stop. The only way I can think to break this off so that I can get some sleep is to simply say "I love you" and then stop.

Love Always,
Leland

Heldra, Germany
June 28, 1945

My Dearest Letty:

It may be that you are tired of trying to read my letters on this rough paper and in the stinted type I use. But the truth is, the one thing the Army teaches is the value of being able to improvise. If you do not have the material the book calls for, simply substitute whatever you have and accomplish the mission with that.

Well, the mission of all my letters is to tell you that I am still dreaming of you all the days and that nothing else can be as important to me as the fact that you keep remembering me and loving me. So, if I do not have the smooth paper Miss Post says is acceptable for such messages I simply roll a sheet of the rough German pulp into the old portable and say the same things I would say on scented linen if that were available. Knowing you as I do, I am sure it would not make the least difference if I used faded newsprint.

The enclosed picture is the result of the same kind of improvisation. There are practically no facilities for developing and printing films over here, and as a result we rigged up our own darkroom and printed a few. At the other place we had a nice setup but were short on print paper. We even rigged up an enlarging machine from a tin bucket, an old camera, a reading lamp and whatever happened to be lying around. I managed to develop this one and it turned out beautifully. I even enlarged one print from it (which I sent to Mother), then we had to move and leave most of the equipment. The paper we got here was poor and the negative was damaged in the move, so it turned out like this.

No, those are not chickens I am holding; they are pheasants. They were killed in the area between Versen and Munchengladbach when we were there last winter. I wrote you that we were eating pheasant and deer regularly then.

Well we are eating fish now. We got about ten pounds yesterday and about the same amount today. We also took pictures of them and I shall send you some samples to make you hungry when they are finished.

Letty, you said you would meet me when I came home IF I WANTED YOU TO. You knew all the time I was crazy for you to do just that. How do you suppose I keep my poise here while I am waiting for the transportation home if I do not think all the time that you are waiting for me? If you could wait for me in New York it would be just a couple of days that I would not have to sweat out, as they say in the Army. If it is at the train, that will have to serve.

But don't get any ideas into your head that you will not let me kiss you there. For you shall. Even if the whole town is there.

The thing that is holding us up is shipping space. The sick and wounded men, the former prisoners and the divisions that are on their way to the Far East have priority over us in the matter of shipping, so we have to hang around until there is room for us to ride. However, rumor has it that we may not be around too long, a few months at most.

However long it may be I shall love you just as much when the waiting time is over as I do now, and that is more than you may be able to guess.

Love Always,
Leland

Heldra, Germany
July 1, 1945

My Dearest Letty:

At the moment there seems to be nothing better to do than to write you a letter. In fact, there is nothing better at any moment unless it is to see you. Now please don't look too closely at that sentence; I know it has an odd construction and that is being charitable. But the fact is, I have been reading a book called *You Wouldn't Know Me From Adam* by one Colonel Stoopnagle. All of his sentences come out something like that, and I hope you will understand that I may have absorbed some of his style. Please don't be alarmed, for I promise it won't stick with me long.

The colonel is a great guy. He takes great pains to describe the Adam that people wouldn't know people from, and the Mr. Updigit who works in the candy factory. It seems that Mr. Updigit's present job is to not touch the candy that is not touched by human hands; however, he is hoping for a promotion to the front office, where he will be in charge of Letting Well Enough Alone.

The book is liberally sprinkled with poetry, which the colonel claims to be a new type of verse. Sometimes the syllables are switched and this he calls Vice Verse. A nice sample is the one on going to church:

> Presiding at our midday fiest
> Is Father Murphy, parish priest;
> But I prefer our local Vicker,
> Because he ends his sermons quicar.

Or

> A mouse in church, I've never seen;
> A church-mouse is a mouse I meen.
> I may as well give up the surch;
> I've yet to find a mouse in chearch.

Then there was one more that I must quote, and then I promise to forget the whole thing:

> Roses are red violets.
> Are blue, Sugar.
> Is sweet and so——
> Are you?

Come to think of it, that is a good question at that. You are always preaching to me to be a good little boy, and I have never once given you a bit of moral advice. Which is a little strange. Why? Because it is you who needs the admonition to be a good little girl. In the first place, no one ever accused me of having been anything but the perfect specimen of morality. Fond mothers used me as the example when talking to their little boys, before the boys were old enough to hear about George Washington.

But what fond mother ever said to her little girl: "Now be good and you will grow up to be a nice young lady like Letty?" Of course, they might have said, "Don't let it happen to you" when they were giving their little girls advice and the little girls mentioned you. And you are always telling me to be a good! Imagine that!

Women usually marry men with the idea that they can reform them. They like men with a colorful past, because to them habits are like furniture: They are made to be rearranged. However, I make no claim that

I am marrying you to reform you; that would be impossible. Besides, I don't want you reformed. I want you to stay like you are, mischief and all. After all, why should I want the girl I fell in love with a long time ago to change into some other pattern?

Love Always,
Leland

Heldra, Germany
July 3, 1945

My Dearest Letty:

Of what shall I write today? It is a good question and I am wondering what we would be talking about if I were at home and there was nothing for us to do but spend the long hours together.

We could go into all the local gossip, of course. I am far behind on that so that now I do not know who is doing the things we would never have thought of them doing. Or you could spend the day telling me all the things that have happened to you since I went away. That could consume a whole rainy afternoon.

You could tell me which is more interesting: working in the city or in the old hometown. I have thought it would be more interesting to work in the town where you knew everyone and could fill in all the blank spots in the picture of the small-town drama. You could guess, with a surprising degree of accuracy, just why Mrs. Smith happened to call Mrs. Wilson at exactly three o'clock on three successive days. The fact that you guessed wrong would not take any interest out of the game.

But in the city it would all be so impersonal that it would not seem to matter who called whom nor why. There the people lose their individuality and become just crowds. In the case of the utilities they are simply a lot of disembodied gremlins that kick out plugs or whatever it is that happens when someone wants a telephone connection.

All this you could tell me and I could tell you a couple of things in return, such as how much I have missed you all the years and how much I love you.

Then it might be that we would not talk much at all. Sometimes we didn't, you know, and those were the best parts of the evenings I spent with you. We didn't talk because there seemed to be no necessity to say anything. There was the quiet, silent understanding that made words superfluous.

But since I cannot talk to you this afternoon I am puzzled as to what I should write about. Perhaps I should tell you that some of the guns I sent home have arrived. They are all old collector's pieces and you will care nothing about them. I warn you that they are one of the many things that will clutter up the house. Many times you will threaten to throw them away, but you will never get brave enough, just as you will never get brave enough to burn my pipes or poison my dogs.

Incidentally, I have a dog that lives right there in Russellville. Yes, a city dog, believe it or not. If you happen to know Murry Colburn and if you should pass his home you could see my dog there. He is a red hound with a white tip on his tail and a white chest. His official registration name is Sunny Valley Spike from the tip on his tail. The name was shortened to simply Spike but I usually called him The Pooch. He didn't seem to object to that, just as he never objected to anything I ever did.

Skipper is dead now as is Lady, Steve, Rick, Ada, Pilot and a lot of other good dogs that once followed me around. But they were a grand lot.

Hattie still lives, or at least she was alive when I had my last report from West Texas. She is a collie I owned when I lived out there. Technically, she is still mine although I have not seen her in almost four years. However, much as I liked her, I shall not claim her when I come home again.

But I must call an end to this and fix myself some lunch. It is now 2:30 and I have not eaten since breakfast. The kitchen is in another town and we are living on field rations, which means that we are doing our own cooking. We can eat when we get hungry, but there can be little variety in our meals. I am ready for the kitchen to move down here and start cooking for me.

Love Always,
Leland

Heldra, Germany
July 8, 1945

My Dearest Letty:

I have been writing all morning and have not turned out a single letter. You see, I have been on an assignment to write a short account of
the activities of the troop for the last year. It is to be the basis of a book
that is to be published on the history of the 85th cavalry.

Letty, I loved the half-dozen letters I had from you in the past few
days. They all came at once and piled upon my desk to be answered. But
I could not answer them all. I could not, for example, figure out an adequate answer for the one in which you announced that in one short year
you had grown a backbone and begun to show people that they could not
push you around. Secretly, I have always wondered why you had to be the
nice little girl who was always getting other people out of jams and helping
them get the things they wanted but never taking anything for yourself.
You were never spineless when it came to defending someone else, but (I
can say it now, maybe) you were an awful flop when the interests of Letty
were at stake. I have often wanted to tell you to chuck the whole bunch
over and strike out for yourself, but I could not. I often wanted to tell you
to marry me and we would grow up together, but I could not do that either.
But suddenly you learned it all without my saying it and that was the best
way. Now I can ask you to marry me as soon as I get home and we can
start right in living without having to grow up at all.

Somewhere at home I have a little book called *Dreams* by Olive
Schreiner. A little allegory in it is called Life and Love. Remind me to
have you read it as soon as we collect our combined literature. It followed
the same line of thought that you have been developing in your letters,
but I know you have never read it.

Yes, there will be hours and days when we will not be so near other
people that we will have to listen to their problems through the walls
and when we can do our own arguing with no one to hear us. I don't
know where it will be, maybe Lake Placid, maybe the Rockies, or maybe
we shall decide that we can only afford the Ozarks, and that will make
little difference. The main thing will be that there will be no one to tell
us what to do. Of course, I shall tell you what to do and you will tell me,

but I have a feeling that neither of us will do it. I think we shall only tell each other so that we may have the pleasure of refusing.

I must write a few more letters now.

Love Always,
Leland

Heldra, Germany
July 10, 1945

My Dearest Letty:

No matter how old you may think me to be, I still have energy enough to get up at three o'clock in the morning to go hunting. I did this morning but I didn't kill a thing.

But I did not regret the loss of sleep, even if I failed to kill a wild boar. It may sound crazy to say that there is some compensation in seeing the world of the woodlands wake up. It is one of those values that defy expression. It cannot be captured in print; perhaps an artist could come nearer expressing it. Since I cannot paint, I do not know about that, but the setting seems to lend itself to canvas more than to black and white.

Now don't be surprised if I should drag you out of bed some morning at three o'clock and tell you to get your brushes and that we were going to trap the elusive dawn. It would be well worth the try. But anything we should decide to do will be fun, if we do it together.

Well, Letty, the War Department got around to announcing the time when the Fifth Armd. Division is scheduled to go home. The plan is subject to change without notice, as are all plans of the Army. Then it is also possible that they might ship me to another outfit. This is not likely so long as they select their men for transfer under the present rules. But rules, too, are subject to change.

The men in this outfit are shifting around quite a lot. They are even taking Modlin, who came in at the same time I did. However, he does not have as many points as I do. He did not get wounded, and that gives me five more points.

Well, I guess the old town is growing dull with the summer heat. It is usually that way at this time of the year. The farmers are busy, the rest of the people are lethargic, and the streets are deserted except on Saturday.

However, so long as Dad and Elmer Rackley have things under control there is nothing to worry about. I can even guess the trend of their conversation, so Russellville is not so different after all. They seem to get along wonderfully.

Love Always,
Leland

Heldra, Germany
July 12, 1945

My Dearest Letty:

Somehow I did not get around to writing the letter I had planned for last night, so I am trying it this evening. The slight delay could not make much difference, for you probably have half a dozen letters in the mail now and would not notice one more or less. Of all the things I do to occupy my time, the letters to you are the most pleasant. They are the nearest I can come to talking to you and the only means at my disposal of making you mad. But, boy, when I see you! I always enjoyed pestering you even when you were a kid. Bertrand Russell could probably offer a scientific reason for it.

Today I had a letter from one of my young cousins. Her dad and I grew up together, and to me she should still be a player with dolls. But she is a sophomore in high school and her letter is mature. Perhaps I should not even know her if I met her on the street. You may have to extricate me from a lot of jams like that. I always tried to remember names, but now I shall be so far behind that there will be plenty of people I don't know. You can stand at my elbow and tell me who they are. It is an old practice among politicians to have a stooge to remind them of names. Want to be my stooge? No? Too bad, I shall have to hire one. And I had always hoped to marry one.

All the time I wanted to marry the most wonderful girl in the world. You see, I have always thought of myself as having excellent taste in matters feminine. Girls had to measure up to a certain standard to interest me seriously. I am not trying to pat myself on the back; I am merely saying that it took you to measure up to all the standards I had set.

I was not trying to see if you would wait for me when I resisted the temptation to ask you to marry me long ago. I tried to explain my reason then as fully and as honestly as I knew how. It was difficult to do without sounding dramatic, and I may have failed. I did not want us to talk of how dulcet and decorous it was to be crippled by a war that was too big for us to fight against; I merely wanted to save you from as much of it as possible. If it were to be done over, perhaps I should do the same thing again. But all the time I was so much in love with you that it was not so easy. Now I am glad you did not object to my behavior too much.

Tomorrow the squadron S-3 has a new job figured out for me. I am to be head of a school in basic English composition. It is all part of the Army's I & E program, and is designed to fill in the gap of slack time before the division sails for the states. Since there is nothing compulsory about the men taking the course, it should not be difficult to teach. They will have a certain amount of interest at the beginning and this is essential in this kind of school. It will mean some extra work but I don't mind that.

One thing that has always puzzled me is that people always insist that I am a teacher. I can never figure it out. My father was the first, or perhaps it was my grandfather. When I was a kid of 14 they insisted that I take the county teacher's examination, just for the heck of it. Out of pity or for curiosity the board gave me a passing grade, with the footnote that I was too young to actually teach. When I was older, Dad insisted that I try the profession. In those days, I thought fathers knew best. I was a terrible flop but the failure marked me with a mark I have never been able to erase. Everywhere I went people took one look at me and said, "You are a teacher, aren't you?" They never accuse me of being a farmer, a salesman, a digger of ditches, a carpenter, a grower of roses, or a hobo and loafer. In fact, the curse still stays with me and they insist that I am a teacher instead of a soldier. It is strange that my grossest failure should be remembered the longest, but such is true.

Must try to rig up something for the boys to do tomorrow.

I shall be expecting you at the station.

Love Always,
Leland

To the Elbe River

Heldra, Germany
July 13, 1945

My Dearest Letty:

Your letter was the only one that came in the evening mail, so there seems nothing for me to do but write you now. The rest of the day's work has been finished.

It was not too hard, even if they did open up a new program on us. In the morning we had to take a road hike of sixteen kilometers (about ten miles). After lunch I had to take over the school in English Composition, which I wrote you about a couple of days ago.

The school seems to be working out OK in spite of our limited equipment. So far, we only have a blackboard and a piece of chalk. There are no textbooks even though they have been on order. The result is that I have to write my own. It takes a couple of pages each day, but it should prove profitable if we have to keep the school going for long. The way I figure it I can save the pages, and after a time I shall have enough to make a complete text. Then when the war is over and I come home I can have it published and live off the royalties. Simple, eh? There is nothing to it.

You should see a sample of the text. It looks something like this: [A long discussion of the proper uses of "shall" and "will" and commas and of Duvall's rules of composition follows.]

Now, please do not get the idea that I am going to start the use of this stuff in my letters to you. It really has no use there, and I do not know how to use it anyway. Like so many men who have attempted to write books, I do not have the least idea what it is all about. The whole trick lies in putting something before the reader that looks good and gives him the impression that it is important. In the Army, the idea is to impress the High Brass that you are doing something, give them a program that looks good on paper, and the colonel will get a letter of commendation on his efficiency report. This is the whole secret.

My letters to you are not in that category. They are supposed to keep you convinced that I am still in love with you until I can come home and keep you convinced the easy way. In order to do this, they should be bright and interesting, and none of this will help make them this way. I can't see how I happened to get off into the dry subject of English classes in an Army school. It just happened that way and I promise I shall not do it again.

Dearest Letty

Your letter today was bright and cheerful. You were elated over the fact that, at last, you had managed to catch up on all the sleep that you had been missing and that you had a new girl working in the office. That and the unmentionable fact that you thought you had discovered another skeleton in my closet. Well, I hate to disillusion you but you are mistaken. Barbara is no skeleton (this is evident, unless she has lost a lot of weight since I saw her) and she has never been in my figurative closet. Nor can my eternal cheerfulness be disturbed by bringing her up, so you failed dismally in making me mad. See, all the time you thought you had me seething and, in fact, offered to give me a pill if I were not, but you only underestimated my capacity for good humor. Some day I shall tell you all about my old girlfriends, but she will not be on the list. I knew her quite well, of course, but never had a date with her.

But you must call this a letter, for I have to write my text for tomorrow's class. It has to be good enough to get the approval of the major in S-3.

Love Always,
Leland

Heldra, Germany
July 15, 1945

My Dearest Letty:

Today I have already written a whole chapter on my proposed textbook on English and have finished a lesson in my correspondence. You might think that I have written enough today, but there still remains the letter to you that I promised yesterday. It may not be such a wonderful letter, for I have exhausted my supply (quota would be a better word) of adjectives and idioms for today. I can at least tell you that I am still in love with you. At the risk of boring you, I could include another page of the book and let you pass judgment on it.

After the usual rules and examples of English grammar, there is the part that concerns itself with the division of composition known as "description." The chapter for today contrasts artistic and scientific description. The example of scientific description, as yet uncorrected, goes something like this:

"This pencil is a wooden cylinder, three-eighths of an inch in diameter and five inches long. Around one end is a form-fitting metal band, one-half an inch long. Half of this band extends beyond the wooden cylinder and holds a red rubber eraser. The other end of the pencil is whittled to a point and this exposes the end of a fine cylinder of lead, which fills the center of the pencil. The entire body of the pencil is covered with a coat of fine-textured yellow paint."

Revision should turn that into a fair sample of scientific description. Artistic description is not so easy. For my sample of that I chose an old living room, which I happened to visit once. It was so impressive that even now I remember details of the finishing. The sample runs something like this:

"The room was dusted meticulously, the curtains were drawn back, and the chairs were placed with precise care as if the place were occupied by two maiden aunts who were expecting company. One immediately felt as if the room should be a part of a conducted tour of the city's interesting places. 'Specimen of Nineteenth Century American home,' the folder should say, for the room was complete and unchanged from the time when some former owner had finished it in perfect taste in 1890. The green curtains, the light-blue walls, the mahogany casements, the wide-open fire, the pattern fire screen: None of these had been changed. Nor could one discern a single alteration in the arrangement of the books in the mahogany-and-glass bookcase. Longfellow, Whittier, Hawthorne (except for *The Scarlet Letter*), William Dean Howells, and Emerson were in complete sets, all bound in soft leather in blending colors. Present, too, in smaller parcels, were Keats, Shelley, Byron, Cooper, and Wordsworth. Apparently, so far as the former owner was concerned, the publishers refused to print modern trivia on presses made divine by the production of the acme of all literature. When he sniffed the faint aroma of lilac in this prim and precise room he felt that he had, through some mysterious miscalculation of the old man who manipulates the eternal hourglass, wandered into the wrong decade, and, indeed, the wrong century."

It is my hope that the contrast is enough to make my meaning clear to the men. It should be, for they are smart boys and with them one can afford to cover a subject lightly. They grasp ideas readily and it is not too difficult to teach a class like that.

Letty, there is still no news of when we will ship out from here. The only thing I have is the story I sent you a few days ago, and so far as I know the plan has not been changed. Remember, you planned to meet me at the station and I'm expecting you to keep your promise.

Love Always,
Leland

Heldra, Germany
July 22, 1945

My Dearest Letty:

Just because I have not written you in a few days, please don't get the idea that I don't love you anymore or that I am on my way home. It is just that we have been on one of those highly secret missions. They gave us no warning that we were going out but simply told us to pack up. Then we were not told where we were going or what we were going to do. When we got there, it developed that the whole Army in Europe was pulling one of those sudden shakedown inspections. The idea was to put the German civilians on the ball and to find any guns that they may have hidden.

It was a pretty thorough job, too. We searched every house and other building in the American part of Germany. All traffic was stopped so that the word could not circulate as to what was going on. It did not hurt the German people, you understand, for there was no damage to any of the property. Of course, the military government dealt with those who had hidden guns, but the others were not harmed.

From your letters I gather that you do not like to be neglected in the matter of writing. Some day I shall take time out and tell you a million reasons why I failed to write at the times you expected letters. If there is one thing I am good at doing, it is making excuses for doing the things people think I should do. Given three thousand miles and a war, I can explain away anything. The nice part of it is, you will never be able to catch up with any liberty I may have taken with the truth.

When the critical score is finally announced, it may be low enough to give me a discharge. It might not seem exactly fair to take one while there is still a war going on. I had not given much thought to that angle, but the fact is that I have grown tired of having someone tell me exactly what to do all the time that I might take a discharge without even thinking about it.

Then, too, there might be a few people who would consider five major campaigns enough. As it is, my luck probably ran pretty low at times and I might not get by Tokyo as safely as I did this part of the world. This game does not contribute to longevity, and I am selfish enough to want to grow old with you.

Love Always,
Leland

Heldra, Germany
July 24, 1945

My Dearest Letty:

In exactly ten minutes I shall have to quit this letter and go on a parade. (You know how I like them.) So I am in no humor to write to anyone but you. I shall have little of this written then, and when I come back the tone of the letter will improve no end.

It is to be a big parade with a general and a band. Our troop is receiving a special citation for alleged outstanding work, and when they pass the reviewing stand the band will play a special salute. The colors will stop before us for a special playing of "To the Colors" and our troop guidon will have a special ribbon pinned on it by the general. I still don't like it. Parades have no appeal to me. I keep thinking of all the boys who helped do the same job and are not there to receive the credit. Formality beats me anyway.

Well, the parade is over and it was not so bad; the general decided not to make a speech and that cut the whole thing short. It was thoughtful of him. Few people would have neglected such a chance to appease their ego, but he did and I appreciated it.

General Oliver is a pretty good Joe, and I have always admired and respected him. He is smart enough to know what the score is, and that is the biggest thing that can be said for a man over here. Dumbness is one thing that is inexcusable in this game. He is a pretty human sort of a guy, too. He understands men well enough to know what they are capable of doing and he does not try to drive them beyond that point.

Another thing in his favor is that he is not afraid. It was not necessarily his job to prowl around where the guns were shooting, but it was not uncommon to see him up with the front men. I should say there are few better division commanders in the whole Army.

Well, Letty, since I try to tell you the straight truth about everything, I might as well let you in on this: Right now, it is a race with time to decide whether I will go home with the division or be delayed. Please don't get all excited about it and don't think I have not been telling as much as I knew. According to the new order, all men who do not have enough points to qualify for a discharge will be shipped out of the division in a few days. The only thing that will keep me in the division until it goes to the states is for the final critical score to be announced before I ship out. If that happens to be less than 83, I shall stay with my old outfit and go home with it; if the score is delayed or if it happens to be higher than 83, I shall be shipped to some other unit. It might be an occupational force, or a unit headed for the Far East; there is no predicting the destiny of a guy in the Army.

That is why you were foolish to fall in love with a guy like that, but no matter where they send me I shall be loving you as much as I always have, maybe more. Anywhere the Army may send me, it will not be long until I shall be calling you on the phone from New York or San Francisco and telling you that I am on my way home. I know if it is two months or four, you will be waiting just the same.

Perhaps I shouldn't have said there was a chance of my coming home early. It has always been my aim to not tell you a lot of rosy dreams that could not come true; this time I let my enthusiasm run away with me. No matter what happens, remember that I shall go on loving you just the same.

Love Always,
Leland

Heldra, Germany
July 27, 1945

My Darling:
While all the boys are gone to the show, I am taking the time to write a letter. It is supposed to be a good show, too. It is a French stage show

called *Oui Oui* (pronounced wee, wee), which means Yes Yes. They say it is pretty good, but I have no taste for it now.

The reason, I suppose, is that I saw the Bob Hope Show yesterday, so I could not appreciate the second-class comedy while I remember him so vividly. He is an excellent showman for the average dogface. Soldiers are easily entertained, anyway, if the cast is plain old American. They applaud the old gags as well as the new ones if they are told well, and Hope can tell a story. He is also good at feeling the pulse of the crowd so that he never lets the show lag. There is never a dull moment when he is master of ceremonies. This show was staged in an old German hangar and the whole roof had been knocked off by American planes. This left the ragged walls around the platform and the boys swarmed over them and perched there so that they could look down on the stage. Hope warned all the actors when they came out that they had better make their acts good, for they were surrounded. Said it looked like a bobby trap to him.

The actors must have taken the hint, for they all did an excellent job. Colonna went over big, as did Jack Pepper. It goes without saying that the boys all liked Patty Thomas, who did several songs.

Letty, I mailed a box to you today. It contained some of the odds and ends that I have acquired since I came over, but there is nothing that you will find interesting. There is a blank picture album that you may want to fill up sometime. There is also a nice tobacco leather folder that one of the boys gave me, and I want to keep it as well as the leather cigar case that another guy gave me. There is also a plate that Shryer bought in Mastrich, Holland. It is supposed to commemorate the freeing of the city from German occupation, but I suspect that some smart pottery maker saw a good thing in the person of the American souvenir hunter. At any rate, Charlie bought it for me and I hope it is not broken in shipping. There are also a couple of books that I managed to pick up at places that I have reasons to want to remember. If all this stuff starts to pile up so much that it is crowding you out of your apartment, let me know and I shall make arrangements for storage space somewhere. I still have a few odd souvenirs that I shall have to ship before I start moving around. I have sent some of the stuff home but I have some odd pieces left.

Letty, there is no news as to what they are going to do with me. If they ship me to another outfit I am prepared to give the Army an argument as to why I should go to school. There are courses offered at Oxford, Paris and some of the other leading schools in Europe for the men who are waiting around and not doing too much work. Right now, I would not think of applying for one of them, for it would mean that I would leave an outfit that is on the hot list. Then, too, it would get me out of Germany and that would please me. You may have gathered that I do not like the place.

You may also have gathered from this letter that I am still in love with you.

Love Always,
Leland

Heldra, Germany
August 2, 1945

My Dearest Letty:

I have been so busy answering letters from men who have shipped out that my typewriter is still hot. If I were a speed demon it would probably be burned up. Several men who have shipped out to other units are writing back to let us know where they are stationed. Most of them went to the Second Armored, the Third Armored and the 104th Infantry divisions, but a few went to smaller units. They are scattered all over Europe, some of them are in America, and a few are on their way to the Far East. The division is not the same anymore.

I also had a letter from one boy who was hit last September and we did not know where he was until yesterday. His car was knocked out by a bazooka and he suffered from loss of memory. He said he could not even remember who was commander of the troop for a month after he got in the hospital. Even now he could not remember my first name. Three other guys were killed in the same action and another had to be evacuated. So I guess he was pretty lucky to get out as lightly as he did.

I am writing all this like I knew I was going home in the near future, but there is still an odd chance that it will be a few months yet. If they happen to get me on a last-minute shipment, I hope that you will forgive me for writing all this stuff. It has never been my habit to do this sort of thing, but I simply cannot resist the temptation of dreaming a little now, and a dream is no fun unless it is shared. The whole job will be, if it happens to not come out this way, to try to explain to you that I was not really trying to deceive you. The Army has taught me to expect anything and to not let myself be too disappointed, no matter what happens, but I shall not expect you to have the same understanding of the situation.

Love Always,
Leland

Heldra, Germany
August 3, 1945

My Dearest Letty:

This letter is going to be a little hard to write because it will consist of an apology and little else. It is an apology that I should not have let myself in for in the first place, for I had been in the Army long enough to have learned better.

But the announcements of the War Department were so positive on the subject of discharges that I thought we could at least depend on them. The way they put out the discharge plan, it seemed that I could not miss getting out of the Army in a few short months; now it is all changed and I am having to try to tell you why I may not be home for a while yet.

You know how many points I have. Well, they are not enough. I am not worried about that, but I regret the fact that my recent letters have led you to believe that I was almost a civilian. Please believe that I did not intentionally tell you all this in an effort to fool you. I really believed it and I loved you so much that I could not resist one little dream.

Have just been notified that I am being transferred to the Second Armored Division, which is now in Berlin. Modlin is going, but Sherman has enough points to go home. His two children give him a break. Guess I should have married long ago. Well, I won't make the same mistake again, for I intend to get married as soon as I get out of the Army, or as soon as I can get a furlough, provided I can find a girl that I love who will marry me. Since there is only one who could qualify, would you mind checking on the matter and letting me know how she feels about it.

Love Always,
Leland

My Dearest Letty:

Perhaps the main reason for starting this letter tonight is to try out the new ribbon on my typewriter. It is too late to hope to finish if I am to get any sleep, but I could not resist the temptation to try the ribbon. It is for a Royal and I have a Torpedo machine. I had to make an adjustment to get it to fit and I was not sure it would work. But it seems to be doing OK and now I can tell you that I am crazy about you and know the words will come out clear enough for you to read.

I can also tell you that I have not gone to Berlin yet. They say the shipment has been delayed for a few days and there is no definite date on which we shall leave. I have not packed my duffel bag yet, so it will not cause me any extra work. Aside from the fact that I have too much stuff to carry comfortably, there is no special job to moving. It takes about thirty minutes to get ready to move, no matter if you are going to the next town or to the next continent.

I saw the Jack Benny Show today. It was one of the best and most entertaining I have had the pleasure of seeing. He had Larry Adler, Ingrid Bergman and Martha Tilton with him. In addition to putting on a good show, they were a friendly group and spent their time while off stage talking to the GIs who could not see the stage very well. It went over nicely with the boys. I only had one shot left in my camera and Martha posed for me at the tail of a B-25 plane.

Letty, this would be a beautiful day to go out on the mountain and see some of the places you have promised to show me. There are so many places that I am looking forward to seeing that it may take us several trips to get to them all. Then there are a couple of places I should like to show you, too. There are the caves and cliffs along Clear Fork, where I fished when I was a kid, and there is the Yellow Rock on Iron Ore Mountain that you have never seen. It will take a bit of hiking to get there, but that will be good for you after the weeks and months of sitting at the switchboard. It was from this mountain that I heard many fox races. From here, too, I got the feeling of insignificance that is occasionally necessary to bring a man down to his proper place in respect to the other things of the universe. Then there are the places in the Ozarks that we shall have to see: the hotel at Eureka Springs, the tiny cafe in Jasper where we put

High Life on a large tomcat one night, the fruit stands along Highway 71 where you can buy the best cantaloupes.

I am wondering how much change there will be in all these things, and how they will look to me now. Certainly they have lost none of their beauty, but I wonder if they will have the same magnificence they once possessed. In those days the Ozarks were the highest mountains in the world, so far as I was able to see. I knew none higher. There was no river quite so clear as the Piney or so large as the Arkansas. I wonder if a memory of the Rockies, the Colorado, the Ardennes or the Alps will rob me of some of my appreciation for them. If you are with me, I think not. That alone will make up for a lot of difference in the magnitude of the hills.

Love Always,
Leland

Heldra, Germany
August 6, 1945

My Dearest Letty:

It is almost time to go to the ball game and I am merely starting this now so that it will be in the machine when the game is over.

I am still with the Fifth and the shipment has been delayed until the tenth of the month. The reason, as they gave it to us, is that the Second is moving out of Berlin and there was no point in having us join it there, only to have to move back to this side of Germany in a couple of days. It will save us a long trip by truck, and that will help, even though I did want to see the city if I had to leave this division. However, they say we will be at Frankfurt and that will be some kind of a break. Ardis is only a hundred or so miles south of there and I shall be able to see him for the first time in almost four years.

I have not had a letter from anyone in several days now, and I am beginning to wonder how things are getting along at home. The end of the war did little to improve the mail situation over here. They do not seem to be flying the airmail now, if one is to judge by the time it takes to get a letter from the states to us. I can see that the ships that are going west would be loaded with troops, but it would seem that those coming this way would need something for ballast. Surely there are only a few politicians and show people who really want to come to Europe now, even if the war is over.

It is not a nice place to see. You could have no idea what a war can do to a country unless you get a chance to see one city that has been destroyed and one country road that is clogged with people who do not know where they want to go. There are literally millions of people now in Germany who have no idea where they are going and what they will do when they get to the end of the road.

In one little town no larger than Dover, there is a park to care for the wanderers. It is a sort of small town Bowery or flophouse where the lost people can sleep and spend a night before pushing on to a destination that is unknown to them. Every night the place is crowded with a new group of people. It will accommodate as many as a couple of hundred at a time and there is never an empty corner. When morning comes, they are on the road again, traveling by every means available. Wheelbarrows, toy wagons, bicycles, wagons drawn by horses or cows and tractors pull trains of anything that will roll, and there are a few automobiles. The convoy lines up at sunrise and moves out in the direction of the Ruhr or toward the southern part of Germany. None of them goes east. In one such convoy, I counted three tractor trains (each tractor was pulling at least two trailers and as many small wagons as the owners could find space to hitch on), sixteen animal-drawn wagons (these, too, had a string of small wagons behind them), five cars of various makes, and at least thirty small wagons that were being pulled by their owners. Each small wagon was piled high with bedding, suitcases and all the goods that the family owned.

It was not a pleasant sight, but somehow I can feel no pity for the people. When Germany was winning, it was they who whooped loudest at the announcement of a new victory. When I see them moving, I think of the boys who had to walk 1,200 kilometers as prisoners of war and of the conditions they were in when we found some of them. Then, too, they always remind me of the fact that if it were not for them I should be at home and doing the things I want to do instead of in the Fatherland.

If it were not for them, I should be telling you this evening that I am crazy about you instead of having to write it. That would be more fun, I am sure, and I could certainly make it sound more convincing that way.

Since I started this, I have taken time out to play a ballgame. Naturally we won, but the score was 6 to 5 and we made the winning tally in the last inning. It is time for chow and I am hungry.

Love Always,
Leland

Heldra, Germany
August 10, 1945

My Dearest Letty:

There was an old letter from you in the evening mail last night but there was no new one, so I am not really trying to answer that one. I am merely writing you today as if I had answered all the questions you have asked. I am merely writing to let you know that I still love you more than I did when I wrote last night.

We have not moved out to the Second yet, and there is no definite date for us to move as yet. The clerk at personnel tells me that it will be the fifteenth of the month before we shall start to move, for it will be then that the Second gets set up in the new area. The story still has it that we shall be in the vicinity of Frankfürt, but that could be changed. Incidentally, if we do go there, I shall try to get a pass into Switzerland.

I am sorry to learn that you still hold the erroneous idea that you are going to throw rocks at my birds and poison my dogs. Will I take pleasure in straightening you out in a hurry. The whole lawn will be littered with birdhouses. I have already figured out some of the designs I shall build and how they shall be painted. Then the swallows, martins, bluebirds and robins will have a nice peaceful place to spend the summer, and Letty will not disturb them.

There will be dogs, too. I have not decided how many or what kinds they will be, but there will probably be an English setter and a couple of hounds. That should be enough to start with, then we can add a new one as we see the need. You will keep the feed chart and see that they get the necessary nourishment. Perhaps you had better read a couple of books on the subject just to be sure you know how it is done.

I shall give you lessons in all that when I see you. Now I must begin to think of going to chow, for they do not wait around for me as you would do. If I am not there at chow time the cooks merely throw the food out. That is one way to induce men to be punctual.

Love Always,
Leland

Heldra, Germany
August 13, 1945

My Dearest Letty:

Today there was no mail at all except the *Tribune,* so I had a dull time reading. It is good to get the hometown paper, but a letter is so much better, even if it is one from one of the school kids who hardly remembers what I look like. Some of them write to me more or less regularly and I always answer their letters promptly, for I enjoy reading them. It helps me to keep up with the normal change in things at home, but it also makes me aware of the fact that I have been away a long time.

It is not hard to do that, for I am aware of it ever so often when I think of you and all the time I have been away from you. It seems funny that you should be such a big factor in all my plans and the way I live when I have had so little of you. It would seem that you or I could not possibly have become so aware of the need we have for each other in so short a time. It would seem that our few days could not possibly have changed the whole course of our thinking.

Logically, in the long months we have been apart, we should have learned the knack of letting well enough alone, but I have never learned. Always when I go to bed there is the same mischievous face, the same impish grin etched in the blackness of the ceiling. Always there is you. I cannot dismiss the face, nor do I want to. It says, "Take things easy, Junior (sometimes it says 'Toots' but it always means the same thing). There is really no need to be serious about all this that you see. The world is a place to laugh in and a thing to laugh at. There is war and suffering, like it says in the papers, but that is only a small part of the picture. There is the mountain where the wind is clean and sharp and where the leaves play a soft symphony in the evening. There are quiet lakes where the grass has been nipped short by the grazing cattle so that it makes a carpet of green velvet. There are white birches for the shade, and thrushes and catbirds for the orchestra. Not all the world is tired and hungry and looking for some place to spend the night under a shed before moving out on a road that leads into the unknown."

"There is still the hometown," the face says to me, "where you meet people who will call you by your first name and who really mean it when they shake hands with you. This is the part of the world that you grew up in. This is the kind of life that you learned to like, and it is the kind that you are going back to. I am marking a little corner of it 'Reserved' and that is for us. I hold the other end of the rope that keeps you from drifting into the belief that all the people of the world are a sordid, drifting herd of animals who have not made any progress in the thing we like to call civilization."

All this the face—that is, your face—says to me. Not in so many words, of course, for you would never be so verbose as all that. But you say it in the way you smile, and the way the smile makes me remember that all this is true.

But, to come to the earth after that long paragraph and finish this off as a conventional letter, we have not moved yet. However, it should not be long. They say that a part of the Second is at Frankfürt now and we shall go down as soon as they get settled there. We shall make the trip in trucks, but the ride will not be too tough. It may be that they will put us out in the field and we shall sleep in pup tents. In that case, I shall have some trouble in setting up my office as I have learned to have it. However, I also know how to live in the field and it should not be for too long. The turn of the war in the east will shorten the time we have to wait for the boat.

Love Always,
Leland

Dearest Letty

Heldra, Germany
August 14, 1945

My Dearest Letty:

After supper I should be more able to write this, for I am a bit hungry now. The dinner was not so good and I did not eat much of it. But they always say that the hungry man writes the best letters, and I am trying the experiment.

Incidentally, it seems that you are not suffering from hunger from the way you write. You always told me how much you weighed until the last letter, and that time you evaded the issue. Now you are telling me all the time to be good and moderate while you are overindulging in shoestring potatoes, steaks and milkshakes—all fattening. It seems to prove a point that I have always contended, viz. that you are the one who needs to reform while I am a model of self-discipline.

You can get rid of the excessive weight, you know, by a simple method of diet. There is orange juice for breakfast, a lettuce sandwich for lunch and a vegetable dinner. It is simple. It is the method I use to keep my boyish figure, and it has proven to be effective. I have often told you what you should weigh; anything above that figure (121½) would make things dangerous for me. See that you get down to that figure at once for I shall be coming home one of these days and I still want to be able to boss the joint when I get there.

There is supposed to be a big parade tomorrow and I happen to be one of the unfortunate ones who were chosen to take part in it. It is for a Russian general who is coming through the area and they want it to be stylish. That means that we are to have to dress in the best military manner and present the best possible salute. It amounts to just that. The whole thing is a lot of bologna to me and to most of the rest of the men. This formality beats me and I shall never like it. However, if that is all they have for me to do, I can take it until it is time to get out of the Army. It's easier than the fighting, but it is unpleasant to have to stand at attention to a guy who is merely placed in a position of command.

Don't forget that I love you and that I shall expect you to be waiting for me.

Love Always,
Leland

Heldra, Germany
August 15, 1945

My Dearest Letty:

My last letter is barely in the mail and here I am writing again. What can be wrong with a guy who does that? What can he be thinking of to waste all the time and paper and envelopes? There is only one answer; he must be in love with the girl.

And that is as good a reason as there is for anything. It is an old answer to all the questions that can be asked. It is the universal explanation for odd behavior, the alibi of the wicked, the pillar of the righteous, and the reason for everything. It is a prism through which the passing light is so distorted that the most unconventional behavior assumes the quality of normalcy. Why, then, should it not explain my writing when there is a letter that has not left the troop mailbox.

One of the men who is leaving the troop tomorrow just came in and we have been talking for a time, so this letter has suffered a slight interruption. They keep shipping the men out so that the old outfit has lost much of its atmosphere. It is not the same. There are only a few of the old men left and most of us are going in a few days. There is no word on when we shall leave, but it cannot be long. There is no reason to keep us around and many ships have been released by the collapse of Japan.

Incidentally, today was the official end of the war. It was announced sometime after midnight, although we knew it last night. The general phoned and said that we had word of the end of the war and we could celebrate. But it was all quiet. The men had not shown too much excitement over the end of the war in Europe, and there seemed no reason to put on a show at the end of a war that was on the other side of the world, even if it did mean that we would get home quicker. After all, there is not much you can do in this country to celebrate. It is still the Reich and there can be no cause for celebration as long as I am in it.

Letty, you should have seen the honor guard we had for the Russian general today. It was raining and he was scheduled to come over into our territory on some kind of business (we are located on the border). International diplomacy demanded that we have a guard of honor for him, so we stood in the rain and he pulled a quick inspection. One comical incident happened that could have caused international embarrassment, if a colonel had not thought in a hurry. When he approached, we came to the position of "present arms," and since he was a dignified old gentleman he snapped a quick salute and held it. In the Russian book of military courtesy, evidently he could not cut his salute away until he had given us the command of "order arms." The catch was that he could not speak a word of English. He stood there in the rain with his hand to his cap, but could think of no way to give us the command that would allow him to take it away. He was beginning to look nervous and was no doubt feeling a little foolish when the colonel sized up the situation and gave the command. If he had not been there we should probably have been standing in the rain until yet with the Russian general standing in front of us at the position of "hand salute."

Letty, I wish I had some way of passing all of my accumulated odds and ends of souvenirs over to you so that I should not have to carry them with me when I start moving around. The duffel bag is built to hold only the Army equipment and I have a lot of stuff for which no provision has been made. But it is stuff that they will not let me mail and I do not want to part with it, so I shall have to carry it along. There are, for example, two pair of good binoculars that I want to keep, for I should not be able to buy them in the states. There are a couple of microscopes, three cameras and a pistol that the rules say I cannot mail. Then there is this typewriter and some books that I could not part with at the moment, so I shall have to take them along. Add to that the usual Army equipage and you have quite a load.

Love Always,
Leland

Heldra, Germany
August 16, 1945

My Dearest Letty:

There should be some way to write an original letter, some way that no one else ever thought of using. You must get tired of reading the same conventional letters day after day with never a change to relieve the monotony.

Perhaps if I should tell you a story it would help to pass the long evening. But what story should I tell? Why, a love story, of course. There is no other kind, really. Now don't jump at the conclusion that I am going to say "I love you" and let it go at that. In fact, I am not going to say that here; it will have to come at the end of the letter. But this is the story of a girl who loved a man and of a man who did not know what to place as the value of such love.

Once upon a time, when the world was much larger and America was many long weeks from Normandy by sailing vessel instead of a few hours by plane, there was a young Norman who loved a girl of his village. She was a pretty girl, young and small and feminine with a manner that hid the determination that was hers. They were poor, as were most of the people who lived in Normandy in those days, but that did not matter to the girl. She was willing to live as her people before her had lived, for she was sure that none of them had known the love that she knew, so she was more fortunate than they. It is a strange fact that no one who is really in love believes that other people have ever felt as he feels. So she was willing to live with this new sensation and was sure that she would have a full life. He, on the other hand, must have had a touch of Gypsy blood in his veins for he could not be content with the pastoral quiet of the Norman countryside. He loved the girl but he also loved adventure; he wanted her but he also wanted to give her the riches that old France could not provide. Such things were to be had only in the new world that was America.

He wanted to make one trip to America and get all the things he had dreamed of giving her. It is also possible that he had the instincts of the nomad and that he simply could not resist the prospects of seeing a virgin country where no white man had ever been. At any rate, he signed up as a member of one of the French explorations into the new world. When he came back, he told her, they would marry and she would be one of the rich and beautiful women of the world instead of one of the country lasses who did not know what was in the next province. She did not want him to go, for she was perfectly content to live her life as a peasant, if she could live it with him.

But when the boat sailed from Le Havre he was one of the exploration party. Also in the party was a small boy who had signed on as a helper. He was to cook for the men and help take care of the equipage. If he had not been so cheerful and so charming they would have paid no attention to him at all; as it was, he was always making himself useful and giving a smile to everyone. He gave his name as Jean, which is the French equivalent of John, and because he was so small the crew called him Petit Jean, or Little John.

They sailed up the Mississippi, which had been claimed for France by earlier explorers, to the point where the town of Helena now stands. The great river that rose somewhere in the west had not been explored so they decided to have a look at it. Part of the party was to stay at the mouth of the river with the larger boats, and the remainder of them was to move up the stream that is now the Arkansas. The Norman was in the exploring party, and they insisted that Little John stay with the boats. But the Norman was his hero and could go no place that Little John did not follow, so Little John was with the party when it moved out.

They followed the river past the place where Little Rock now stands and as far up as the present town of Morrilton. Here, malaria gripped many of the men and the whole party was stopped because of chills and fever. Little John did what he could to make the other men comfortable, but there was no medicine that would combat the disease.

At last, Little John was a victim. But he was not as strong as the rest, and it was soon apparent that he would die. It was then that he called the Norman to his tent and told him that he was not really Little John at all. He was the girl who was supposed to be in the orchards of Normandy.

Because I cannot write of strong emotional scenes, I shall not try to reconstruct this part of the story. It is enough to say that Little John died and was buried at the foot of the mountain near the bend of the river above the Morrilton bridge. The grave is unmarked and the exact spot is forgotten, but there is still a monument to her memory. It is more imposing than the monument of Napoleon or the statue of Joan of Arc. It is the mountain of Petit Jean and it tells a story that has more truth in revealing the strength of love than the story of Romeo.

Letty, this is only a bit of local legend that you may have heard many times, but it is really an attempt to break the monotony of always trying to tell you what we are doing here and when I am not coming home. For that part, we are still doing the same (nothing) and there is no news of when we shall move.

But, whenever we move and wherever we go, I shall always love you the same, and it should not be many weeks now until we have a definite idea of when we will come home. As soon as I learn I shall let you know. It will give you a chance to dispose of all your old boyfriends and fix the place up the way you want it to be when I get there.

Love Always,
Leland

Heldra, Germany
August 19, 1945

My Dearest Letty:

Every day something new springs up and I have to write you another letter to let you know what is going on. Today they canceled our shipment to the Second Armored. They also told us that we would stay with the division and that the division had been alerted to leave here the first of September and that it would sail around the middle of the month. If we stick to the schedule I should be in the states by the twentieth of next month. After that, there might be some delay in getting out of the Army after I get there, but it will be much easier to sweat out a discharge in the states than in the Fatherland.

Letty, I have been writing around the country to see how the job situation is. (This is on the level and I am not leading up to a joke about you supporting the family.) I think I can go to work in Little Rock when I get out. It is not the best job in the country nor the pleasantest, but there are many advantages to it. The pay starts at $160 a month. It is an eight-hour day with 5½ working days in a week, and there is a paid vacation. Above all, it is a permanent job even if there should be a depression. What is your idea of such a setup?

Maybe I am a little hasty with all this, for I am not out of the Army yet and I have not asked you to marry me. Lots of things could happen, but there is no harm in doing a little planning and hoping. We could fool around for a while before taking the job, you know, but I might go broke. My cash reserve will be limited to about $1,000.

This may sound like a mercenary letter to you, for I have never thought seriously of what I was going to do next week or next year, but you seemed interested and there was no point in keeping any hint of a plan that I might have from you.

You may have always thought of me as a sort of a hobo who never worked at a job for more than a few weeks at a time. You were right about that. I never did. I was always drifting from one job to another, not because I had to every time but because there was no special reason to stay with one job. In those days it was more fun to drift. There was always something lacking, and you may have guessed that it was you. With you there should be nothing that would make me want to wander more than the usual hobo trips we would want to take.

You should be here tonight. One of the boys who moved in with us brought a big accordion and they are having a jam session downstairs now. He plays well and some of the boys think they can sing, so they are making plenty of racket. They had a guitar last night and they really went to town. It is too bad that no one can play the piano in the next building. If they could, there would be no chance to sleep at all. As it is, they cannot make enough racket to keep me awake.

I am still managing to make straight A's with my course from the university, believe it or not. They think if I could learn to spell I would be a fair student, but that is one thing I could never quite manage. I always kept a dictionary on my desk, but one of the men who shipped out took mine with him. Perhaps I should have gone to school.

Love Always,
Leland

Heldra, Germany
August 21, 1945

My Dearest Letty:

There seems to be no point in wasting a perfectly good evening when I could be writing you a long letter and telling you that I love you more than you may imagine. I could be out walking in the rain, but there would be no point in that now. If the sun were shining and you were here we might go for a long walk on the mountain and see if we could find some of the wild hogs that roam around here. We could climb to the top of the point where the hikers' clubhouse is and take a look at the whole country from here, or we could be lazy and simply stroll along the river and watch the geese paddle against the current.

But there is no fun in doing all this alone. Sometimes I talk some of the boys into taking a stroll with me when the sun shines, but that is not too often. Then I have two girls who go with me on special occasions. But they are lazy and will not go far. Elizabeth is my favorite of all the girls I have seen in Germany. She has blonde hair and blue eyes, but she is coy and mischievous. Ingred is more serious but she is also nice. I shall send you their pictures as soon as I have a chance to have them developed.

In spite of the fact that they both insist that I am their favorite, I still suspect that there is a catch. They seem much more affectionate on the days when I have a fresh ration of chocolate, which leads me to believe that they are after my wealth. You will understand that at their age (Elizabeth is 5, Ingred is 6), chocolate represents the greatest wealth they can imagine, and I must seem like a captain of industry when I have my 14 bars of Hershey's milk chocolate with almonds. When the chocolate is all gone they do not come around so often, but they still manage to keep contact so that they will not miss anything. I often accused them of flirting with the other men, but they deny it vehemently and insist that I am the only one they really care about.

I saw in the paper that the Fifth was scheduled to stop in the assembly area on the way to the port. Letty, you should see one of these places. It is where they collect units for the purpose of getting them ready for shipment. You never knew that we ran an area such as that in England, but we did. We were in the Third Army and the First Army was to make the landing in France. They sent us to the southern part of England to operate the camps from which the First Army struck into Normandy.

At the time, our troop was stationed at a little town called Ivy Bridge. It is not too far from Plymouth, and is one of those sleepy English towns that you read about in such books as *Forever Amber*. Our job there was to see that the assault troops were fed, housed and supplied. When they left, we got ready to follow them across the channel. But where they stayed for weeks, it only took us a few hours to get ready to cross. They were supplied down to the last detail, but we were short several items when we crossed. They told us we would draw the equipment from stocks on the other side, but we were even short a couple of mortars when we went into combat. However, we soon learned that this did not make a great deal of difference and that the shortage was just that much less to haul.

It seems funny that all this could be more than a year ago and that so much could have happened in that time. The only thing that has not changed is the fact that I am in love with you.

Love Always,
Leland

Heldra, Germany
August 22, 1945

My Dearest Letty:

By this time you are probably sitting down to a good supper and dreading the job of washing the dishes. It is that time of the day.

We had an inspection of clothing today and there are signs of activity that always precede a move. The whole atmosphere of the division is one of anticipation, and it seems that we are really getting ready to move. The orders are definite and the present plan calls for us to leave here the first of the month. There will be a short stop in the assembly area and we are supposed to board the ship around the fourteenth of September. These plans are definite but they are subject to change, as are all plans. Anyway, they sound good and I like to repeat them as often as there is an excuse to do so.

If all this works out, I should be home early in October, for a furlough at least. It will only be a short time after that until I get a discharge, for they do not need me in the Army any longer.

Our colonel is leaving tomorrow for the Second Armored Division, and I have been seeing him off. He was not a bad Joe, especially when we were situated as we are now. He gave us all the breaks that he knew how to give us. In combat, I must say that the reports were that he was not too aggressive, but that had nothing to do with me. We worked under another command then, so I would not know about that. There has been no reason to complain of his treatment of us, and I hated to see him go. But for the end of the war, I should have been going with him, and many things could have been worse than that. I had him pretty well snowed and could have taken advantage of it in a new outfit where I was not known.

Just had a letter from a man who spent three years with us and is now in the Second. He claims that it is not at all like this outfit, for they spend a lot of time in the job of spit and polish. It is the one thing that all soldiers hate most, and the one thing we have managed to avoid best.

Love Always,
Leland

Heldra, Germany
August 25, 1945

My Dearest Letty:

It is just now that I learn that you have been in Lubbock and that Bob was sick. Three of your letters came in the evening mail and two of them were mailed in Texas. Of course, I was glad to learn that the boy is better now and that you were able to come home. Tetanus is a dangerous disease, and no one can pass it lightly. It is not a bad idea to keep constantly vaccinated against it, even if the shot does make your arm feel like a toothache for a few minutes. I do hope that you got brave enough to take the shot as soon as you got home.

Well, it begins to look as though we are going to leave this place at last. The present schedule calls for us to leave a week from tomorrow, and there is no hint of a change in the plan yet. I am keeping my fingers crossed.

I had a letter from home telling me that my automatic shotgun had arrived. That is the one thing that I was particularly anxious to have get there. It is a good new gun and I wanted to have it to shoot, if I should find the energy to go hunting. The other guns were more in the relic class and I shall never shoot them anyway. Now you will have to find spaces for a lot of old rusty guns, and they will clutter up the whole house.

There is no need to write to me again here unless you hear that our plan is changed. The letters that are in the mail will have to follow me around now and some of them might even follow me home. Our post - office is due to close in a couple of days. I shall continue to write as long as there is a place to mail the letters, but it will not be long.

I do not know where we shall go, but the story is that we will pass the AAC and go directly to a port. The ship going back will not take so long as the one we rode over here. There will be no circling to avoid subs and no waiting for slow ships to keep up with us.

Love Always,
Leland

Heldra, Germany
August 26, 1945

My Dearest Letty:

By this time next Sunday I hope to be on the way home to you. Perhaps I am too optimistic and it may be much longer than that, but that is the present plan. There will be a long train ride and a slight pause before we get on the boat, but once we get started there should not be much delay.

It will not seem right to have to move. We have been here so long that it is like we are part of the landscape. The bridge over the railroad does not look dressed if there are not as many as half a dozen soldiers hanging over the banister looking wishfully down the tracks. It would not look like Heldra if there were not a line of GIs standing around waiting for chow or the chow truck. But I, for one, am perfectly willing to give the place back to the Krauts and let them see if they can make something of it.

Letty, I am beginning to wonder just what kind of civilian I am going to make. It will not seem right to be able to decide just what I am going to do and what time I am going to get up in the morning and the color of the tie I wear. The Army has decided those things for me for so long that I am not sure of my taste in clothes or of my ability to make decisions. I do not say that it will bother me but it will seem odd at first, just as it seemed odd to have them make those decisions when I first came into the Army.

A drastic change in routine always appealed to me in a strange and intoxicating way. Even the little change like the days when I changed jobs and got into something new. I even got a thrill out of the day I finished the crop at home. It was like a new experience to drive out at the end of the last row and know that I would not have to be back in the field the next day. Go on and say that was because I was lazy, and I shall agree with you, but that was not the whole reason. There was always the prospect of doing something different that thrilled me. Now, I have the same thrill.

Then there is the prospect of getting married, and that is something I never did before. It is so remote from anything I ever did that I shall not know how to go about it at all. I shall probably violate all the rules set down so carefully by Miss Post, but it is going to be fun anyway, and I am not exactly conventional.

Perhaps I am going at this backward to wait until this part of the letter to tell you that I love you and expect to see you waiting for me at the platform when I come home, but that is the way it is. The talk of the love usually precedes the talk of marriage, but I did not happen to put it down that way. The two subjects are so closely related that I find difficulty in separating them in my mind, so you never know which of them is going to pop out first.

Love Always,
Leland

Heldra, Germany
August 28, 1945

My Dearest Letty:
You will not hear from me again for a few days so I thought it would be a good idea to tell you one more time that I am still crazy about you and that I do not want you to forget it until I am able to remind you of it again. We are to leave here Sunday and the postoffice will not be open after today so that I cannot write again.

They say now that we will stop at one of the assembly camps and I may be able to write from there. I have no idea what it will be like and we may not have a chance to write, but if we do I shall let you know what it is like there. I do not think we should be there more than four or five days, so it will not matter what it is like. I can hold a bear for a little while.

From there we are supposed to go directly to the boat. That will be the biggest thrill that they could offer us in this country.

We are having some nice weather for a change, and I am taking advantage of it to try to put on a tan. All my life I never thought of such a thing, and then last winter made me see what I had been missing. Gazing at the frosty tent or riding down the road in a frozen fog, I began to wonder how it would feel to be warm down to my toes again. Any kind of heat would have been welcome, but I wanted the sun more than any other kind. I wanted to lie in the grass and soak up the rays of the sun until I was almost blistered, and I have been doing just that. The sun has been shining for a few days now and it has given me a chance to warm up a little.

If there is time to write at Camp Atlanta I shall send you a letter from there. If not, I may be in the states when you hear from me again.

Love Always,
Leland

Camp Atlanta, France
Sept. 5, 1945

My Dearest Letty:

This is in no sense a real letter. It is merely a note to let you know that I have started on the long trip home at last and that you need not be disappointed if you do not hear from me for a few days. We left Heldra Sunday and arrived at this place yesterday. It is about forty or so miles from Reims, and about one hundred miles from Paris. This puts us about one hundred fifty miles from Le Havre, which is where we are supposed to catch the boat.

This is not a bad place to loaf. There is nothing special to do in the way of entertainment except a show every night and a little softball, but I am not hard to entertain in a place like this. In fact, I have acquired the habit of loafing until it has become an art. It is the one thing that I can do most gracefully. Plenty of people think they are loafing when they are play-ing games. The real loafer is the guy who can lie for hours with nothing to entertain him but his thoughts while he stares toward the tent roof.

It is then that I think of the girl at home and the fact that it will not be long until I can see her again. It is then that I realize how much I have loved her all this time.

Love Always,
Leland

Camp Atlanta, France
Sept. 11, 1945

My Dearest Letty:

There is still no way of knowing when I shall be able to get this into the mail or whether I shall be able to mail it at all, but I shall take the chance and write a note anyway. I may be in the states before this gets out of the mailbox, but I can have the pleasure of writing it anyway and then racing it to the boat.

Well, I was in Paris on a pass a couple of days ago. It is still the most beautiful of all cities, and there is no other place like it. However, I did not have time to see the new parts of town. I did manage to pick up a bottle of Chanel, which I hope you will like. I know no more of perfume than I know of art, and it may not be the type that suits your personality. There is supposed to be a rule to the effect that perfume is suited to personalities by some mysterious association, but I know nothing of those things. It is a pretty bottle anyway.

Must sign off for now and get my duffel bag packed and ready to move out before daylight.

Love Always,
Leland

Dearest Letty

Camp Twenty Grand, France
Sept. 18, 1945

My Dearest Letty:

Rather than get out of the habit of writing, I am pecking this out even if it may not get into the mail. The mail service is terrible, for troops do not ordinarily stay here long and there is no special need for mail.

There is nothing to do but sit around and wait for the boat. There is a show but the tent is so small that it will hold only a few men, and they start lining up two hours before showtime. The Red Cross Club is so crowded that the coffee is not worth the time it takes to get it, and the ballgames are dull. We spend the time lying in the tents and reading or playing the old Army game of griping.

All the time I think how nice it would be if we could spend these Indian-summer days together. It is still warm enough to go fishing, or take sunbaths or loaf through the woods as I have always dreamed of doing with you. There are the bluffs on the mountain that we shall explore and the pine forests on the old farm at home that I want to see again. There are the creeks that I fished and the mountains where we will hike together.

Love Always,
Leland

POSTSCRIPT

Leland Duvall was separated from the army on October 18, 1945, at Jefferson Barracks, Missouri. His train arrived at Russellville the next day. Letty Jones was on the platform to meet him and allowed the public kiss that he had insisted upon. They were married two weeks later.

Upon his retirement in 1990 at the age of seventy-nine, they returned to Crow Mountain, where he built a cottage down the road from her family homestead. There he wrote three novels and packed them away, and she painted. He died there February 18, 2006. Letty moved from the mountain in the spring of 2010 to the Wildflower Retirement Residence at Russellville, where she lives.

LELAND DUVALL was a member of the 85th Cavalry Reconnaissance Squadron from 1942 to 1945. After the war, he pursued a career in journalism and wrote for several Arkansas newspapers, including the *Arkansas Gazette*.

ERNIE DUMAS is a columnist for the *Arkansas Times* and former associate editor and reporter for the *Arkansas Gazette*. He is the editor of *The Clintons of Arkansas* and cowriter with Tom Glaze of *Waiting for the Cemetery Vote*.

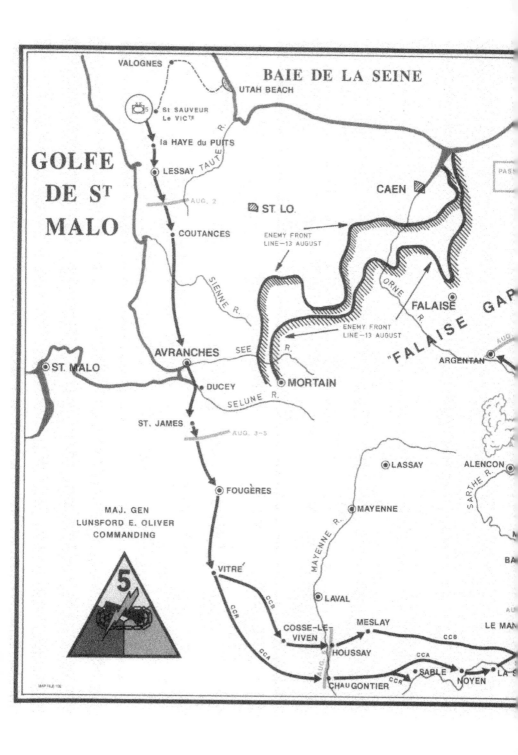

VALOGNES

BAIE DE LA SEINE

UTAH BEACH

St SAUVEUR
Le VIC^{TE}

la HAYE du PUITS

GOLFE
DE S^T
MALO

LESSAY

TAUTE R.

AUG. 2

ST. LO.

CAEN

ENEMY FRONT
LINE—13 AUGUST

COUTANCES

SIENNE R.

FALAISE

ORNE R.

"FALAISE GAP

ENEMY FRONT
LINE—13 AUGUST

AVRANCHES

SEE R.

ST. MALO

DUCEY

MORTAIN

ARGENTAN

SELUNE R.

ST. JAMES

AUG. 3–5

LASSAY

ALENCON

SARTHE R.

FOUGÈRES

MAJ. GEN
LUNSFORD E. OLIVER
COMMANDING

MAYENNE

MAYENNE R.

VITRÉ

CCR

CCB

LAVAL

COSSE-LE-
VIVEN

MESLAY

LE MAN

CCB

CCA

HOUSSAY

CCA

CCR

SABLE

LA S

NOYEN

CHAUGONTIER

MAP FILE 100